D1629598

Ivory Knights

NICHOLAS GORDON

Ivory Knights
Man, Magic and Elephants

CHAPMANS
1991

Chapmans Publishers Ltd
141–143 Drury Lane
London WC2B 5TB

BRITISH LIBRARY CATALOGUING IN PUBLICATION DATA

Gordon, Nicholas
Ivory knights : man, magic & elephants.
1. Tanzania. Ivory, hunting (commerce)
I. Title
364.16209678

ISBN 1–85592–521–4

First published by Chapmans 1991

Phototypeset in Linotron Palatino by Intype, London
Printed and bound in Great Britain by
Butler & Tanner Ltd, Frome and London

For My Mother and Father

Acknowledgements

This book was inspired not only by the fate of the elephants in Tanzania, but by the extraordinary response that *YOU* magazine readers gave to the initial article that was published in the magazine.

Without their support, I would not have written the book.

I must also thank the authorities in Tanzania for their assistance; Costa Mlay for his frankness and hospitality; Gerard Bigurube who piloted me for many hours and for thousands of miles across Tanzania; and Ireneus Ndunguru for his enthusiasm, imagination, and wicked sense of humour.

There are many other people in Tanzania I wish to thank: Markus Borner at Serengeti; Chris Fox at Ruaha; Paul Marenga of the Wildlife Department, who so stoically looked after me in Beho-Beho when I was stranded without a plane; Mr Minja who so capably guided me in the northern sector of the Selous; Erasmus Terimo, also of the Wildlife Department; Chief Nsalamba at Katavi, a tiny park, isolated and unloved, and in need of support; and the man who started it all, Charles Kibasa.

The Wildlife Conservation Society of Tanzania assisted me too. Neil Baker and his wife Liz provided me with an invaluable briefing on the politics of the ivory wars.

In Germany, my thanks to Dr Faust of the Frankfurt Zoological Society which has played a major role in protecting wildlife in East Africa for over a generation, and to Peter Esterts at GTZ.

In America, to Professor Richard Barnes for his advice on elephant behaviour in Tanzania.

In England, thanks to 'Steve' Stephenson, Tony Mence, and Bruce Kinloch, all of them old East Africa hands, each with a rich bag of memories of the way it was; to Allan Thornton and Dave Currey of the EIA who told me about the way it is today; to Lulu Appleton for her advice, Mark Crean for his guidance and Vivienne Schuster for her patience and encouragement. Lastly, thanks to Matthew McCabe who accompanied me on two of the trips I made, a travelling companion who made sure that even when we were in the worst of places, we always had access to Safari beer and a bottle opener; to photographers Alistair Morrison and Harvey Mann; and to Jackie Holland, without whose deft touch on the typewriter and empathy with the subject this manuscript would never have been completed on time.

Contents

Illustrations

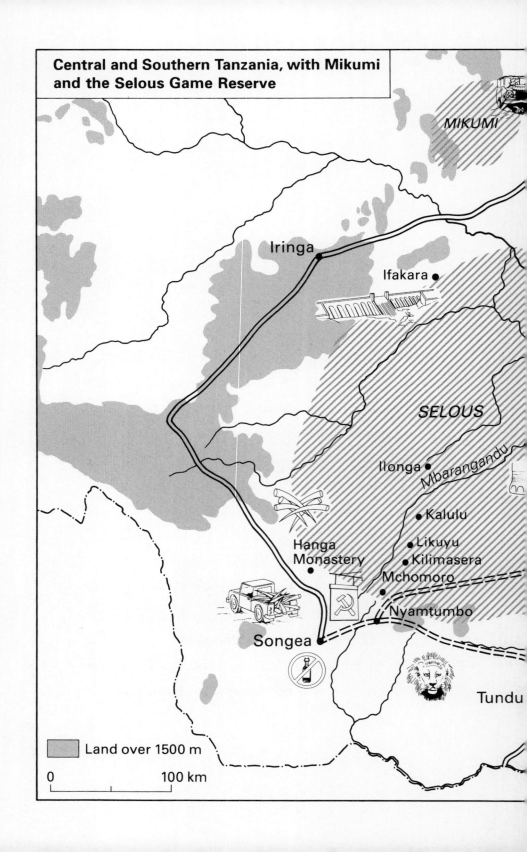

Central and Southern Tanzania, with Mikumi and the Selous Game Reserve

MIKUMI

Iringa

Ifakara

SELOUS

Ilonga
Mbarangandu

Kalulu

Likuyu

Hanga
Monastery

Kilimasera

Mchomoro

Nyamtumbo

Songea

Tundu

Land over 1500 m

0   100 km

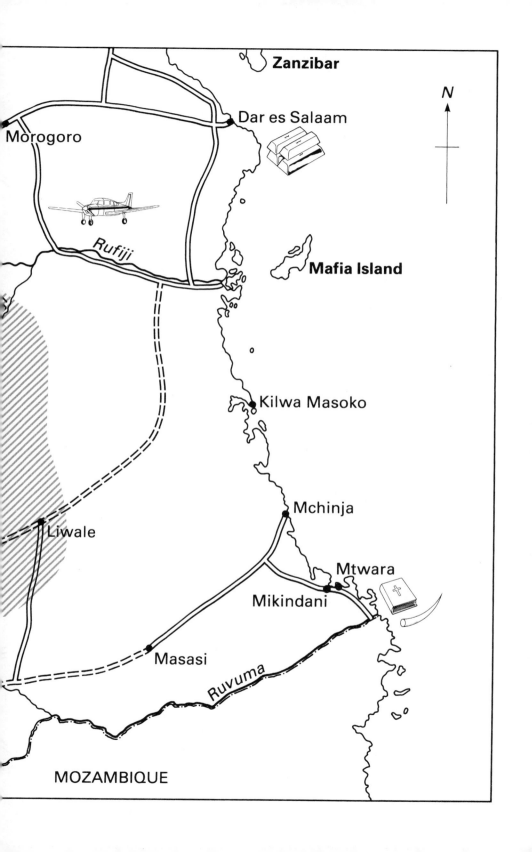

Zanzibar

Dar es Salaam

Morogoro

Rufiji

Mafia Island

Kilwa Masoko

Mchinja

Liwale

Mtwara

Mikindani

Masasi

Ruvuma

MOZAMBIQUE

N

ONE

The Palace of Night

There's a nervousness about nightfall in Africa. The shadows are long but brief. The curtain of darkness descends with a thump, blanking out, until dawn, all the new ways of the continent. Men who work in city offices in white shirts and flared trousers cast off their grey-flannel inhibitions. In the villages, a quite different Africa, it is the same. By day the women till the fields, or make their contribution to the greenhouse effect as they hack down a tree for firewood, or squat uncomfortably sifting maize. Children play next to them in the hot dry dust. Only the headman affects the sharpness of city life in his shirt and trousers. Somehow it doesn't quite work. No shoes, you see.

At night, instinct, freed from the shackles of sunlight, reasserts itself. Africa, the Africa nurtured by the genes, is feeding on a centuries-old appetite of atavism, a heavy feast of magic, custom, legend and fear.

The Mchawi has no shoes. He is not a headman and he is dressed in a particularly hideous maroon and purple sweater. It's the sort of garment that could once be seen on the rummage counter of British Home Stores hopefully waiting for a chest to warm. Terence Conran would be ashamed, but in Kilimasera, a community of just sixty-three dwellings, it cuts a certain dash. This tenth-generation hand-me-down makes a grubby match with the trousers, yet the Mchawi is far better dressed than anyone else in this village. The Mchawi rents a small *shamba*, a meagre patch of land a few hundred metres outside this one-street village where his two wives grow sunflowers for their oil, and maize so the Mchawi can survive. He keeps a few raucous chickens

1

which crow and cluck and pick at the dust around his hut. He doesn't have much else in the world, but then no one else in Kilimasera has what he possesses. The Mchawi is an old man and with his age and the knowledge he has accrued, he has earned the respect of this village perched on the rim of a terracotta-red escarpment overlooking the Selous Game Reserve in Southern Tanzania. The Mchawi is the village wizard, and his judgement, the word of the Mchawi, the interpreter of the old ways, is far more potent than that of the headman, Dar es Salaam man, the man the Party appointed to ensure that Kilimasera behaves the way that Dar believes it should.

The Mchawi owns the past. The past is his country. It is a rich land and he is a wealthy man. Memories in Kilimasera, in this village so near the Selous, are as precious as elephants' tusks. People come to him at night. They come to him to seek the blessing of the spirits, for it is the spirits and the night that guide them. The *jangili*, the poachers, the men who kill elephants for money, come to him. They require good omens and they will not hunt if their Mchawi deems that it is not right. Night rules and these men, these *jangili*, are its slaves. The Mchawi is their link with the night and the past, yet he too is its slave. Now he immerses himself in the blackness and prepares for the task ahead.

Alensio Bero is a *jangili*. He does not live in Kilimasera, but he knows the village well. The fame of the Mchawi travels easily in this land without roads. He too has often consulted the Mchawi. Alensio Bero has spent his life in Hanga, almost two days' walk from Kilimasera. His village is larger than Kilimasera. There is a monastery with its own electricity generator, a football pitch, a bar, and 138 houses. Alensio Bero is renowned for his skill in hunting. He is fifty-two years old and learnt the ways of the bush at the age of eleven. He shoots elephants. Sixty-two in one safari last year. Two of them were tuskless. He owns his own house and does no other work but poaching. He has three wives, a Chinese bicycle, two Japanese radios and a cheap watch.

He, too, is respected in Hanga, but now he is a worried man. The world is changing even in this last redoubt of the old culture. The army has been making poaching difficult. There are many soldiers around the village and inside the

Selous, too. Only recently his half-brother was killed in a fire fight with them. He is beginning to wonder whether to quit while he has his wives and his bike and his radios and his life. But then he stands outside his house and sniffs the dusk and watches the sliver of moon tickle the mountain tops to the east. His mind follows his eyes to the Selous, beyond those purple-flecked mountains. He sees the reserve not as a giant wilderness, the largest left in Africa, but as a giant sweetshop stuffed full of delights. Buffalo, eland, antelope, crocodile, warthog, puku, giraffe (though he knows this does not eat well and should only be cooked in desperation), hartebeest, wildebeest, any beast, hippo, and, of course, *tembo*. The elephant. The villagers of Hanga, and Kilimasera, and all the other tight communities that ring the Selous, see it the same way. They stand on the sandy banks of the twisting Mbarangandu river which forms the border with the Selous and press their noses up the plate glass, and they leave it to men like the Mchawi to sanction *jangili* like Alensio Bero to bring home the bull's-eyes.

Three hours' drive from the Mbarangandu river, which is a trickle at Hanga and wide and brown and lethargic when it reaches Kilimasera, there's a market town called Songea. Once the capital of the warring Ngoni tribe who conquered much of southern Tanzania, later the administrative head-quarters of the German colonists, it is now the hub of the southern interior of the country. Songea is a quiet town whose red dirt roads lead to the cool promise of blue hills. The calm is beguiling and false for it is here that the nerve centre of the operation to defeat men like Alensio Bero is situated.

Ireneus Ndunguru is the man who is charged with stopping the *jangili*. If this battle is to be won, then Ireneus Ndunguru must conquer not just the hearts and minds of the *jangili*, but their stomachs too. He works from a rickety desk covered in snooker-green felt. His office is painted civil-service green too, as if Opal Fruits (lime flavour) had been smeared by naughty children all over the walls. On his desk is a telephone that must be cranked to obtain the exchange and a tin lid with a hole in its rusty bottom. It is an ashtray (for visitors only).

Ireneus Ndunguru is the Regional Game Officer for the

Southern Selous, a title that any bureaucrat could empathize with instantly, but it masks a man whose intellect and actions have proved equal to that of the *jangili*.

Ndunguru is preparing to go up country. To Hanga, the village that is the home of Alensio Bero, just seventeen kilometres off the main Songea–Iringa highway, an hour's drive if the bridges across the Mbarangandu are not down. He pulls open the drawer of his desk and takes out a shallow tin box. He handles it very gingerly. As he opens it on the desk, his lips part to reveal a gap-toothed smile, which, somehow, doesn't quite match the automatic pistol, black and gleaming with oil, which lies inside the box wrapped in a plastic bag.

There are few high-rise buildings in Dar es Salaam, the capital of Tanzania. It is an unspectacular town whose paint-peeled dwellings are a fusty reflection of modern African decay. Overlooking the harbour which the Arabs called the Haven of Peace, is a nine-storey concrete tower. On the sixth deck in a corner office that gives splendid views of the harbour with its flat cocktail of the old and new, rust-bucket container ships and rotting dhows at anchor, is the head-quarters of Costa Mlay, Tanzania's Director of Wildlife, Ndunguru's boss.

This office, which overlooks this idyllic Haven of Peace, is anything but. An official called Erasmus Terimo knocks and enters. Four per cent has been lopped off the budget of the Department. He joins the Director who is gazing out of the window, not at the harbour but at the traffic bustling by on Ocean Drive, a piece of California fast lane transplanted rather unsuccessfully into this equatorial town. Terimo counts the Mercedes slowing down, changing gear to avoid the potholes.

'See down there,' Terimo says, pointing to the Drive which leads to the docks of Dar. 'Thousands of new Mercedes come in here every year. There must be 10,000 in East Africa.'

There are 10,000 elephants being looted for their ivory each year in Tanzania and Costa Mlay and Terimo both know it. One elephant for one limo. A simple equation . . .

Six floors below them, down on the Drive, they are observing the other end of the chain of corruption that quietly

4

twists and grips its sinuous and secretive way from Hanga village, from Kilimasera, from the Selous, until it reaches Dar es Salaam where what was begun under the blanket of the night is transformed into a lurching cavalcade, a status symbol, something gleaming and potent, a piece of machinery whose horn can be blown in the face of poverty and all those potholes. For two years Costa Mlay has sweated to chop that chain. First he engineered Tanzania's campaign to ban ivory trafficking. Then he persuaded the Government to declare war against the poachers, the middlemen who fund them and the politicians who enjoy the fruits of corruption. It is a dangerous business. Twice he has had to vanish, leaving his wife and children in Dar es Salaam, while the police investigated the death threats he had received. Today, with the morning mail stacked high in his in-tray, he is about to receive another.

Elephants get drunk. Elephants have size 45 feet. Elephants suffer from corns. Elephants find private places to make love. Elephants sing. Elephants teach their young manners. Elephants punish anti-social behaviour. They dance, they court, they stroke each other. Elephants bathe languidly and long. Elephants are choice piano keys. Elephants are billiard balls. Elephants are bad false teeth. Elephants are a problem. They trample down *shambas* and carelessly crush crops and fences. They uproot trees. They destroy man's work. In one night a year's living can disappear. Elephants are made of flesh and blood and gristle and dentine. Elephants are meat. The trunk is said to be delicious, the heart a delicacy. Smoked elephant, where the flesh is cut into strips and dried in the sun or over a fire, can sustain a village for a month.

Elephants are big. Far, far bigger than Man. They uplift the spirit of humanity by their very size. They serve to remind us that we do not possess the sole rights to this earth. But Man and Elephants need space.

There were 50,000 elephants in Tanzania's Selous Game Reserve two years ago. Now there are just 30,000. In 730 days, 20,000 elephants were killed, hunted down like dogs for their ivory. That makes 30 a day, 60 tusks, and the slaughter wasn't aimed only at the bigger tuskers, the bulls whose trophies would fetch the highest prices. The killing was indiscriminate; where once only the choice bulls

5

carrying tusks of over fifty or sixty kilos were tracked down and hunted, now any elephant was a target. Size of ivory just didn't concern the *jangili* who were sure that, however small the tusk, they would obtain a good price.

There is a vast, grey stone warehouse on the edge of Dar es Salaam which bears witness to the massacre. Inside it is cavernous and gloomy, reeking the atmosphere of the morgue. In the dim light it is difficult not to trip over the rows and rows of objects littering the floor, and as the eyes become accustomed to the darkness, these things begin to catch whatever light they can, almost as if they are crying out to be noticed. They are tusks, dozens of them, neatly laid out in long, long lines that vanish into the interior dusk. They are tiny, most no more than two feet long. Some are even smaller, less than twelve inches, a pathetic reminder of the infant animal, still warm when they were gashed out of its body.

These are the trophies that have been seized by Costa Mlay's men: Ireneus Ndunguru has sent hundreds of tusks here under armed guard. But thousands more pieces of ivory have escaped Mlay's dragnet only to be fashioned into ornate sculptures and cheap trinkets, the sort you see on an airport quick-change counter.

Here in this tropical charnel house it is difficult to comprehend that these orderly rows of remains were once creatures who ate and loved and scratched their backs against trees, who wallowed in mud and showered each other with fun. Now they are exhibits. This room, backing on to the railway line that leads into the interior westwards, following the identical route that was trodden by the slavers one hundred years before, is the Auschwitz of the Elephant.

TWO

Shaking the Dollar Tree

Iam sitting drinking Safari beer in the mezzanine lounge of Dar es Salaam's finest hotel, feeling the sweat trickle down my neck and trying not to surrender to impatience. Why am I impatient? Surely this is idyllic; the heat, the turquoise pool in the garden where languid United Nations staff splash for hours in the algae, the palm-shaded bar beside it, serving steak *à la* Firestone and rice, the torpid ambience of the Kilimanjaro Hotel, where I seem to be the only guest.

When will I see an elephant? When the Director of Wildlife, Costa Mlay, answers his phone, opens his door, clears his desk and flashes the green light that will allow me to leave the city for the bush so that I can meet the men whose job it is to protect the decimated herds of elephants in the country.

But no message arrives. I try to retain the casual air I have so laboriously constructed round myself and decide whether or not to order another Safari. It's a weak, schmaltzy beer which is full of bubbles and causes problems after the third bottle. I am on my fourth. I wriggle in my seat for the sake of propriety and at the same time my eyes attempt to penetrate the shadowy and inert mass of room that is sheltering itself from the sun behind its dense brown curtains.

I am waiting for a messenger. I do not know in what shape he will materialize, only that he will be black and as smart as a frayed collar allows. I have visited Africa enough times to recognize a civil servant.

Another gulp of Safari. I must make them last. More sweat, another Benson, a further furtive check.

A man approaches and introduces himself with the wide

7

grin that says sorry I've kept you waiting, here are all your permissions, you can leave immediately, and don't worry about transport – we're providing you with a Land Rover, a driver and a plane.

This man is not clad in civil service regulation white shirt and grey flannels. He is wearing a khaki shirt with epaulettes, lots of buttons and olive-green trousers bagged out below the knee by bulging pockets. There are more zips on his legs than you'd see on a varicose veins case.

'Hello, I am Juma. You are here by yourself?' He looks at the empty seats drawn up hopefully round my table.

'Are you from the Wildlife Ministry, Juma?'

Juma laughs and sits down, fingering the half-empty bottle of Safari.

'Is this your first time in Dar es Salaam?' He helps himself to a swig.

'No. I was here twenty . . . do you want a drink?'

'That would be nice.'

Silence. I wait for the waiter to decide that the time is right for him to make an approach.

'Do you want a woman?'

'Go away.'

'Have you ever had an African woman?'

His head swivels away from the beer to the silent girls with loris eyes who wait in the gloom by the door of the gents toilet on the other side of the mezzanine.

'That one in red.' Juma's eyes are lasering her, willing her to stiffen herself out of the slouch she has adopted to while away the hours so that she can offer herself and her military red dress all the better.

I am here in Tanzania to write about ivory poaching. My time is short. There is a deadline drowning in Safari beer somewhere inside my skull. I am anxious for information. Any leads which I can fasten upon – like ivory. I decide to ask.

'You want some ivory, now?' There is a look of pity in his eyes. 'Go downstairs to the hotel shop. They sell lovely ivory carvings there.'

Juma is not to be diverted. He asks me my name. He asks me what I am doing in Dar. Unashamedly he brings up the subject of women again.

8

'They grip you so you will never forget. I tell you, you will never want a white woman again.'

'Have you ever had a white woman, Juma?'

'I am the father of a girl in America.'

'*America?*'

'Yes, America. I was a student there. Accountancy.'

'So why are you selling girls in the Kilimanjaro?'

'Because it pays me to do so. Do you know what I earn as an accountant? Only a few thousand shillings a month.' A Safari beer costs 250 shillings. Juma raises his glass, drains it and looks at me hopefully.

People are drifting into the bar, and I am anxious not to be missed. I calculate that it is better for me to be sitting alone. That way I will be conspicuous, but I do not reckon with African lassitude. It is now well into the afternoon, and my phone calls to the Director's office have gone unanswered. Juma leaves me to be absorbed by the shadows with just the humhum of the air conditioning units in the bar to converse with.

I had visited the Kilimanjaro Hotel before, twenty years before, when I had finished a year of voluntary service, teaching in the Sudan, with a three-month vacation in East Africa. What a place this hotel had been then, a Mecca to a youth starved of life's little luxuries. There was a breakfast bar, self-service, with cornflakes and milk, bacon and eggs, fruit juice; there was beer, and English cigarettes and the Archies singing 'Sugar Sugar'. There were men in wild tropical shirts straight from Notting Hill Carnival, bar girls who danced and drank and looked as though they were enjoying it; there were Asians, cooking rice outside tiny rooms on curried corridors, waiting for permission to leave for a corner shop in Leicester.

Today that breakfast bar is still there, downstairs and across the lobby to the right. But there are no cornflakes, no bacon, no eggs, no Asians, gone to Leicester every one. Inside, running my finger along the self-service counter, and making patterns in the dust and grease, I realize it's not me that's changed, but Tanzania. Twenty years ago, the roads were reasonable, the city was growing up, literally, the Kilimanjaro Hotel worked, even though the air conditioning units in the bedrooms leaked at night and made you wish you'd brought a pair of gumboots with you. The trains ran,

9

not quite on time, but at least they departed and arrived; the food on the railways was simple, owing much to the old-style British Rail fare – Brown Windsor, braised steak, fruit cocktail, that'll be 7s.6d., thank you very much sir.

Now the trains seldom run at all, and if you travel as I did in 1970, from Dar to Moshe, you would be well advised to stay awake all night, and however hot you may feel, on no account open the steel-shuttered windows to take the air. Thieves prey upon this line, running alongside the train as it crawls past trackside settlements, and hopping into any open window to steal whatever is at hand.

The roads in Dar may have been designed, as roads are, to make communication within the city efficient and quick, but after a generation of independence they are pockmarked with craters and serve only to destroy vehicles, even Land Rovers and Landcruisers.

Twenty years on, the Kilimanjaro, like Tanzania, has not improved. The chair in which I sit is further evidence of the time warp I am trapped in. It is a low-backed, short-legged creature which owes its existence to some fashionable designer of the sixties. It gives me backache so, in return, I give it some essence of Safari.

I decide this chair is exactly the piece of furniture that Julius Nyerere would have created if he had been into furniture instead of politics. If only this man, this great and revered Tanzanian, had dealt in wood instead of people! Inside my briefcase, which is nestling beneath the chair, and which I find difficult to retrieve thanks to my discomfort, is a piece of paper that records one of the founder-President's most infamous speeches, grandly entitled 'The Arusha Manifesto' of 21 September 1969. This is what it says:

> The survival of our wildlife is a matter of grave concern to all of us in Africa. These wild creatures amid the wild places they inhabit are not only important as a source of wonder and inspiration but are an integral part of our natural resources, blah, blah, blah . . .

The Nyerere-waffle amounts to an empty shell of puffed-out dreams. He goes on to promise:

> . . . We solemnly declare that we will do everything in our power to make sure that our children's grand-

children will be able to enjoy this rich and precious inheritance.

Oh, really? Now, unlike the former President, I don't profess to be an expert on elephants. I'd never fed them buns as a child. In fact, I couldn't stand those visits to the zoo, when parents would cling to my hand as if they feared the animals might catch something from me, and force me, up in their arms, to lick the rustiness of the cage steel and inhale the pungent fumes of stale excrement. As for the animals, they looked out of sorts and out of place, and decidedly bored and unhappy. I suppose I was an odd child. I know the Latin name for the African elephant, but maybe the Swahili would be more useful out here. *Tembo.* Sounds more like the seaside resort I was brought up in in South Wales than this great lumbering beast whose uncertain future had caused acres of rain forest to be hewn down and on whose broad back many of Britain's leading trendies had clambered, some because they simply couldn't bear to be out of the papers and others because they genuinely believed that elephants were good and should be saved.

One hundred years ago, Alfred J. Swann passed through this city. Of course, Dar was just a staging post then. Zanzibar was the gem where the money and the power and influence resided. Alfred J. was a sailor (ret'd) who was either foolish or brave, but more probably unimaginative. He answered an advert placed by a missionary society who required an experienced sailor to transport a steam boat in sections from Zanzibar right across the interior to Lake Tanganyika where it would be used to patrol the waters and spread the heavenly word upon them. Swann was equal to the task. He recorded his adventures in his book, *Fighting the Slave Hunters in Central Africa*, and a more mordantly observed snapshot of those grotesque times you would not want to read.

Swann meets a mile-long chain of human misery. The slaves are manacled, some have their necks fastened together with six-foot wooden yokes. There are women, too, carrying in one arm a baby, in the other a tusk. Their bodies are scarred by the *chikote* (a piece of hide used as a whip); their feet and shoulders are covered in flies, feeding on the blood that runs from their festering sores.

11

And here am I, six miles from Dar es Salaam International Airport, and all I've seen is one pimp, a few prossies, and a tableful of empty Safaris, growing misty as the condensation inside the bottle rises to the neck of each one. I glance over at the girls in the bar. They are coming to life, opening their petals, reacting not to light but to the sudden increase in white expatriates who are crowding the tables, gesturing for drinks, and causing the whores to raise their expectations along with their skirts.

The girl in the red dress, Juma's choice, is joined by a florid white, who has clearly been so long out of Africa that he doesn't know sideburns are now *de trop* in England. Perhaps he was a long-distance trucker in the UK, or the proprietor of a travelling brothel operating out of the back of a furniture van in lay-bys from Shap Fell to Scotch Corner. Whatever he was, he's chatting up the girl, though it is plain he cannot speak Swahili, and her English amounts only to 'beer' and 'sterling'. They rise, he first, then the girl, and walk towards the lobby. The couple vanish behind the lift doors. I see it is going up.

If Tippu Tib walked into the Kilimanjaro, there'd be some changes, I'd put money on it, a fat wad of greasy Tanzanian shillings, which wouldn't be worth the paper they were printed on. In Tippu Tib's day, a girl could be bought in Zanzibar for a handful of beads. A beautiful girl at that. Tippu Tib – the name translates as 'The Man with the Flickering Eyelids' – was the most ruthless exponent of the ivory trade that ever lived and a sworn enemy of Alfred J. This was not because Alfred J. disapproved of the taking of tusks from elephants. Alfred J. was not a muscular Green, he was an Englishman, a Christian and a sailor, in that order. What touched his tripartite heart more than anything was the slave trade, but, as Tippu Tib knew well, slaves and ivory go together wrist in manacle. You couldn't transport ivory without some wretch to carry it, because ivory was bulky and heavy, and the markets where it would be sold to European and American dealers far from the killing grounds. Indeed as more and more elephants were killed, the caravans were forced to venture further into the interior to find their raw material.

But that was a hundred years ago. Girls in the Kilimanjaro

are less beautiful, and more dangerous, the slave trade is crushed, the Arab dominance a memory, Tippu Tib's eyelids flicker no more, Alfred J. Swann is an entry in an antiquarian bookseller's catalogue, and elephants, despite what the former President vowed in 1969, are still being slaughtered.

I didn't know why. But then I hadn't met Costa Mlay, or Ireneus Ndunguru. I hadn't flown over the Selous in Gerard Bigurube's tiny Cessna and watched his tiny eyes silently pleading to see just one elephant. I hadn't met Vincent the *deriva* or Boniface. I hadn't drunk with Captain Katali in the New Super Moscow Bar. And, as for Alensio Bero and the Mchawi, who were they?

I didn't know that another form of slavery was strangling Tanzania, a far more insidious and subtle form than ever the Arabs had practised. I didn't know the country was running out of hard currency, that the men who fought the poachers were armed with old-fashioned weapons, not the semi-automatics the *jangili* possessed. I didn't know that a moral vacuum existed in Tanzania, and that the death of one elephant was leading to the extinction of a nation. Nor did I know about the night. That it was another country, which I would find impossible to enter.

All I knew was that it was past eight o'clock in this seedy city and I was doing what most journalists do all their working lives. Drinking. Waiting.

THREE

The Trouble with Kibasa

First I stared at my watch. It was six o'clock and the dawn mist was struggling to get past the windows of my bedroom on the third floor of the hotel and lick me awake. The bedroom door was talking to me, an urgent message. Not another proposition! Girls had been knocking on it all night, a gentle feminine tap-tap-tap, followed by a sweet voice saying: 'I am your friend, please let me come in. I will be good to you.'

But at six o'clock that morning, the voice behind the knocking was calm, and deep, and persuasively called out my name.

I padded across the lino floor, missing the pools of tepid water that the air conditioning unit had mysteriously produced overnight, and slid open the bolt. It was Juma.

'You say you are interested in the elephant, Mr Nick?' Juma rested his arm on the doorpost.

'Not your sort, Juma.' I thought of all the long, fizzy hours of yesterday.

'Now, really, Mr Nick, I have moved the earth to help you. I am here to take you to Kibasa.'

'Oh God, not another taxi.'

'Kibasa is a man, Mr Nick. He knows about *tembo*. He is the greatest anti-poacher in Tanzania.' He would fetch Kibasa, Mr Nick, bring him to the Kili, Mr Nick, for breakfast, if he could find him, Mr Nick. I could see that he was embarrassed and that he genuinely wanted to help me. Why? Because he was a hustler and he needed the money. I'd met his type before in Africa. They see a white man as a tree, laden with the fruit of the dollar or sterling. Their whole *raison d'être* is based on the whereabouts of that tree.

Wherever the tree goes, they must follow. Every few days, the tree must be shaken vigorously and the fruit gathered up and pocketed.

As time goes by, and less and less fruit appears on the branches, the frequency of shaking must be increased. So too must the effort made to dislodge the fruit, for by this time, which is often too late, the dollar tree is aware it is being attacked and it tends to protect itself from the parasite which is clinging to its branches by whatever method it can. Often these dollar trees have been known to wreak cruel and vicious revenge on their enemies, so Juma be warned.

Still, I'd known him for less than a day and he had not yet extracted any money from me. Only beer.

Kibasa was a stout, powerfully built man with receding hair and a dignified expression. He rose to receive me in the hotel's lobby, upright as an assegai. He was bulging out of an immaculately pressed chocolate-brown Kaunda suit. His brown shoes were spotless. He was in his early forties. His face was round and polished. Someone, his mother maybe, had been busy with the dark tan.

'Who told you about me?' he asked.

'Only Juma, Mr Kibasa.' He grinned, disarming me so early in the morning as he slapped his knees, a habit I was to see much of in the next few weeks, a habit that I later found papered over the deep resentment he harboured. When Kibasa smiled, the eyes, cheekbones and mouth, working together, lit up the face and transformed the man. The seriousness had vanished for a moment.

'That Juma, he is a devil, but he is not just a pimp. Let's have some coffee downstairs.'

Over the Kilimanjaro's self-service breakfast, Kibasa – his first name is Charles, his middle, Wickson – told me he had been a game warden in a number of parks and he had been dealing with ivory poaching for almost eighteen years. He wanted to show me what was going on in the parks, how elephants were being killed, and why the park wardens and rangers were often powerless to stop the slaughter.

It seemed to be all that I needed, but then I didn't know that Kibasa wasn't telling me everything.

'What about my appointment with Costa Mlay?'

Kibasa smiled for the second time that day. Again he

15

slapped his hands on his knees and said: 'He is a very busy man. He is leading the fight to persuade the world to place the elephant on the endangered species list. You won't see him today. We are going to Mikumi.'

Kibasa sat back, holding his coffee cup in one hand, the other gesturing out of the window, waving me away from the ocean, the city, and into the bush. Mikumi was the nearest national park to the city, a few hundred kilometres to the west. He knew it well. He had once been its chief game warden.

'Juma will take us there.'

'Oh, no.'

'He has a very good Land Rover.'

I agreed. I had no choice.

The pimp-accountant-seducer of American womanhood, and now driver, was flinging the Land Rover from side to side as we negotiated one of the worst pieces of road in Africa. I hesitate to call it a road. It runs from Dar es Salaam to Chilesi, over 100 kilometres of craters and chasm, joined together by meagre strips of tar. Besides the state of the roads, Juma had to read the pitiless minds of the bus drivers, truckers and cyclists coming his way. They were more unpredictable than the road, playing macho games much to the pleasure of their passengers who cheered each time Juma was forced to give way.

I sat in the back, gripping the handrail in front of me, sliding from window to window, with my bottom firmly planted on the bench seat for never more than a minute. The kamikaze seat next to Juma was empty. Kibasa crouched behind, nursing a shiny black executive-style briefcase between his knees.

This wasn't a friendly piece of road. Granted it was metalled, but that was about the only concession it made to the Land Rover, which fought it every inch of the way from Dar. The vehicle was built for punishment, but I doubted whether it would be capable of surviving the spite of the road and the brainstorming quirkiness of Juma's driving. At every opportunity, and he contrived to find many, he would sink his weight onto the accelerator pedal, drilling his body down to the depths of the vehicle's floor as if he was trying to crush a particularly loathsome creature. Potholes, cyclists,

plodders were ignored. So too were those warning clouds
of dust that floated slowly and inexorably towards us, each
one signifying, with a thunder that filled the choking sky,
the approach of a 44-ton lorry on its way to the city. As he
grew more confident, the speed increased, and as the speed
increased, so he became cock of the road, often turning
round to grin foolishly at me. Juma liked grinning. His teeth
were fine and white and even. Or he would crack his hand,
slap down against the leatherette seat, empty beside him,
to emphasize, I am certain, his lack of respect for those
passengers, Kibasa and me, who were too intent upon survival to perceive his skills at the wheel.

All this time, Kibasa and I were being tossed from one
side of the vehicle to the other, and try as we might to retain
some stability, it was impossible. Our conversation was pep-
pered by sudden involuntary lunges to the left and right, to
the front and back. As I swung from the straphang, trying
to ignore the agony of a shoulder that was continually being
wrenched from its socket, I forced myself to talk to Kibasa.
He was telling me, between the rolls and the swerves, the
dust and the hooting, that he had worked for over twenty
years in the Wildlife Service. He had studied at the Wildlife
College at Mweka and had continued his education at the
University of Arizona in Phoenix. He was an experienced
game warden and had arrested many poachers. He was
married to a teacher who lived in Iringa, some 200 kilometres
north-west of Mikumi. He had worked in Ruaha National
Park which was further away to the west, beyond Iringa,
and had then been transferred to Mikumi.

I asked him where he was working at present and he said
nothing, looking down at the floor of the Land Rover. I
thought that maybe he was feeling sick, maybe his stomach
had had its fill of Juma's capricious skill and so I waited and
asked him again.

'I am not working at the moment. I am suspended from
my duties.'

I asked him why, sensing a story here.

'It is difficult to tell,' he said, looking up from the floor.
His briefcase was still wedged between his knees, despite
the battering that we were both suffering. He wiped his
brow with a white handkerchief and muttered into it. I
couldn't hear what he said and decided to wait. It was no

use pressing him, especially as the roar and whine of the engine made talk so difficult. But I thought. I began to ask myself questions. Maybe Kibasa had problems. Drink? I hadn't seen him touch a drop of Safari or anything harder. Was he a failure? That didn't seem to fit either. Whatever the reasons for his suspension, this man possessed a profound sense of dignity. He was, I could see, a neat and proud man. He looked me in the eye and had a firm handshake. Now I know this sounds public-school, but it is the basis often for sound judgement, and Kibasa, I knew, met these criteria.

Juma decided he would stop in Morogoro, halfway to Mikumi, not to ease our bottoms, or rest our spines, but because the market there was renowned for cheap and fresh food. We had no choice. As he went off with his straw basket looking for bargains, I wandered round the market, which a chipped inscription in English revealed had been opened in 1953. The market place had been built in the style of another, older, empire, not British but Roman, but by the look of it, no lick of paint had been applied in all those intervening years.

The town itself had seen better times. The mud roads were awash with water from the rains of the night before; the one imposing building, the three-storey wooden-balconied Rathaus where the German military had planned their campaign during the First World War, leaned on the street dolefully waiting for the past to reassert itself, for snappy soldiers to bark out orders, for a brass band to salute the officers who over seventy years before had paraded each day and then clanked into the mess to pastry their moustaches.

'You think this town is dead?' said Kibasa. 'It isn't. Far from it. These people in Morogoro, they are poachers, *jangili*, and if they are not actually killing elephants, then they are on the side of the poacher. You will never persuade a jury to convict a *jangili* if he comes to court here.'

'What about the magistrates?'

'They, too, are sympathetic.' Kibasa looked at me sternly but said nothing more. He walked on ahead, briefcase clasped in one massive hand.

The Land Rover was full of bananas, potatoes, rice, grape-

fruit, beans, corn, a mobile greengrocery. I asked Kibasa
what Juma was going to do with all this produce.

'He'll sell it in Dar for a small profit.'

'Won't it go off?'

'That won't worry Mister Juma.'

Mikumi is the show-piece park of southern Tanzania. It is
not large, nor within its 3,250 square kilometres of flood
plain does it harbour an extraordinary array of wildlife. It
owes its prestige to its proximity to Dar es Salaam. Ambassa-
dors, visiting diplomats, conservationists, royalty, all make
the bumpy trek up the Chilesi–Morogoro road to stay in
Mikumi.

One VIP who didn't quite make it was the Russian
Ambassador. I saw his coffin on its way back to Dar that
afternoon on my way to the park. He had made the fatal
decision of ordering his driver into the passenger seat so
that he could drive. The accident happened a few kilometres
beyond Morogoro, when the front wheel of the embassy
Mercedes caught itself in a particularly deep pothole and
forced the car to career off the road and into the ditch. An
army Land Rover, its lights blazing weakly in the afternoon
glare, signalled the approach of His Late Excellency. The
corpse was in the second car. I suppose all they could find
to carry the coffin comfortably was a long-wheelbase Toyota.
As the cortège, full of its grisly self-importance, sped by,
back to Dar and the first available flight to Moscow, even
Juma slowed down, not, I believe, out of respect, but
because, like us, he knew these roads were truly democratic,
a tribute to Socialist thinking, and that it was right and
maybe fitting for the representative of such a country to die
this way. Potholes do not pick out the rich or the poor.

It wasn't until we entered the park boundary that Kibasa
told me he could not accompany me any further. The closer
we were to Mikumi, the quieter and more withdrawn he
became. I thought this was because he had been touched by
the sight of the makeshift hearse, but he said that he would
explain at dinner that night at his house in Mikumi village.

'It is best I am not seen in the park lodge. There are
troubles. Juma will bring you to my house.' He got out, still
clutching the briefcase, and walked into the bush.

Troubles? Who had troubles? Already Juma was making tentative movements in the dollar tree direction, suggesting that his Land Rover 'might ride smoother with a new shock absorber and I know a man in Dar who could fit it fast', and now Kibasa vanishes into the elephant grass.

I had a story to file to London, I had missed an opportunity of meeting Costa Mlay, the most important man in wildlife in the country, by agreeing to come on this journey. I was miles away from any contact in Dar, not that I had any, and now the man I had come to see, the man with all the information, had done a runner.

As the Land Rover slides and grinds and bumps from pothole to pothole, and finally pulls in outside the Park Warden's HQ, I see the rangers in their green fatigues and forage caps idling outside their headquarters. A Tanzanian flag lolls at half-mast. The Ayatollah is dead, I am told. 'And Mr Salman Rushdie is sipping champagne in London,' laughs the newly appointed Warden, Mr Mtaiko. He is small and neat in white shirt and cream trousers and this is his first posting as a warden. He looks like a schoolboy, a specially enthusiastic and uninspired plodder who has been instructed by the headmaster to show the visitors all the brownie points the school is proud to exhibit.

His men parade before me, a Dad's Army platoon, ranging from Corporal Wilfred, 6 ft 3 in and armed with a Chinese SAR (semi-automatic rifle), to Private Alex, flabby and unshaven, jolly and a father of six. Alex is suffering from high blood pressure and asks me, as soon as he can contrive to find me alone, whether I have a Walkman for him.

There is a ranger without boots, just cheap trainers, and a ranger wearing flip-flops, because his boots rotted and could not protect his feet from a thorn bush. He limps to the parade ground, a gravelled clearing round a flag-pole, carrying a muzzle-loader seized the previous year after an 'exchange of fire'.

There's a ranger shouldering a twelve-bore that was made in Birmingham by Wesley and Scott. It looks a hundred years old. 'You see,' says the Warden, 'these men are not armed well. The poachers have SARs.'

Alex Byatti, the ranger with a yen for a Sony, has been in the service for eighteen years. He enters the Warden's office and salutes surprisingly crisply for such a sloppy-looking soldier, setting down his huge boot with a shudder. His uniform is too frail and worn to hold in his Kilimanjaro-sized gut. Bits of Alex Byatti are appearing from it everywhere. I can just make out, beneath all the blubber, the remnants of a well-trained and disciplined askari.

'Yes, the *jangili* have better weapons than us. In 1974 when I was in the Serengeti, they were using bows and arrows. I know, I was shot by one. An arrow hit me . . . here.' Alex Byatti points to his shirt. Mercifully, he does not attempt to disrobe. 'It went through my shirt.' He pats his gut. 'If I were the size I am today, the *jangili* could hardly have missed me.'

'What happened to the poacher, Alex?'

'I had to shoot him. Broke both his arms.'

Alex motions me outside. 'Mr Nick, I will show you what we do to poachers.' Two young wretches are plucked from somewhere round the back of the Warden's office – Africa is a continent of extras, there is always someone ready to enter the scene – and they are pushed, pulled, jabbed and frogmarched to the scene of the would-be arrest.

The rangers swing their rifle butts at the boys' heads and throw them into the grass. The rangers smile. They are enjoying this. The boys, well, they are not so certain. Alex fixes his bayonet and his snaky eye on the youths, both now on their knees in front of him. He has to be reminded that this is only an exercise. Only a charade, Alex.

'Who was the warden before you?' I ask Mtaiko.

'Kibasa.' Alex too has heard my question. 'He gave us incentives,' he murmurs.

The Warden butts in quickly. 'Kibasa is a troublemaker,' he says, trying to exclude Alex from the conversation. 'He's been suspended. Ask Mr Babu.' Mr Babu is the head of the National Parks.

'Incentives?' I turned to Alex.

'If we recovered ivory, or if we arrested *jangili*, then we would get extra pay.'

'What do you earn?'

Alex's belly erupts. He is laughing. 'Not enough to live on. About 2,000 shillings a month.' Ten Safari beers, £10.

'Let me tell you about *tembo*, Mr Nick.' Mtaiko moistens his lips, eager to change the subject. 'Do you know how many there are in Mikumi? Less than 2,000. And have you noticed how small they are?'

I hadn't, because I had yet to see an elephant. But I don't let on. The Warden continues. 'There were 13,000 elephants here at the end of the seventies. We have lost 11,000 in ten years.'

One thousand a year. Thirty a day.

He takes me to the motor pool where I see the carcasses of Land Rovers. It's more like a graveyard than a garage. None of the vehicles is working. Three of them slump, gutted in the dirt, their front wheels splayed out in a kind of mechanical rigor mortis. I leave Mikumi with all the colour I need. I can gauge how demoralized the men are. This is not the way a park should be. Even I can see that, and Mikumi is my first. The park is a shambles, the men demoralized, the Warden out of his depth. And then I think, it is only a year since Kibasa left, so why if he is telling me the truth has everything gone downhill so fast? Why was Kibasa suspended? Is he a troublemaker? Or does he know too much?

It was eight o'clock when Juma found Kibasa's house at the third or fourth attempt. We drove from the Park Lodge to Mikumi village and then Juma admitted he was lost. He turned the vehicle up the escarpment that leads to Iringa, and after thirty minutes of icy silence between us with only the grinding of gears and the tinny rattle and thump of the Land Rover pitching and tossing on the dirt road to conceal the tension, we reached his house.

Actually it was no more than a hut with a yard. Kibasa sat on his verandah, watching a child, his nephew it turned out, play in the dust.

'We'll eat outside,' he said, flicking at a squadron of mosquitoes circling with intent two inches above his head. I fished for the anti-mossy cream in my bag and started to smear any part of my body that was exposed. Kibasa dismissed Juma, telling him to pick me up at eleven.

We ate rice and chicken, and drank coffee. There were hard-boiled eggs, and then fruit which I refused. Instead, I took another egg. Better for the logging, or rather, I hoped, non-logging. I decided I would try first an obsequious approach and then follow up with attack. Sycophancy had served me well in journalism, and I prided myself on how accomplished a toad I had become.

'Well, Charles, I've seen Mikumi. It's a shambles, isn't it? I'm surprised there are any elephants, let alone 2,000.'

He looked at me for a long time before speaking. When he opened his mouth, the words came out deep and considered. He was touched with the dignity of an Old Testament prophet.

'Nick, it is a great shame. I spent almost ten years of my life over there,' he said, nodding towards the park, 'and I had a good success with it. I didn't stop the poaching, who can? But I arrested it.'

I needed to know how. Kibasa sat back in his wooden-armed chair with its ethnic rug cast over the back like an antimacassar in an old folk's rest home. This could have been Cheltenham except for the heat, the flies, the dust and the colour of Kibasa's face.

'You really want to know? Those askaris earn nothing. They've got *shambas*. They keep chickens, they grow their own maize and rice . . . '

I agreed. They were running out of ways to make a living in the bush.

'Nick, they poach. They have to survive.'

'Why didn't you stop them?'

'I did.' Kibasa rapped the arm of his chair. 'The first move I made was to sack seven askaris. They were poaching, no doubt at all. So I got rid of them. They can earn 200 shillings for a tusk from the middleman in Mikumi village. A few days' poaching,' Kibasa jabbed a finger at me, 'three years' wages.'

'Tell me about the go-between.'

'Oh, the *bwana mkubwa*. He's still here, still working. He's a farmer, only he doesn't farm, if you see what I mean.'

I'd dropped the obsequious tone by now; in fact, I couldn't remember adopting it. I liked Kibasa. He was talking from the hip.

'So, Charles, why isn't he behind bars?'

'Why am I out of a job?' Kibasa looked out into the darkness, his face now lit up, now in shade as the breeze pushed and pulled the flame of the hurricane lamp first one way and then the other.

'I've told you once,' he began slowly, 'and I'm sure I'll

tell you again. This is a war and sometimes the enemy is on our own side. I suspected this when I came to Mikumi, and I decided to make spot checks on the askaris. There was not even a patrol book there to log their movements. My deputy, Mr Balosi, was on patrol one day and saw elephant carcasses near a rangers' post. The patrol book which I had introduced made no mention of these dead elephants. The rangers couldn't explain it, so I sacked them. I believe they had sold the tusks already.'

That night I learnt of Kibasa's extraordinary record in anti-poaching and later I confirmed it both in Dar and in Frank-furt at the headquarters of the Zoological Society who were monitoring the poaching situation in Tanzania.

In November 1986, he seized 46 tusks weighing 209 kilos after ambushing a *jangili* band; between January and October 1987, two tusks were found and six firearms ranging from muzzle-loaders to a .375 hunting rifle. At the same time Kibasa introduced the incentive system that Alex Byatti was asking questions about.

He told me how the askaris were rewarded for their loy-alty, so that every time they found a tusk, he found some extra money for them. He paid out between 10,000 and 20,000 shillings in that way. It made a great difference, he felt. It raised morale, the askaris felt that for the first time they were valued, and the poaching figures took a sharp turn downwards. So they had. Between 1986 and 1989 500 elephants were killed in the park. The figures for the ten years before that, between 1976 and 1979, showed that 7,000 elephants were slaughtered.

'You know, Nick, when I was warden of Mikumi, more and more elephants came here. I swear that once an elephant crossed the boundary and was grazing in my park, that elephant knew he was safe. You only had to look at them, feeding, or looking after their young. They were relaxed.'

We looked at the dregs of our coffee, but Kibasa wasn't going to stop now. He told me about the Mikumi he loved, about its elephants and the great game reserve which it borders: the Selous, with not a single village inside it, the home of 30,000 elephants, Africa's last hope for the species. For centuries elephants have migrated between Mikumi and the Selous.

'My whole life revolves around a single object.' Kibasa turned towards me. '*Tembo*, Nick, elephants.'

'And now you are no longer here?'

'Mikumi' – he sighed – 'is like the elephant without the matriarch. Once she is taken away, killed for her tusks, then the others in the herd, the young, sit around and mope. They do not know what to do. They become badly behaved. Or they starve and die.'

I had two questions, but I wasn't certain Kibasa would answer. What was patently obvious was his anger and dismay at what was happening to the elephants in the park he had so painfully reconstructed. His park, his elephants. I decided to try. 'You know too much, Charles, don't you?'

'Yes.'

'Will you help me?' Kibasa nodded.

'Have you heard of Mama Tombo?'

'No.' But I had. Mama Tombo was the District Commissioner, the Party boss, in Ifakara.

'Whose side is she on?'

'Not mine. Not yours.'

I asked Kibasa if he would take me to Ifakara, but he shook his head and said it would be pointless. The Mama would give nothing away, and even if I did manage to see her, what would I ask her? It was far too dangerous to go to Ifakara, he said, his voice pitched low rather as if he thought that every word he spoke was being swallowed by the shadows and sounds of the African night.

It took me over half an hour, a hot and increasingly sticky half-hour, to fix my mosquito net and crawl into bed. The net I had bought in London did not have a wooden bar to hang from the ceiling; just a series of loops and hooks and net (like a bra or a corset you'd once see in a Soho sex shop) and, as there was nothing on the walls of the bedroom in the Safari Lodge on which to attach them, I had been forced to do a Pickfords in my room and move the bed into the centre of the room, climb up the curtains and knot them to the rail, anyway you get the drift.

I was lying there in the usual ocean of sweat, about to fall into a doze, when there was a scratch on the door. I ignored it. Maybe it was a rat. I could do without admitting rats into

25

my room. Then the scratch became a knock, less inhibited this time.

'Yes.'

'It's me, Juma. Is that Mr Nick?'

'No, it's President Nyerere, and I'll have your balls for disturbing me.'

'You must not say things like that, Mr Nick, you will get into big trouble.'

'You'll be in trouble, Juma. What do you want now?'

'I will tell you about Mama Tombo and Ifakara. It will cost money, a lot of money.'

I told him that there was no point in making the journey. Juma, however, sensed money and was not to be put off. Here we go, the old dollar tree is about to receive a good shaking.

'No, no,' he urged. 'You will feel differently in the morning.'

'Well, tell me in the morning.'

'I must tell you now. They are bad people in Ifakara. They are all of them robberers.'

'They're what, Juma?'

'Robberers, Mr Nick. They are bad.'

'So are you, Juma, you are a robberer as well. How much?'

I was not, on any account, going to let him enter my bedroom, not because I suspected he was after my body – well, he was, but only in the capacity of a go-between – but because I dared not untangle myself from the arcane system that held up the net. To do so would literally bring down disaster upon my head. So the business had to be conducted between half an inch of plywood, with probably the whole Safari Lodge party to the ebb and flow of negotiation.

'No.'

'Why not?'

'Because I can't. That's why, Juma. Now *go to bed.*'

'I must not.' His use of the imperative confused me. Was it that serious? I struggled out of the net, doing my utmost to avoid the web of intricacy that secured it to the curtains. I tripped, pulling it down on top of me.

'Fuck!'

'Not here, Mr Nick. We are not in Dar now.'

The bugger was out there laughing at me. I opened the door and put on the light at the same time.

'My God, Mr Nick, what have you been doing? Have robberers been in your bedroom?'

Juma sat down languidly on the easy chair in the room which was tied to the leg of the bed. Now he reverted to his accountant's mode. He unzipped his trouser leg, and withdrew a notebook and pencil, which he proceeded to tap on the chair arm.

'I have made some calculations about petrol, wear and tear on the vehicle' – he always referred to the Land Rover as 'the vehicle' – 'my time as your guide and driver, food and overtime pay, and I say you owe me . . .'

I kicked him out. It was easy. Then I started to repair the damage in my bedroom.

Elephant grass. Just look up at it. Kibasa was standing fifty metres off the road outside Mikumi village. He had joined me early in the morning for breakfast at the Lodge and had suggested that we go looking for elephants. But all we could see was concealed by the elephant grass, ten-foot-high tendrils that wove across the path and smacked against the cheeks and thighs. There was further punishment here too. Tsetse flies, horny-backed bandits that flew out of the trees and targeted any flesh that happened to be within their range. They met their match in the stack of red-backed notebooks that I was carrying, little red gems they were, whose covers, when wielded in my hands, soon ran red with the blood and black with the eviscerated carcasses of any tsetse unfortunate enough to feel their wallop. Don't be fooled. Killing a tsetse is far from simple. Tsetses are no ordinary fly. They are the ninja warriors of the breed. They are fearless, armour-plated against all retaliation but for a direct hit followed up by a whacking crunch. The tsetse has to be manoeuvred to a hard surface, a vehicle windscreen, a tree, or, if extremely lucky, Juma's skull, and then pummelled to death with the force of dementia behind you.

I had told Kibasa of Juma's willingness to take me to Ifakara, and then of his attempt to extract more money out of me. He laughed at the first piece of information, and shook his head at the second. He wouldn't pay him another shilling. Already Juma had taken too much out of my wallet, and as for Ifakara, there was no point in going there. He reminded me of the advice he had given me last night. I think he was surprised that I could be swayed.

'Ifakara is a town that does not welcome strangers, but it is a haven for some.' This was Kibasa to a tee. Powerfully concise. The man wasted no words. His description was direct, simple and loaded with the menace of the place. His portrait of Ifakara was peopled with mosquitoes and middlemen, the *bwana mkubwa,* who both thrived on the greasy green swamp that edged the town. For it was the climate that made the place inhospitable for ordinary men and paradise for the mosquitoes. Ifakara, he said, was low and mean, and built by men who lived on ivory. There was a railhead there, too, which made transport to and from the area relatively easy, but for all that, no one ever went there unless they were on government business or they belonged to the *jangili.* Soldiers manned roadblocks all round the town, not to keep out the ivory dealers, as I thought they would, but to protect the hydro-electric dam nearby.

This dam was Mama Tombo's means of isolating the town, the key to her ascendancy. It supplied the electricity for Dar es Salaam. It was a national asset. It was strategically vital. Without it the enemies of Tanzania would rejoice, Dar would revert to hurricane lamps and the bush would claw itself back on the wide streets and into the high buildings of the city. That was why soldiers guarded the dam and the roads that led to it. Strangers were not wanted in Ifakara.

I asked who would go so far as to blow up the dam. Kibasa laughed and said 'No one'. But then, he continued, still smiling, that was not the point. The point was the threat. The Mama had sold the idea that her dam, yes she had adopted it as if it were a son, a first-born at that, was a top target for the South Africans, who were not at all pleased with the way the Tanzanian Government had oh-so-enthusiastically embraced political refugees from their country and issued them with blankets, rations, the Thoughts and Speeches of Julius Nyerere, the odd pound of plastic explosive and, of course, that guerrilla's vade mecum, the Kalashnikov.

The dam had been pumping out electricity reasonably efficiently for over twenty years now, and not one hostile finger, let alone a gun barrel, had been pointed at it. By now, Kibasa was roaring with laughter. 'Do you see the irony?' he asked. I nodded. For it was in those twenty years when generation after generation of servicemen had lounged at the side of rickety roadblocks waiting in vain for desperate men in combat trousers and jungle camouflage to destroy their dam that the plundering of the great herds had turned to massacre.

'These roadblocks. Are the soldiers trigger-happy?' I asked.

'No, they are bored. They ask for your papers, pretend to read them, but you can see by the sweat on their brows that most of them cannot read.'

I asked Kibasa about the Mama, what did she look like?

He ignored me, or perhaps he had not heard my question. His eyes were wandering through the screen of grass over to the mountains to the east of where we stood. He sniffed in the air, but I realized this was not for his well-being. He clutched my arm and pointed silently. I followed his eyes but saw nothing, heard nothing. I began to talk, trying my question again. He put his fingers to his lips, and turned away to the east.

'There! There!' he whispered, but by the time my eyes reached the point in the distance he had fixed upon, it was too late. All I could see was grass, tall, spiky elephant grass.

He smiled, shaking his head from side to side. He clapped my shoulders and said that I had missed the Mama by a fraction of a second.

'You asked me what the Mama looked like and there, out there, I saw her.' He paused, milking the moment. 'An elephant. A Mikumi elephant. Short, portly and feeling very relaxed. Just like the Mama.'

He didn't laugh for long, though, on that closed-in trail of bush. That elephant, the one I had failed to see, was an orphan. Most of the little elephants in Mikumi had lost their parents. For them the park was a haven, as Ifakara was a haven for the Mama. But Kibasa told me not to be fooled by sentiment.

'She controls the judiciary, the army, the police, the middlemen. They use her because she is politically safe. Now you know about the dam. That dam keeps everyone out. Almost everyone. I'll tell you, a few years ago when I was at Mikumi, I was driving towards Ifakara with an English official of some conservation body, and I said to him, look, there's a big middleman. I pointed out a brand new Land Rover coming our way. He asked me, like you did, why I did nothing about this man, especially if I knew what he was doing. I said nothing. He went back to Dar and reported this middleman to my boss, the minister in charge of our division. He was told that nothing could be done and, anyway, why should the word of a junior civil servant be taken?

'You see, that's what they see us as. Clerks. Well, I knew this middleman worked for Mama. The fact the minister did nothing proves nothing. The minister may or may not have known Mama, and let's assume he didn't, but what I'm trying to say is that whatever you do, it doesn't make any difference. People like the Mama will survive.'

'How are the police involved?'

'There have been cases where the ivory has been transported in government vehicles with police protection. This ensures the middlemen will be able to cross the roadblocks and reach Dar without any interference.'

I hadn't seen one elephant yet, but now I was aware of the extent of the problem. Mikumi had surrendered to incompetence, been overwhelmed by lack of resources, poor leadership; Mikumi was pitiful; what was needed was a stiff injection of money and moral courage. Then there was the Mama, the matriarch with her obeisant herd of henchmen, all of them chained to her purse and politics, each one of them – policeman, soldier, middleman and *jangili* – dedicated to the death of the elephant. And Kibasa? Kibasa was a warrior, but was even he resolute enough to win his personal battle?

I turned and made my way back along the path to the Land Rover where Juma was waiting. Kibasa followed and we sat in the vehicle, waiting for Juma to drive away. But not to Ifakara: 150 kilometres across unpaved roads was out. There was no point in going there, even though Juma was convinced the journey would be a success. He had even selected a hotel where we could stay the night.

'The Garden Guest House. It is on the edge of the town. Ten bedrooms.' He smiled and paused, turning to me in the back seat and throwing a wide, proprietary grin over his shoulder. 'So we will not have to share, Mr Nick. I know this place. It is on the road leading out to Viwanja 60 and I know also that you will pick up much information there. The Garden will be full of ivory men.'

But Kibasa shook his head and thumped his fist on his black briefcase and said that we should return to Dar. We had seen Mikumi and now I should meet Costa Mlay, the Director of Wildlife. 'I know him, Nick. Don't go. He won't like it.'

I had no choice. I had to go back to Dar and, in any case, there was the story which I had to file. My journey was over, and I knew that I now had enough material to write an article. I would contrast the chaos in Mikumi, the junkyard vehicles, the threadbare uniforms, the arsenal that went out of fashion with Rorke's Drift, the promises that were never fulfilled, the morale that was as weak as my Auntie Anne's tea, with the determination, strength, vitality, experience and vision of Kibasa who, through some ludicrous decision, was no longer allowed near an elephant.

With all his success I would have imagined that Kibasa would be automatically given a major role in mobilizing Tanzania's game wardens. I'd have expected that Kibasa's management methods, his strategies, his day-to-day tactics, his motivating influence, would be adopted right across the country. It would be surprising if Kibasa hadn't been appointed to lead the fight. But things are not that simple. This is Africa. Kibasa was not promoted. As I found out later, he was sacked. Today he is a general without an army.

'What will you do when you go back to Dar?' I asked him.

'I will see if my appeal has been granted and, if not, then I think I must give up.'

I couldn't understand why the National Parks Department were being so stubborn. Surely there was a way they could compromise and make use of this man's talents and experience to fight the poachers? But Kibasa was as obstinate as his bosses. He didn't tell me whether there was a conflict of personalities between himself and Mr Babu who was in charge of the National Parks, but I guessed there must be some element of personal animosity. Like Kibasa, Babu was a difficult character too, a stickler for discipline which, I am told, is often seen as a character defect by the majority of Tanzanians. Babu's grandfather was said to have been a German, and perhaps this mixing of blood so far back contributed to the unpopularity of the man.

'Babu is a good man to have in charge of the Parks,' said Kibasa, 'but he has moved me from place to place and then back again for many, many years. I do not know why he does it, but it happens regularly. He is stubborn. I have refused a transfer to Kilimanjaro. Why should I go? There are no animals there, only tourists. Now I am tired and want to stay either in Mikumi or Ruaha. No one can say I have not done my job, but still they move me. Elephants need me. Babu doesn't.'

'What will you do if your appeal fails?'

'I need money. My children cannot afford to go to school and I have to live off the earnings of my wife. No man should come to this.'

'They all seem to in this village, Charles.'

'This is a village. These people here are not the same as the townspeople. I am a Hehe. I am a fighter. My tribe defeated the Germans a hundred years ago. My tribe defeated the Arabs. We have never been slaves. The Germans cut off our chief's head, but we made them return it. You can see it in Iringa.'

'And what about the elephants? Are you going to abandon them?'

'No. I would never do that.' For the first time since I had met him, he raised his voice, and I glimpsed his vulnerability. 'Every time an elephant is killed, every time a poacher strikes, it is as if I have been personally attacked. I have spent my professional life looking after game. If there is none left, there is no reason for me to have lived and worked here.'

I told Kibasa what I was going to write, and he agreed. He knew it would be tough for him but already, I believed, he had made his decision to leave the service. I went silent in the Land Rover as it rolled back the bush on its way to Dar. I was already working out the times of the planes to London. Could I make the BA flight on Saturday? Possibly, if Costa Mlay agreed to see me when we reached Dar. But Kibasa was reading my thoughts.

'Look,' he said, 'I will arrange for you to see the Director, and if it is at all possible I will try to persuade him to let me take you to the Selous. This is the place where the poaching is still going on. There is a man there you should meet, a

32

good man. Ndunguru. You will get on well with him. Then I will have to leave you. I must return to my family.'

There were no knocks on my door in the Kilimanjaro that night. I had settled the bill with Juma, and I slept soundly. But the dollar tree had shed many, many leaves and much fruit.

As for the flight to London, I never made it. But then I didn't understand Africa.

FOUR

Tusk Force

Hippos do not often visit Dar es Salaam. Nor do many other wild animals unless they happen to be dead. This hippo was uproariously alive, grunting through the grass at the side of the road and causing the families who lived in the suburb north of the airport a deal of commotion. To begin with, few had seen such a beast before, and here was a *kiboko*, a hippo, who had no business to invade their street, disturbing the peace of the morning and scavenging the grass their goats chewed without interruption all day long. Hippos should know their place, and their place wasn't the city. How this one had arrived on the tin-can fringes of Dar, no one knew, but most people there that morning blamed the spirits of the place, and once they had apportioned culpability, they sent for the police.

The police thought it was a joke, and then they saw the *kiboko*, munching its breakfast absent-mindedly. And then the police did what police do everywhere when they realize that a considerable gap exists between the problem itself and finding the solution. The police sealed off the area with barbed wire, called for reinforcements, and surrounded the hippo, who may now have begun to regret this saunter into the city, with a detachment of elite troops, each armed with a sub-machine gun. And then the officer commanding this bristlingly nervous platoon called the Director of Wildlife.

When Costa Mlay took the phone call, he had just started to explain to me how isolated his position was, and why, if nothing radical was achieved in the next few months, the elephant crisis would be finally solved. 'There just won't be any left,' he was saying. 'You've glimpsed in just a few days what we are fighting and you've seen the lack of equipment, and the low morale. Imagine how I feel.'

It was then the phone rang. Costa could not believe the news either. He began to laugh. 'Do you want to see a sight that Dar es Salaam has never seen before? Nick, this is not a joke. There's a *kiboko* in town. It's most probably starving. My guess is that it followed a water course that filled up after the rains, and it lost itself, got hungry and followed the river into Dar.'

It was true. The hippo was grazing away, unconscious of its size, or proximity to urbanization, and equally unconcerned by the bedlam its presence had provoked.

The police chief and his army counterpart were conferring some distance away from the cordon of soldiers. When they saw Costa Mlay's Land Rover pull up they sprinted over to it, and demanded to know what he was going to do.

'This hippo is outside our jurisdiction, sir. We haven't got much time,' a major explained.

Costa took in the scene, the hippo, the barbed wire, the grass it was devouring, the men with their handbag-sized killing machines, the audience of shack dwellers, relishing the unexpected, and then he turned towards the two officers and said: 'What do you expect me to do about the *kiboko*? I can't take it back to its home. Have you asked it where its mama is?'

'Well, we can't leave it here,' said the police commander.

Costa signalled me away from the scene and we both climbed back into the Land Rover.

'What will they do?' I asked him.

'I think they will kill the *kiboko*.'

Back in his office on the sixth floor of the Ministry building, the phone rang again. It was the chief of police. Costa put his hand over the mouthpiece and whispered to me: 'I was right. They have killed it, and now do you know what they are asking? They want to know what to do with it.' He picked up the phone once more and shouted: 'Haven't you ever heard of *food*?' Then he slammed down the receiver.

'It's strange for you, Nick, to think that Africans do nothing about their heritage. Those people you saw there today, for them it was the first time they have seen such an animal. They are unlikely to see another. They will never be so close to nature, yet when it happens, what do they do? They destroy.'

'What will they do with the carcass?'

Costa shook his head. 'That's the really odd thing. They don't know what to do with it. These people are starved of meat, so I told them to eat it. I guarantee you there will be nothing left of that *kiboko* by tonight.' (He was right. That evening every shred of muscle, tissue and bone had disappeared; now the *kiboko* was merely an outrageous memory and a warm, full stomach.)

'Nick, you can now gauge the extent of the ignorance of the people that I am fighting. If they can do this to a hippo, what will they do to an elephant? And these are city people, not villagers. They would have dealt with this instinctively there and then by themselves.'

This was the first meeting I had had with Costa. It had taken me some days after returning from my visit to Mikumi to effect and in the end I gave up and strolled the few hundred yards from the Kilimanjaro along the ocean front, littered with broken-down wooden dhows pulled up on the shore to rot, to the Ministry. I walked through the iron gates, and waited with a crowd of civil servants, messengers and visitors for the lift to take me to the sixth floor. I was on familiar Fleet Street territory, a doorstep. I would wait for Costa outside his office. He had to notice me. It worked. I waited for thirty minutes and was shown inside. At last, I was facing the man who had been saddled with probably the most important and urgent wildlife problem in Africa. Costa was small and tidy in his Next double-breasted suit, and he was framed inside his tiny office by a pair of polished tusks, curved and shiny and cool. They were about four to five feet tall. His eyes brimmed with energy and intelligence, but there was also a streak of melancholy there, a trickle of sadness in the intonation that served to remind me of his problems.

Costa was a diplomat, smooth in the arts of political manipulation. He was no novice when it came to dealing with governments. He had spent most of his career at the side of Nyerere who had chosen him to be one of his presidential aides. He had been as close to the President as his hand luggage, conferenced the world with him, drafted his speeches on wildlife and conservation. Often, he told me,

36

he had reminded the President of his promises from all those years ago enshrined so floridly in the Arusha Manifesto.

'So what happened?'

'You know what politicians are like. You can present them with a problem and a solution, and they will equivocate, and say they are interested, and yes, this does concern them, but finally, they will do nothing. They seek refuge in complaisance.'

'You mean the easiest answer is not to answer.'

He nodded and shuffled through a mess of papers on his desk. There were more files, brown cardboard piling up on the shelf to the right of his desk. They overwhelmed the little room. He pushed the papers to one side, and crumpled up one particular sheet on which he had been doodling. He aimed for the bin in the corner, and missed.

He stared at me, then stood up and looked out of the corner window overlooking Ocean Drive. It was a favourite view. He spoke to me, still facing the window, gazing out over the harbour where rusting container ships were at anchor, waiting to unload.

I watched the back of his neck, glistening above the collar of his shirt as he recited the problems of the Department. No weapons. Obsolete weapons. No ammunition. No vehicles. Broken-down vehicles. No spares. No tools. Just like you saw in Mikumi. Aircraft. Two, but often one or the other is grounded. Fuel, stocks low, and fuel was expensive. Man-power, weak and untrained. Money. Not enough to pay the men well, pay them so that they would not be tempted to poach.

The recitation stopped, and he turned to face me. 'Do you know what the salaries are here?'

I said no.

'Here, look at this list.' He opened a worn, bound file and leafed through it, thumbing the fragile pages until he found what he was looking for. The page read:

Salaries
Game scout: salary per month – 2,000 shillings.
Game warden: salary per month – 6,000 shillings.
Senior game warden: salary per month – 8,000 shillings.

There was, I could see, a neat and niggardly symmetry about

the payments. I worked out that they ranged between £8 and £32 a month.

'What about you, Costa, how much do you earn, or is that a state secret?'

'It's no secret, for sure.'

His embarrassment was showing. I kept my mouth shut. I waited.

'About 10,000 shillings.'

'How do you manage? You are married and you have three children.'

Costa nodded. '10,000 shillings is not enough, but it is a treasure chest to a man in the bush.'

'So is an elephant, Costa.'

'Of course, Nick, I would like more money, so would you, but that is not possible with the way this country is run.'

Costa was one of Nyerere's children. His elder brother was independence and he had shared his youth with the peachskin blush of those early days of freedom. Now he was middle-aged and his illusions had been bruised by experience, and yet it was he who had to clean up the pile of mess that had accumulated over the years. He shared his problems with Tanzania, yet Tanzania had no intention of sharing the answers. He saw ivory poaching as a cancer that afflicted all classes from peasant to policeman, small-town merchant to middleman, whore to game warden. Poaching respected no one and no place. It attacked a weakness, gained a grip, and gathered so much impetus and strength that it had now destroyed the rotting remains of the moral fabric that had once hugged this country in a tight and breath-squelching embrace.

The politicians had admitted that mistakes had been made in the past twenty-five years and that the country was now emerging from the slumber and sloth of Nyerere's dogma, that private enterprise was being encouraged, that foreign exchange would soon come trickling in, that that trickle would burst into a flash flood of dollars and marks, that tourists would follow; but I was sure Costa knew better.

'Is there anything you can do?' I asked.

He shrugged and stretched once again across his desk for another sheet of paper, and sipped the tepid coffee his secretary had brought. 'She is a good girl, but when will she learn to make *kawawa*?'

Costa asked me whether I had ever heard of 'the Chain of Corruption'. 'Let's start with the village *jangili*. And then the *fundi*.'

The words coming out of his diplomat's mouth sounded curt and appallingly direct. He recognized my blank look and explained that the *fundi* were the gang who worked for the *jangili* chief. They could number up to fifty or more, but usually they operated with about six or seven. Their purpose was to cut out the tusks and transport them to their hiding place or handover point. Their other role was to carry enough food and water for the poachers to stay in the bush for as long as it took them to kill enough elephants. That could be up to a week, but more likely a month.

'How many elephants can a *jangili* kill in a month?'

'About 100. And that's on the conservative side.'

I worked it out. Three elephants a day, which makes six tusks a day, which makes about 180 a month.

'Yes, but most of those 180 tusks will be very small, maybe under five kilos.'

Costa wiped his brow and stroked the ivory tusks on the wall of his office. He pulled at his eye, as if to remind himself where he had got to. There was the village headman who, he said, would possibly know where the tusks were buried and more probably who in the village had killed the elephants. He would have to be paid off. Silence was a commodity. And there was the district commissioner.

'Mama Tombo,' I murmured clearly enough for him to hear.

'So you know about our famous Mama, do you?'

'A little.'

'I am told you know a lot more. You met her?'

'No, but I heard about the dam and I learnt how difficult it is to kill a tsetse.'

Costa laughed when I told him about the notebook I had converted into a lethal weapon. 'You see, Nick, we have DCs like her who have been in their districts for so many years that nothing, revolution, earthquake nor disease can move them. She has made this part of the country her own, and she has achieved it by digging in, as it were, and paying off her friends in Dar. You will achieve nothing by seeing the Mama.'

'Why did you mention DCs?'

39

'Nick, if I can't be honest with myself, then who can I be honest with?'

He waved me silent and his voice, cool and quiet in that late morning, invoked a roll call of corruption. The police, because they could move ivory at night without alerting suspicion and because they possessed the means to move it; the game warden, who was poor and tempted by easy pickings; the game scout, ditto; the middleman, who provided cash and arms and bullets; the exporter, who 'bought' the permits to overcome legalities; the customs official, who saw that everything ran smoothly at the docks; the docks superintendent, who made sure the ivory was sent on its way.

'Are there any more you can add?'

'Yes,' he replied, 'but I'd be very foolish to go higher.'

'What about this department?' I had heard that a former official had been involved very heavily in the poaching racket, and had been protected for years by someone in the Government.

'He was moved.'

'Was he ever prosecuted?'

'There was no evidence. He was transferred within the civil service. Now he is living upcountry.'

I asked Costa what sort of house he lived in, this official who had been part of the ivory poaching racket.

'I have never been there, but I hear it is quite spacious.'

I was told later how he worked. A licensed dealer would come to him seeking a permit to deal in ivory which weighed more than the legal limit of 10 kg. The official would ask how much he wanted. The dealer would suggest 30 kg of ivory and then the official would suggest he made it 50 kg – 30 kg for the dealer and 20 kg for himself. The permit, though, only related to the dealer. So the official stood to gain 20 kg of ivory, secretly, tax free and, for official purposes, perfectly legally.

Another method was for him to sign complementary slips to dealers alleging lack of transport at headquarters and asking regional and district game officers to sell ivory to them (the dealers). That way he managed to keep the price of ivory at 350 shillings per kilo unchanged for ten years, even when the world market price was US$100. Even at 17 shillings to the dollar, he and his collaborators stood to split

1,350 shillings a kilo. When the consignment was 7–10 tons, the loot was colossal.

This was how the official operated. A paper trafficker. A man who signed away the lives of elephants in a calculated bureaucratic way. It was almost as if his very office was one that endorsed not the enduring protection but the rapid destruction of the species.

Costa's information was an all-embracing accusation which reached out and touched every part of the country. It pointed to a highly organized, carefully structured hier-archical ladder, which rewarded everyone whose foot and hand clung to the rungs. I was beginning to grasp that the killing of one elephant, just one, was also contributing to the destruction of the nation. I kept repeating to myself the question I had asked Costa earlier that morning: how could one man with no money and paltry resources stop this massacre? How could one man persuade people to put aside their greed and self-interest, curb their natural instincts, and stop the killing, the dealing, the profiteering?

'I think we are at a turning point in this war,' he said. 'I think we are about to see the worst.'

'More carcasses?'

'We have the army on our side now.' Costa smiled warily. 'Since this month. Operation Uhai has begun. It means that the army are moving into the reserves and game park areas and they will be policing them. You should visit Major-General John Butler Walden.'

The Major-General was in charge of Operation Uhai. Costa picked up the phone on his desk and spoke to him. He told me I could see him tomorrow at the military HQ in Dar es Salaam.

'You said the worst from both sides.'

'The army, Nick, especially in Africa, have been known to act rather enthusiastically in their pursuit of the enemy.'

He rose from his desk, yawning, and suggested in his calm way that we take a trip downstairs to the fifth floor. 'We have had a small success in anti-poaching, and I thought you should meet our latest hero.'

The office is windowless, and catacomb-dim. The single light bulb buzzes annoyingly, competing with the clack of the

41

fan. Two men are hunched over a wooden trestle table, facing each other. One is smoking, gasping in the nicotine and blasting the smoke out of his body in violent heaves. As we enter, I see he is jabbing his finger with what looks like a degree of impatience at a map that is stretched out between them.

I catch the words 'Tabora' and 'middleman', and then their concentration vanishes as abruptly and silently as our entry. They rise and stare. It is not a friendly stare. I watch their eyes dart from the Director, their boss, to me and back again.

'Carry on, Terimo,' says Costa. His tone is half imperative, half polite. He introduces me and pats a seat against the wall. I sit and say nothing.

Terimo is not satisfied. He is worried and puzzled by my presence. He walks the three paces from desk to door and whispers to Costa. The Director pats Terimo on the shoulder, glances in my direction, and introduces me to the two men.

'This is Terimo, Erasmus Terimo, and this,' he says pointing to the small man who has just stubbed out his cigarette with his Bata boot, 'this is Musa Lyimo. He has just returned from an undercover operation. Now, why don't you continue? Ignore us.'

They don't. They stare. Costa, Mr Mlay, nods. The nod is an order. Terimo takes his seat at the table, turns to me, and says nothing.

Lyimo goes back to the map. He jabs his finger down hard. He looks uncomfortable. It must be me. Or is it the Director? No one likes their chief coming too close.

'I met him here.'

'Did he work out your accent?' says Terimo.

'No, the original briefing worked well. I said that I was on the staff of an embassy here in Dar and that I was a driver for an ambassador. I was speaking Swahili with a Dar workman's accent. He agreed to meet me that night.' Lyimo pulls an envelope from his breast pocket. He opens it and produces a black and white photograph. It is crumpled. 'Here. It's a village four or five kilometres outside Tabora.'

The photo shows a white-washed, single-storey house, with a tin roof and rickety verandah.

'What then?'

42

I am so absorbed I do not notice that Costa has slipped out of the room until he has gone. It is clear, though, that Terimo and Lyimo have.

'I ordered the back-up team to surround the place after dusk, and I went in alone.'

'Were you armed?'

'Yes, I took my pistol. Then I entered the house. The middleman recognized me and said that we would have to make a journey into the forest.'

'Why?' I am sure that Terimo already knows the answer. He is a trained interrogator and he is following procedure. They are always taught, always, to ask the absurd question, the one that you think is unnecessary.

'Because,' says Lyimo, 'the trophies were buried there.' I can measure the weariness in his voice. He plays the game well. He has prepared himself for a debriefing as nerve-racking as the operation itself.

'So what did you do? How did you inform the back-up team that you were moving out of the house?'

'I didn't.'

'Why not?'

'Come on, Terimo, you know what it's like.' It is clear to me that Terimo doesn't.

Lyimo pauses, giving Terimo an opening which he knows will not be pressed home. I can see him, sitting there, with the map and the satisfaction that he has survived an operation about which Terimo can only ask questions, separating him from his interrogator, smiling to himself. He has touched a nerve and gained an advantage.

'Look, Terimo, all I could do was hope the boys would realize that the trophies were hidden in the forest and keep an eye out for me.'

'Did you see any trophies?'

'Thirteen tusks.'

'Weighing?'

'Fifty-one kilos.'

'Small elephants, then?' Lyimo demonstrates the pitiful inadequacy of the tusks, flexing his hands so that they are about eighteen inches apart.

'How did you pay for them?'

'With fake money. God knows how they fall for it. I handed over a pile of paper with real notes top and bottom.

Must be my honest face. No, Terimo, remember it was dark. There was no moon, luckily for me.'

He's talking too much. Lyimo's nerves induce him to light up another Sportsman. He sucks in the smoke.

'So, Musa, what went wrong?'

'Maybe they knew something. I was weighing the tusks when one of them . . . '

'Which one?'

'He was thin faced, almost blue black, could have been a Somali. I was weighing the ivory and this man starts asking me questions about the embassy. Where it was, how long had I worked there, what was the ambassador's name. He wants to know who I drive for. I answer him. Then he gets even more interested, saying His Excellency's car is a grey Merc, and how new it is, and so on.'

'So what.' Terimo is aggressive. 'You answered his questions.'

Musa Lyimo remains silent. The clack-clack-clack of the fan breaks the heat of the room. He draws a breath, and puts his hand on Terimo's shoulder.

'I pulled my pistol out of my pocket and I fired.'

'Idiot!'

'Terimo, I didn't kill any of them.'

'More fool you.'

'I aimed as near to this man's head as I dared, and I pressed the trigger. He was deafened and blinded for a few seconds. I hit another with my fist.'

'I expect you think you deserve a medal.'

'No, but I reckon we'll get a conviction. This one I knocked out was employed by the Government. He deserves nine years.' Lyimo spits out the words. 'That man. He was a teacher. And up to his arms in ivory.'

'And maybe he knew something.' Terimo is not really listening any more.

Lyimo follows his interrogator out of the room. As he passes through the doorway, I get up, and offer him a Rothmans. He takes it, and walks away.

Was the Department leaking? Costa said nothing. He scowled at the cold coffee on his desk and walked over to the corner window and watched the limos flash down Ocean Drive. He turned to me and said: 'I don't know, but I trust those two men. They are brave, but they are right to be suspicious. There are not many whom I can trust.'

He sighed and stood up, and walked over to the map pinned to the wall opposite his desk. His finger sought out the Selous. It was a huge green area spreading from the south-east of Dar and the ocean, down to the Mozambique borders and west almost as far as Lake Malawi, and criss-crossed with the spindly blue lines of rivers and the purple of highlands. He told me that I would be going there tomor-row, to the south of the Selous, to a town called Songea, where I would meet a man called Ireneus Ndunguru. I realized then that Kibasa had kept his promise and contacted the Director. He returned to his desk and hastily scrawled a letter for me to give to Ndunguru. This man Ndunguru had been working with the villagers, the *jangili* themselves, attempting to persuade them to abandon elephant poaching. I would learn a lot from Ndunguru.

I looked at the map, trying to take in the vastness of that sheet of green ink. I asked Costa how I was going to get to Songea.

'That's easy,' he smiled. 'Captain Gerard Bigurube will fly you down there. In the Cessna. If it is working, that is.'

He flung a fat wad of papers at me, a file, marked 'Selous Census 1989'. I saw it was a final draft and was decorated with an ink sketch of five or six elephants drinking peace-fully at a water-hole. All the creatures wore their tusks proudly.

'Will I see many like this, Costa?'

'Nick, you're going into the Selous. It's the finest, largest game reserve in the world. There are 55,000 square kilo-metres of wilderness down there. But you'll be lucky to see any elephants.'

'There are 30,000 left, aren't there?'

'Yes, but never forget there's a war going on too. Don't expect too much.'

FIVE

The Black Mamba in Brogues

I'm lounging against the back of an easy chair in the Officers' Mess of the Tanzanian Defence Force just a few minutes' walk from the Army HQ in Dar es Salaam, listing so critically that I am in danger of disappearing, slipping off the broad seat of the easy chair and on to the polished wooden floor. Nothing, I feel, can stop the slide. I'm going to end up under the table, under the regiment of empty Safari bottles that line the table top, at the feet of the Black Mamba.

The Black Mamba is perfectly aware of my condition, but he is, I believe, far more interested in the glass of Konyagi – it is pungent and tastes like neat gin – that he is nursing so affectionately with both hands. The Black Mamba is partial to Konyagi which he mixes with soda. Already this afternoon he has drunk the best part of a bottle. I too have had my fill. Not of Konyagi, but of Safari beer which the Black Mamba's henchmen have insisted I drink out of litre steins. Maybe I'm drunk. And this mess, with its hunting rifles and muzzle-loaders, expertly and lovingly fashioned by hand, that decorate the walls, is swirling round inside my head. I am drunk. I've been here three hours now and I can hardly keep my eyes open. The men around me, the officers, are dressed in their number ones, green tunics, green trousers, creased with a broad, gold stripe. No one is singing a soldier's song. There are rules of behaviour in this mess like any other, and even in my condition I realize that Rule One is to follow the Black Mamba down the Konyagi road. So drink when the Black Mamba drinks, listen to the Black Mamba's jokes, laugh at the Black Mamba's jokes, drink and never sip. Rule Two: show respect. Rule Three:

never buy your round. This is the kingdom of the Black Mamba. He is the President of the Mess, and he makes the rules and Rule Four is: a guest fiercely obeys Rules One to Three.

I had been with the Black Mamba since 1.30 that afternoon. When I met him in his office at the Defence Force HQ in Dar he was a mere Major-General. Major-General John Butler Walden, a shortish, stocky man, maybe 5 foot 7 inches in his carefully polished brogues. He was pale, a milky coffee-mug with a pockmarked rumpled skin on top, and the lower part of his face was bisected by a stiff-winged black moustache that had taken much training, though now this unruly relic of Blimp was in need of a deft rescue, a little waxing, a snip here, a tug there. Two heavy chunks of gold, his medals, glinted on the front of the green tunic hung up behind his desk. We shook hands.

He sat upright and full of business and waved me towards a chair at a large oblong table covered in green felt. Round it, waiting for me to take my seat, were three other officers, a colonel, a captain and a lieutenant. The General did not introduce them. Between these soldiers and me, a large map lay unattended upon the table. I could see it was a map of the Selous and stuck on it were large arrows sweeping across land and river and mountain: Operation Uhai. It reminded me of those diagrams illustrating the German advance in the First World War.

The desk the General sat at was glass-topped, with one cracked corner destroying the illusion that he was completely in control. He took me in with a brief dark gaze while his fingers searched out a cigarette from the king-sized Embassy pack lying in front of him. There was already one, half-smoked, in the Top Club ashtray to his right, next to the two Thermos flasks, one red, one grey, and the tin of coffee. To his left were three phones, one green, one black and one very British Telecom, ivory coloured and with masses of buttons. Behind him, next to the tunic and the medals sleeping on its breast, was the Tanzanian flag, green for the land, yellow for riches and blue for the ocean (slightly different in its tone from the version coined at Independence which goes like this: green for envy, yellow for cowardice and blue for the mood), furled and quiet in the shade. And

next to that the face of the President, smiling benignly upon
our gathering.

The General twisted the cigarette into a shiny black holder
and proceeded, in a quiet and purposeful way, to tell me
about Operation Uhai. He told me how many troops were
involved and where they were based, and he told me about
all the arrests that had been made. Yes, there had been
a few complaints about ill-treatment but these had been
disproved and the soldiers concerned vindicated. He told
me about the number of trophies recovered and how his
men had searched village after village, confiscating thousands of muzzle-loaders and hundreds of semi-automatic
rifles. And all the time he talked, the General's black eyes
drilled into me. I was staked out in front of him on a target
board and there was nothing I could do about it. So I took
out my red notebook, and as I wrote, so did the lieutenant
sitting across the table, behind that map. I wrote about the
General's moustache as he was firing another stick of high-
velocity statistics, and I watched the lieutenant slyly. He
was transcribing statistics.

'What is the most notorious place for ivory dealing?' I
asked.

'Ifakara.' The General paused. The lieutenant looked at
the captain, who looked at the colonel, who pointed to a
town on the map bordering the Selous. 'Ifakara. The people
there, well, 90 per cent of them, are hunters. And its sister
town Mahenge. You see, there is a road and a railway link
to Dar es Salaam from Ifakara. There are Somali traders there
and it is reasonably simple for the middlemen to smuggle
the trophies out of the country. The river too, the Kilombero,
is navigable and the smugglers use this route as well.'

'How many did you arrest in Ifakara?'

The General did not answer me. I waited and then I asked
him again.

'We made many arrests,' he said, 'but I am not sure there
were so many convictions.' He leant forward, both hands
plumped firmly on the desk as if he had the whole of the
Selous within his grasp. 'There were leaks. It made me
angry, but people in Ifakara knew that we were coming. So
many of the poachers hid away their tusks and their
weapons. It put our operation back by months.'

On the map I read the success rate of Day One of Operation Uhai:

Ya shortgun na risisi: one shotgun with ammunition
Watuhumiwa 12: 12 suspects arrested
Shortgun 2: two shotguns seized
Rifle: 3
Gabore 12: 12 muzzle-loaders
Risari shortgun 44: 44 shotgun cartridges seized
Risasi rifle 22: 22 rifle bullets seized
Vipande 46 meno ya tembo: 46 pieces of ivory seized
Vipande 4: 4 rubies seized

Forty-six tusks. Only 46 tusks, but this was Day One of Uhai, to be fair to the General, and the middlemen and *jangili* of Ifakara had been tipped off.

The General sat back, satisfied that I had been told enough. But I hadn't. 'What about your name, General?'

'Yes?'

'It's hardly Tanzanian, Sir.'

A puff of the cigarette, an inhalation, a smile, a silence.

'You want to know about my father, do you? Well, he was British.' The words came fast. I looked to see if the lieutenant was writing them down. He was.

'An Englishman, and my mother was a native of Tanganyika. Stanley Arthur Walden. He worked for the colonial government. He was born in Henley-on-Thames in 1909. I have an auntie there, you know. She is still alive. I saw her last year. She has a lovely garden.'

He stopped as abruptly as he began. The eyes levelled themselves at me, as if down a barrel. He leant over the desk and said: 'What size shoes do you take?'

I started. 'Seven and a half.'

'Here, take these.' The General reached into a desk drawer and pulled out a pair of well-polished dark tan brogues. 'I am going to trust you. Take them. No arguments. In return, when you go back to London you will send me another pair. A size eight and a half. 43, I think.' He looked across at the silent colonel and captain and they nodded. 'That's right, 43. These are too small for me. They pinch. Good.'

The shoes had barely been worn. Furtively pushing them into my briefcase, I asked the General if he considered himself as English as his shoes.

He scratched his head. 'A German speaks of the father-land, but the British, they always talk of the motherland. I have ties with the land of my father but Tanzania is the home of my mother.'

His father, Stanley Arthur Walden, had been a district commissioner in the south-west of the territory in Mbeya, a town near the shores of Lake Nyasa. Stanley Arthur Walden had met a local girl and married her. At that time, in the late twenties and early thirties, it was a courageous and even foolhardy decision to defy convention, not that taking a bush wife was uncommon or even frowned upon. What was outrageous and extraordinary was his decision to marry the woman.

So the boy who took his father's name and half his colour was brought up the English way, only with antelopes and goats and eland instead of sheep to stare at or buses to catch. But the General did not care to talk much about his father. All he would say was that Stanley Arthur had divorced his mother. 'Did your aunt make a fuss of you when you visited Henley?' I asked him.

'No.'

'Why not, Sir? Surely she must have been proud of you?' He played with the buttons of the ivory-coloured phone. He didn't answer. I was beginning to fear that I would lose him.

Later, when I was back in England, I visited his aunt. She lived on the edge of Henley in an old folks' enclave, a neat bungalow at the end of a long, wide silent road. She wouldn't let me in, even though I had telephoned her the day before and said that I had news of her nephew and some pictures of him. She stood implacable at the door with a tan-coloured dachshund sniffing round my ankles. She said that she had nothing to say about the 'black boy' and knew nothing about him either. She had visited Africa only once for a holiday. I asked her about her brother, the father of the 'black boy', but she was relentless and unmoving. 'It's all in the past,' she said. I asked her about the General's visit last year. She nodded her white head and said he had come. 'He drove up. There were three of *them*.' The frosted glass door shut, closing, I suppose, a chapter of her life that she had no desire to examine. I didn't know this when I first met the General that afternoon at his barracks in Dar es Salaam. I later learnt that none of his father's family knew anything about his marriage and his son until 1964. But whatever the old boy had concealed for so many years, he could not bury the blood and all that it contained. The General was as English as steak and kidney pie, fashioned by all that his father loved and knew.

The General chatted on to me amicably enough, occasionally glancing towards his three subordinates, who shared with schoolboys that admirable chameleon-like facility to appear interested and even rapt when the unpredictable eyes of the headmaster happen to glance their way.

He'd seen action in the war to liberate Uganda from the tyranny of Idi Amin. The General leaned back in his chair, cigarette holder in the side of his mouth, and recalled the time when he entered Kampala to find Amin had fled.

'There were many starving peasants' – he said 'peesants' – 'in the city and the only enemy troops were the suicide battalion that Amin had ordered to stay in the city and destroy the place. I saw terrible sights in the State Research Bureau.' But he wouldn't elaborate, not until later, that is.

The General sprang to his feet. The interview was over. He smoothed his shirt with its scarlet tabs and its scarlet epaulette on the left shoulder, turned and flicked his tunic off the hanger. He pushed back his shoulders as he slipped into the jacket. Then he buttoned it slowly, carefully fitting the brass studs through the holes.

'Now,' he said, addressing the room, 'I would like to extend an invitation to you. Please be my guest in the officers' mess.' I followed him to the door of his office and all but cannoned into his back as he halted in mid-stride, turned, sidestepped me and marched back up the room to his desk. He reached over it and picked up one of the Thermos flasks. 'I must not forget my porridge,' he said. We laughed, me, the colonel, the captain and the scribe lieutenant. So did the General.

It is in the mess that I come to know the General. The meeting in his office is fencing practice. His mood lightens the moment he enters the single-storey room with its wood-panelled walls, polished lino floor and small bar neatly tucked into one corner opposite the door. Here, surrounded by his officers, he is expansive, a leader among his men, capable of relaxing with them and putting them at ease. He orders the drinks and sits me down at his table – proprietorial as any pub regular – strategically sited near the bar and with the advantage of a commanding position of the door.

'I am,' the General announces to no one in particular, 'the President of this Mess. It is now 4.10,' he says, looking at his watch. 'You see I wear this watch on my right hand. Why?'

I am mystified.

'Because I do things differently.' He flourishes the watch. 'It is now 4.10,' he repeats, 'and this mess closes at 3.30. But because I am here, the mess will stay open.' He stops the orderly who is pouring Safari into my glass and reaches over and tilts it. 'No, this way,' he instructs. Then he lifts his Konyagi to his lips and sinks it. 'Better than Gordons.'

I sip it and wince. It isn't better than Gordons.

But the President of the Mess is undeterred. 'I am a diabetic and I tell you this Konyagi is good for the health. You know I received the last rites last year. I had amoebic dysentery and the priest and the doctor, they both said I was a goner. But I had the will to survive. The *will* to survive. I never lost it. I didn't lose it in Kampala and I didn't lose it in Dar. I am still here. Let's drink to that.'

One of the General's cronies introduces himself to me and slides down to sit at our table. He is in mufti and is a lawyer in the army with the rank of brigadier. I ask him how long he has known the General.

'Since he was the Black Mamba,' he replies.

It is difficult to follow this conversation because this officer has a high-pitched voice that is either a by-product of an overdose of Konyagi or points to some more profound physical defect. I cannot imagine him delivering life-saving speeches at a court martial. But the 'Black Mamba'? The General doesn't look like a snake. He's short and plump and balding and the moustache and cigarette holder make him appear as affable as Terry-Thomas.

'We were in Uganda together,' the brigadier shrills. His arms are flailing, and it is sheer luck that his glass of Konyagi does not land on my trousers. It's moving faster than a series of left-hand jabs, and all the time I am riding the punches.

'General,' I say, raising my fifth litre of Safari, 'General John Butler Walden, alias the Black Mamba.' He turns to me, perfectly aware of my conversation with his brigadier.

'Yes, I am the Black Mamba.' He pulls the ends of his moustache, one at a time. 'I was given the name when I took Kampala,' he explains. 'I drove Amin out of the city.'

'Why were you called that name particularly, General?'

He looks at the brigadier. The brigadier waves over to the table another couple of officers who have been staring at CNN news on a large television set on the other side of the mess. 'He,' the brigadier's arms swerve and swoop around me, 'he wants to know why the General is called the Black Mamba.' 'The General is a hero,' a colonel tells me.

'Yes, but what did you do?' An orderly is now applying the sixth litre of Safari to my glass.

The General grins. 'Let us say that I ended the war very quickly, very efficiently and very quietly.'

He semaphores both his arms at one of the mess orderlies and shouts in Swahili at him. The orderly salutes, turns on his heel and goes off, returning a few seconds later with a varnished wooden box about two feet long and four or five inches wide. He hands it with a degree of ceremony to the General. The General places it upon the table, waving away the empty beer bottles with the back of his right hand. Then he opens the box. Inside it is a shining Gurkha knife, eighteen inches long, and curved to a point. The General takes out the knife and runs his thumb along the blade. He is careful not to draw his own blood. He hands me the knife. It is cold and quiet and the reflection of the lights of the mess dazzles my eyes.

'*That* is why I am called the Black Mamba.' He takes the knife from me and puts it back to bed inside the box, which he pats. 'My friend in Uganda.' The General stands up. 'Gentlemen, it is 6.35.' A flourish of his watch.

I stand, or try to, to thank the General for his hospitality but he brushes me aside, draining the last of his Konyagi. 'Now to my house. For dinner. My wife is not expecting a guest, but she will cope.'

Three Alsatians flung themselves at the General as he lurched out of his Land Rover and walked through the double chain-link gate inscribed with the initials J.B.W. The house was small, single-storey, surrounded by a wall. I waited for the carpet roll of tongues to vanish inside the Alsatians' smiling black snouts before I followed. The invite for dinner was not just restricted to me. The brigadier-lawyer with the laughing-gas voice and unpredictable arm movements and the colonel had joined us. As soon as he was inside, the General disappeared, leaving me with the officers. I sat down in his living room, staring at the SAS calendar and the banks of shooting trophies. East African Champion 1959. Six other trophies, each of them manufactured from cheap plastic, the antithesis of the skill and determination which won them, stand on an exquisitely carved Zanzibar chest, next to a video recorder and TV set.

Food was served by the General's wife. She had prepared a buffet and we washed our hands in a plastic bowl of water she had brought to the table. We served ourselves. Rice, chicken meat, beef, spice, bananas. She was shy and knew her place. I glimpsed her – plump and short like her husband, but with mid-length, shiny Asian hair – for a moment, but it was enough to thank her for the hospitality. The officers she must have been used to, for they did not so much as acknowledge her presence.

Then she floated off to another part of the house, leaving the men to eat. After dinner, the General disappeared again and returned carrying tenderly in his arms a large, brown, highly polished leather belt. Hanging from it were two holsters, and in them were two silver guns. He gently extracted them and handed one to me. It was a Colt .45, long-barrelled and inscribed 'To the Black Mamba, Brigadier J. B. Walden. Kampala 1981'. The other gun was inscribed in exactly the same way, with a flowing copperplate that somehow turned the pair of pistols from two lethal weapons into those snug and respectable items you see now and again on *The Antiques Roadshow*.

I gave the Colt back to the General. He buckled on the rig, carefully tying each holster round his thigh, swaggered up and down the room, whiplashed and drew double-handed. A flash of pistol twirled Billy the Kid style round his fingers before slipping effortlessly back inside the holsters.

'These Colts,' the General, who could have been handling Sèvres porcelain, drew from the right thigh and fanned the cocking lever with his left hand, 'belonged to Idi Amin. I took them from his palace. It was the next best thing to him. He'd gone, but I got the guns.'

The audience of brigadier and colonel, who had clearly seen this Dodge City charade many times before, applauded.

'You must be a good shot, General.' I had thought it prudent to applaud too.

'Yes. See these trophies. I am a *Marksman First Class*.' There was cordite in the voice, the flash and bang of gunpowder mixed up with pride. The General loved shooting and he loved meat. I had seen the relish with which he attacked the pieces of chicken and beef that his wife had left for us. But I didn't know which he loved better, the shooting or the eating. I think they would probably rate equal. He talked that night in his home about hunting, and how when he was a young man he would shoot game. I would guess that no animal was safe with the General in the vicinity. In fact, a few days later I was told by one of the wardens in the Selous that when the General was visiting the Operation Uhai troops who were stationed in one of the northern sectors of the reserve, he spotted a hartebeest, called for a rifle from one of his entourage, levelled the weapon, aimed and fired. The beast fell stone dead. One shot. But the General was not finished, nor was he satisfied. As soon as he had dispatched the animal, he spotted another four hartebeest. Four more shots rang out.

But now, legs apart and weighed down by Idi Amin's guns, the Black Mamba was frustrated. He had the skill and the means to hunt, but, he said, to much nodding and rumbles from his fellow officers, hunting in the country today was in the hands of the corrupt. The hunting blocks are owned by many gangsters, he said, and some are even not hunted at all. 'These people apply for the hunting blocks' – he says blokes – 'and then they do nothing with them. Purely speculative.' He told me that sometimes the men who owned the hunting blocks would hunt out of season, beyond the months of July to December when it was legal. This was unfair to the animals who weren't clever enough to know when it was dangerous and when it wasn't. Hunting out of season interfered with breeding too. In the north of the country, round Arusha, there were farmers who cultivated crops on the land, crops like maize, bananas, pumpkins and beans, all of them particularly appetizing to game, purely so that this irresistible food would attract certain animals. The farmers would allow the animals to eat the food for a time and then they would shoot them. They made money out of it. They gave nothing to the villagers. Not even the carcasses.

'These block owners should give at least half the money to the villagers. They make thousands of dollars from each hunter who comes here from America or Germany or England. I think they charge around 30,000 dollars for a month's hunting. The villagers have nothing. Maybe that is why they hunt illegally. But it is their country too.'

He talked contemptuously about the corruptness of some of the organized hunting businesses in the country, yet I could see that he longed to be in the bush himself, his eye glued to the sights of his rifle, with a wild animal a breath away from death.

'You are going to Selous?' he asked me.

I nodded.

He pulled one of the Colts onto his lap and sat there stroking the barrel. 'I could show you some *wonderful* sights.' He looked me in the eye, his tongue rolling out the word as if he were making pastry. 'And maybe,' he winked, 'we could have done some hunting.'

What on earth was the Black Mamba suggesting? He had been charged with protecting elephants in their last great stronghold in Africa. He was convinced that there was nothing immoral in what he was doing. Certainly hunting was no crime. In fact, it was a right. I couldn't understand his attitude at the time, but then I had never been in the bush, never felt the night wrap me close in its velvet smock, never been startled by a nightjar as it thrust itself up and through the undergrowth a foot in front of my face, never watched a snake curl along the path, forgetful of human footsteps and intent only on vanishing into the elephant grass, never listened to the complaints of villagers who had nothing. It was later, so much later, when I began to grasp why the General thought the way he did.

'Remember,' he said as I climbed into the Land Rover, 'the shoes. Size 43. Brogues. And another thing, before you go. Remember this well. I have received the last rites. The Black Mamba never dies.'

SIX

Kissing the Selous

Bigurube is piloting the Cessna 182 over a mass of green, all shades from lime to pea to emerald. The lushness appears to have no limits. Down below, five thousand feet below, an empire of green is silently on the move, a shifting mass of shades, constantly changing as the cloud shadows stray idly across the vastness of the *miombo* woodland. Lime green, moss green, emerald and sea, pea green, turquoise, grass green, grey green, forest green, and olive, putting green, Wimbledon green, village green. This is anarchy in one colour. No one shade can ever hope to tyrannize the other. Only night will put an end to the nudging and pushing.

Down below us, five thousand feet down, among the swamps and clumps of rock and brachystegia, along the sand rivers, each of them impressed with the pattern of a snake, between the ragged edges of the redstone bluffs, is the Selous.

It looks to me as if this is the day that God chose to create it. Down there, there are no *shambas*, no wisps of smoke, no people, no discarded Coke cans, no cigarette ends. But there are animals. Impala, puku, reedbuck, sable antelope, water-buck, warthog, wild pig, giraffe, leopards, lions; there are mighty herds of buffalo intent on keeping fat; there are hartebeest and hornbill, and zebra. And there are elephants, somewhere, 30,000 of them.

I'm strapped into the co-pilot's seat, dripping with perspiration, staring down at the Selous, and I've been in this little wasp long enough to have settled down and not be over-concerned by the way the arrows inside the mess of dials seem to swing wildly in the wrong direction. Please, God, don't let my eye catch the oil pressure gauge again, block up my ears and shield me from Kibasa's vomit. He sits behind me, not looking anywhere, not breathing, his hands are strangling what life there is left in the sick bag. Kibasa is not a happy flier. He finds nothing amusing or remotely ironic when I point out the stark red letters of the notice in front of him that absolve the manufacturer of the aircraft from paying out a large cheque should we crash or injure ourselves seriously or die.

The Cessna booms along, single-enginedly, telling me in its club bore of a voice that there's no hurry, we'll reach Songea, you'll meet Ndunguru.

I look again down at the land beneath me, and I realize that I haven't seen an elephant, not even a hint of grey, not a wave of a trunk, or a shiver of an ear, and I realize that my thought that here was God's own garden was high-octane romance, journalist fantasy. No, down there among those foetid swamps, in among the *miombo*, humans have been at work. They are there, possibly now, upsetting nature's imperative. They are down there, in the Selous, killing. They are killing elephants with automatic rifles rolled off a production line in Eastern Europe. They are emptying thirty 7.62mm assault rifle bullets at a time into each elephant, and then they are hacking out the tusks. And if they haven't a Kalashnikov at hand, then they are down there with their home-made muzzle-loader, and if that jams or the breech explodes, they are down there, lurking round the water holes, waiting for their prey to feast upon the pumpkins that they have that day filled with poison.

We've been flying now for an hour. Kibasa has just vomited again. None of it escapes the sick bag this time. I remind him that he is a Hehe and must accordingly uphold the nobility of his race. He chokes and then looks up from his stomach and says his tribe never needed an air force to win their wars.

Another fifteen minutes pass. Beneath us, the Mbarangandu river slithers and slimes round bends, effortless and careless of direction. The Mbarangandu doesn't know the way to go. Nor is it worried. It's wide and shallow, sandy and turbid. There are buffalo grazing earnestly by the sweeping banks, two feet in the mud, shaking their tails at flies, or perhaps stirred into some minor revolt by the irritating buzz of the Cessna. But the Mbarangandu is indifferent. It has seen it all before, since time began, so it passes by the herons and fish eagles, the simper of crocodiles, flat-bellied in the heat, and steps up its pace. A speck of white water, a ripple round a rock tumble, tell their tale. Now the earth is redder, as if it's been fired in a kiln, the trees more dense.

Another five minutes. Then Bigurube shouts. He is pointing. He banks the plane sharply to the left. He circles. There below us is a solitary grey figure. Its tusks are catching the white of the sun. It is nuzzling the bark of a brachystegia. An elephant. But only one.

Bigurube has pulled back the stick and pushed the nose of the Cessna into a dive. We are coming down to kiss the Selous. The river has suddenly lost its langour. Bigurube tells me over the engine noise that the Mbarangandu is now the Ulanga. It is wider, some 200–300 metres between each bank, altogether more stately in its progress, and it is choking with hippo and crocodiles. I can see them very clearly because Bigurube, much to Kibasa's unease, is taking the plane down to within a few feet of the shining brown water. The Cessna levels out at about fifty feet, skimming the river which rushes past on either side of the windows. Crocodiles can hear its whine and are doing press-ups before shimmying like some broad-tailed bar girl for the safety of the river. Four fish eagles fly above the Cessna, certain now of their superiority over machines. Bigurube is enjoying this. I look at him and see the small, neat head, the mischief implicit in the grin, the toothbrush moustache, and I don't see Bigurube any more. This aircraft is being flown by Eddie Murphy.

Another fifteen minutes. The Ulanga is left to recover. The crocs and hippos are at peace with only each other to gaze at.

Bigurube points again. Elephants . . . one . . . two . . . three . . . then another, a little one. He banks the Cessna and wheels the wings round. Then there are more, this time a threesome, and over there to the right, Bigurube, it's me, my voice, I've spotted how many, twenty, more, thirty. The mood in the cockpit has changed. Even Kibasa is smiling. In all we count over sixty on this flight. Bigurube is satisfied with the total. It's not a particularly good area for spotting them, this part of the Selous, he says.

What about skeletons? Did he see any? Kibasa is asking

the questions, leaning over from his seat behind the pilot. Bigurube nods. A few, but their colour was grey, and this meant the remains had been there for some time. There is, he thinks, little evidence to show from this flight that elephants are being killed.

I ask where they all are.

He shakes his head. 'I wish I knew.'

Sixty minutes later the tin roofs of Songea winked at us shamelessly as we circled over the town's airstrip.

The green of the Selous was in the distance now, sheltering behind the powder-blue mountains that protected the town. As we waited by the Cessna for Ndunguru to meet us, Bigurube busied himself with refuelling the plane. He was balanced on the wing, legs apart, filling the tanks with kerosene. He finished and patted the plane as if it were a well-behaved child, a younger sister, and said to Kibasa and me: 'She's done well, considering her age.'

'Just how old is she?' asked Kibasa.

'This 182? We've had her for ten years but she's probably been flying since the late sixties. 1968, I think.'

'Have you ever been in a really dangerous situation, Bigurube?'

'I've had a few close ones.'

'Crashes?'

I could see Kibasa had moved away, though not far enough to miss what was being said.

'Yes, it was back in 1982 when I had just started flying. I had taken off from the Selous for Dar es Salaam, and I noticed that the fuel gauges were showing the wrong amount. My battery was flat, so all I could do to check the amount I had in the tanks was to tilt the wings, and that showed that I was losing a lot. I had to land and I did not have much time to pick a place because it was almost dusk and the fuel was now very low. I was flying over those mountains between Dar and the Selous, the ones we crossed this morning, and after I had passed over them, I dropped down to take a look at the ground. It was forest, so the one place that I thought was suitable for landing was a small clearing. I put down the plane and the wheels sank into a swamp. There was no one around, and as my battery was dead I was unable to radio Dar or the Selous.'

'Weren't they looking for you?' asked Kibasa who had drawn nearer as the story unfolded. 'Wasn't the alarm raised when you failed to show up?'

'No,' said Bigurube. 'Dar was unaware that I was coming, and the people in the Selous had no reason to believe that I was not there already.'

'What did you do?'

'I decided that all I could do was sleep the night in the cockpit and then walk to the next village at first light. I couldn't sleep. Mosquitoes.'

'How far was the village?'

'I had no idea, but I was lucky because this swamp was the place where villagers came every month to collect clay to make their cooking pots. The next morning was the day that they were due to come, and they found me, and brought me to their homes.'

'What happened to the plane?'

'It couldn't take off because the swamp was too sticky and the wings of the plane were damaged. So it stayed there all winter, and had to be unbolted and dragged to the road, put on a lorry and repaired in Dar.'

'Exactly what plane was that?' murmured Kibasa.

'This one,' said Bigurube, pointing to the Cessna, 'the one you've just got out of.'

Kibasa stood, feet apart on the firm, red earth, tapping the soil with his feet, scuffing the ground. He could not quite believe he had survived. He looked at his watch, then walked towards the edge of the airstrip, vanishing into a jungle of dense tall grass that covered his head. I thought he was going for a pee, or to be sick again, and perhaps I was right, but when he reappeared a minute or two later, both his arms were laden with a sheaf of golden sunflowers. 'For Ndunguru,' he said, smiling. 'I haven't seen him for some years. We worked together, you see.'

When Africans greet each other, and I don't think it matters whether they are friends, non-acquaintances or even enemies, I advise you to set aside some time. Bring a book. Start a painting. Take a sleeping pill. This was one of those long and complex hand-wringing, back-bruising, palm-slapping rites that can absorb you for an afternoon. When it was over, my arms were sore, my shoulder blades hug-happy and my palms smarting, but at least my cheeks and lips had not been touched. That is something you can say for British rule. Now if the French had been here . . .

I handed Ndunguru a letter of introduction from Costa Mlay which he had difficulty in opening because he was using one hand. In the other he clutched a tin box. He read the note, folded it, all with his right hand, and tucked it away in the breast pocket of his shirt.

'Welcome to Songea,' he said to us, sweeping his left hand in a wide gesture that took in the airstrip, the mountains faint in the distance, and the few buildings we could see that signalled the beginning and end of the town. 'Songea, queen of ivory towns. You are my guests here and I will do my best to show you what we are doing to stop this killing.'

As he said this, he smiled, a gap-toothed grin, that made him look like an idiot. In fact, he was anything but, with a Masters in Terrestrial Ecology from the University of New Mexico and a lectureship at the Mweka Wildlife College on the slopes of Kilimanjaro, the major training ground for all the men who worked in conservation in the country. Ndunguru, with his silly grin, was not just a man with an impressive c.v. who answered to the title Regional Game Officer of the Southern Sector of the Selous Game Reserve. His intellect was fired up by a steely streak in his character that allowed his mind to create a vision of what he could achieve and the means to bring it within his grasp.

The town was tucked up, sleeping soundly under the worn white sheet of afternoon sun. Few people were to be seen walking along the middle of its ochre streets. In fact, from three to five, the roads of the town returned to that era before the motor vehicle spluttered into the south-west of the territory when a man was more likely to direct a stream of angry words and saliva at a bullock cart than a Land Rover. Songea, all of 1,000 kilometres distant from Dar es Salaam, had deceived me. Ndunguru saw my yawn and said as much. He told me not to be fooled. Far from being a backwater where nothing remotely interesting happened, this town had seen two big ivory trials in the past twelve months, the arrest of its major citizen on charges of trafficking in trophies, and the exodus of at least forty Somali families suspected of involvement with the *jangili*.

The Angoni Arms where we stayed that night was built of brown brick and stood a few hundred metres away from the old German boma from which they had administered the area during their brief colonial rule which ended with the defeat of the Central Powers in 1918. The hotel looked promising. It stood in its own grounds, sheltered from the road by giant Flamboyant trees whose chorus of scarlet flowers swayed to a rhythm choreographed by the most delicate of southern breezes. Beneath the trees a woman brushed small clouds of dust from the earth, and when she had finished she sprinkled the heap she had collected in her pan back on to the ground. Scattered around were a number of red mud huts. The walls of most of them were crumbling, desperately in need of a mud fix. The tin roofs had lost their shine. It was only when I noticed that each faded green door bore a number that I realized these were bedrooms for the hotel guests. Inside the main hotel building a man was eyeing the darts board. It too was decaying with wire spokes missing or dangling from their attachments. I asked the board-gazer whether there were darts to be had at the bar. He shrugged.

Nor was there any beer in the Angoni Arms. No Safari, no Tusker, nothing. Unless, said the manager, managing his face to look even rounder than it was, unless, tilting his blue-black head onto his white collar, unless . . . I put my hand inside my pocket and felt around long enough for him to hear the rustle of money. I'm sure he didn't really hear it, because much of the currency is so old and decrepit that the rustle has long since vanished. Tanzanian shillings slither, slide and stick together. Money that tends to do this is not reassuring. It does not excite. It possesses neither the cachet nor the confidence that comes with crispness.

Begrudgingly he produced three bottles of Safari. No more, he said, shaking his head. Kibasa and Bigurube didn't mind, because both of them were teetotallers, so that left Ndunguru to fight over the odd bottle with me. The dining room was further inside the hotel, a few steps away from the bar and its invalid dartboard. We were served chicken and rice, Kibasa's favourite. By the time we had finished, the plates looked fuller than when they first arrived. I pushed to one side the still heaving mound of uneaten rice and chicken bones and skin and asked Ndunguru, who was now toying with the metal top of an unopened Safari bottle, whether he would like to try some brandy.

'There is no brandy here. Konyagi. Try that.'

I told him about my day at the officers' mess with the Black Mamba, and then I pulled out of my flak jacket pocket a plastic half-bottle of Hine.

Ndunguru was interested enough to push the Safari in my direction. He demanded a glass, unscrewed the top of the Hine, and carelessly slung half its contents into a deep tumbler. I apologized for the brandy's warmth. I had been carrying the bottle around with me for a week or so, just in case, but Ndunguru didn't seem to care. His lips licked at the glass and it was drained almost immediately. He tapped the glass, expectantly, on the black metal box which he kept on the table, within his reach.

I asked him about the two trials in Songea, the ivory cases. He looked up at me, with the glass in his hand, passed the glance down the table to Bigurube and Kibasa, almost as though he were seeking their approval before he spoke, and received what I took to be a reassuring nod from the pair of them. He said that he had been involved in both the cases, but the one concerning the MP for Songea was extremely sensitive and he was not sure if he could tell me much about it at the moment.

'MP?' I asked.

'Yes, Ali Yusuf Abdurabi. He was the MP for Songea.'

'Was?'

'Yes. Now he is in prison,' said Bigurube. 'Twelve years.'

'He was caught with many tusks.' Ndunguru fixed himself another drink. I could see that if I was to succeed that night and over the next few days in extracting the information I needed, I would have to bring into play the bottle of Hine which was sweating next to my socks inside my bag.

Ndunguru said he would tell me about the other case, but not now. Instead, he picked up the glass, rose at the head of the table and said: 'We will drink to the end of the middlemen. We will toast them in their cells.' He drew his lips to the brandy and drained the glass. Kibasa and Bigurube followed his example with Seven Up.

'Death to the *jangili*,' I said. The three of them laughed, raised their glasses and emptied them. Ndunguru was pulling his silly grin, and I wondered how many times that MP or any of the other middlemen of Songea had seen it and underestimated him. As the spirit infused his blood and his brain, he discovered his reserves of fluency. He told me that when he first came to Songea in 1972 the ivory business was a 'common thing'. People expected the authorities to do nothing about it. Ivory poaching and ivory dealing were not considered crimes. They were a way of life. Ivory poaching and the activities of the middlemen were accepted by the police, the magistrates and the Department.

'I'll tell you,' he said, 'that in the villages where we are going tomorrow, you'll see men who would go hunting for elephant and leave the ivory in the bush. We would often find a skull with the tusks intact. Then they were only interested in the meat.'

As he talked, he looked not at me, but at his glass, which I made sure was brimming all evening. By now I had produced the second bottle from my hut and was debating whether to move on to Konyagi from the bar once the Hine had disappeared. Ndunguru's fingers drummed on the table, his head down, pushed on to his chest, as if he was exhausted with the talking.

When he recalled the atmosphere in Songea and the villages in the seventies, he was doing his best to portray an unruffled world, largely untouched by outside influences, a world shaped, for the most part, by the traditions that had been infused in mother's milk from generation to generation. But that was before the war with Amin and before the price of ivory hit a high on the world markets. Suddenly those villages were riven apart as soldiers who had fought for the Black Mamba strutted back home, flush with excitement and all the promise that victory had offered them. Many came back from the front with their weapons. Overnight the villagers found that their *gabores*, the muzzle-loaders they had relied upon for so many years, were obsolete. Now they had access to AK-47s and ammunition, and their combat training meant that these ex-soldiers, soon-to-be *jangili*, were formidable opponents for the game scouts who too often relied upon single-shot rifles and poor-quality ammunition when they could obtain it.

I asked him about these villages and he told me that they lay on the edge of the Selous, his southern sector, where there was a huge concentration of animals. If poaching was to be stopped, then it was the people in these villages who had to be persuaded that it was not in their interests to kill elephants. 'Tomorrow I will take you to see the work we have begun in Mchomoro, Kilimasera, Nyamtumbo, Nambecha, Likuyusekamaganga . . . ' It all sounded like the wrong end of a British Rail announcement.

'Likuyuwho?' I said.

'Just call it Likuyu,' suggested Kibasa. 'None of us can get our tongues round these strange southern names.' I'd see it all tomorrow anyway, so I didn't bother to ask Ndunguru to repeat them. Instead I asked about the other trial, the one he'd said he'd tell me about.

He hadn't heard me. Or he wasn't ready. He looked up from the table, and shushed me quiet. He moved the sauce bottle in front of him, crushing the grains of rice flat onto the pink tablecloth. What, he said, do you think happened to the villagers when peace came, when the war was over?

'You've told me already. The soldiers came back.'

Ndunguru was insistent. 'What else happened?' He stopped playing with the sauce bottle and looked me in the eye. 'Peace brought inflation.'

'So?'

'So every time there was a crisis with the economy, the villagers found it more difficult to buy seeds to grow their crops. They starved. My father is a coffee farmer. He had bad times, very bad times, but he didn't suffer as much as the villagers in the Selous.'

All this time, he said, from the early seventies up to the mid eighties when he returned to Songea, the price of ivory was increasing. When he came back in 1987, he found there were great differences. Ivory poaching was still accepted by the people. Indeed it was seen as a reasonably easy way to make a living. But there had been a change of attitude among the authorities. Now they would no longer tolerate it. It was obvious to him on his second posting who in Songea was behind the organized ivory trade, and he decided that the time had come to wipe it out.

Ndunguru squeezed the last dregs of Hine from the plastic bottle into his glass – then shot out his hand. He was reading my mind. He'd seen my fingers tapping across the stains and rice that now decorated the table top. His hand beat mine to his black tin box and covered it protectively.

'What's in there, Ndunguru? It must be precious.'

Bigurube stood up and shook Kibasa awake. Perhaps he was embarrassed by my behaviour. More probably he realized that this was Ndunguru's territory. Either way, the pair of them said goodnight and left us alone. Ndunguru waited until they had left the room, and then he nudged me with his elbow, winked, took a key out of his breast pocket and unlocked the box.

'I don't like too many people seeing this. Especially,' he paused and looked around, 'in a place like this. It is far too public.' He raised the lid a fraction, then a little more, until the light caught the snub, squared-off barrel of a gun. 'A Walther PPK .762.'

'Why on earth have you got that?'

'My job is dangerous.' He said it matter of factly, with no hint of fear. I asked him if he had ever used it.

'There have been times when I have been under fire. There are many people in Songea who do not want me around.'

'You've been threatened?'

'I sleep with it,' he said, lowering the lid, and locking the box.

Ndunguru pushed his chair away from the table, rumpling the pink cloth as he moved, dislodging sticky bits of rice and scrambling the flies that were feeding on the leftovers towards the safety of the ceiling. I looked at the mess that we had left behind. The tablecloth was littered with sticky glasses and half-full plates. All except the space in front of Kibasa's empty seat. That was as immaculate as the lime-green Kaunda suit he had changed into for dinner.

Now Ndunguru had left the table, I thought this was the signal for bed. I wasn't really relishing a night in the hut I had been allocated. Number 2 was just a stumble across the dark yard from the Angoni's main building. Inside there was a narrow bed, a shelf for luggage, an electric light, and an en-suite toilet and shower. It sounds luxurious, especially for somewhere as remote as Songea, but the bathroom floor was running with mud and the shower water was cold, there were cracks in the walls and holes in the windows. I rejoiced when I saw the mosquito net, curled up on its hook above the bed, waiting to be unfurled and tucked under the mattress. Even so, I could see this was the sort of place that required either a great deal of nerve or a dose more of alcohol to ensure a peaceful night.

I needn't have worried. There was a knock on my door and Ndunguru pushed his head into the room and suggested that we get some air.

As we walked in the cool of the night, through shadows that turned out next morning to be cashew nut trees, I couldn't believe that I was approaching the hub of an ivory town whose chief citizen, its MP, was now serving a prison sentence for trafficking. Apart from some drumming and ululations, which Ndunguru said was a wedding party, Songea was comatose. I couldn't hear a dog bark or a night watchman's snore. Only the shadows kept us company. Even at night, Songea looked neat and polished with not a speck of litter on the streets. I remembered the woman in the hotel yard, brushing the dust and then scattering it into the breeze. But lurking in the darkness behind this façade, according to Ndunguru, was a highly co-ordinated network of ivory traffickers who had been allowed years of near-official freedom to establish themselves, build up their contacts across the country and beyond its borders, and accumulate enough money and influence to protect their investment.

Ivory, he explained, was a means of laundering money. Ivory was a hard currency. He had noticed men driving around Songea in the last year in new Japanese cars and pick-ups. He had asked the police to investigate and they told him that one of the drivers of these new vehicles had said it was a present from a Japanese businessman who was thanking him for all the assistance he had received from him during his business trip the year before. But that was a lie. It was ivory money.

'You know, Nick, it is not just new cars that are being exchanged for tusks. You are sure to see radio cassettes hanging off people's ears in Songea these days.'

'Up north,' I said, 'they stuff their ears with torch batteries.'

'What can you expect of the Masai?' he replied, and immediately the street filled with his laughter.

'Who are the poachers, then, in Songea?'

'Somalis and Baluchis. Or were. God's first nomads. There

used to be fifty Somali families in Songea and all of them were poaching. Since the arrest of our admirable MP, they have quit the town. No one knows where they have gone. Maybe Ifakara, or Kenya, or far away from here.' But there was one family of Baluchis left in the area, he said. 'The Ishmaels. They run a transport business. They are so rich, these Ishmaels.'

There were lights ahead of us, an attempt at neon, and a sign that read Serengetei Bar, with a picture of a lion, swinging lazily in the warm breeze. A vehicle was parked outside, but in the bar there were just two girls, leaning against it, not bothering to talk to the barman. Maybe it was like this every night. We ordered beer and sat at a table against the wall facing the bar. The girls joined us. The barman followed. I nodded at him. The girls relaxed as he brought them two beers as well. He charged us for six. They opened their bottles and settled their bottoms into the worn plastic of the Serengetei chairs. They stared. It was certainly too late for a smile. The barman turned up the music. Country and Western. One of the girls wriggled her hips against the plastic seat bottom. The other was concentrating on her beer. They both wore flowery dresses, tucked, African style, into the folds of their bodies. These were not attractive women, even at that time of night, so far from home.

Ndunguru ignored them, drawing himself closer to me in an effort to defeat the music. He was shouting at me now, endeavouring to tell me about the next day's plans. We would set off for the Selous, 55,000 square kilometres of territory of which a quarter was vital for elephants. We would visit the villages which bordered the Selous, the pockets of men from whom the *jangili* were recruited.

He wanted me to see what he had done to involve these villagers in actively helping to protect elephants and not, as they had done for centuries, destroy them. To succeed, these people had to be persuaded not to kill, not to hunt. It was easy, relatively easy, I could see, in Songea where men could be jailed or driven out of the town, but the bush was different. The men who lived there had hunted for centuries. *Tembo* belonged to them, and so did the lands the *tembo* browsed on. Elephant hunting was seen as a right. Elephants could be eaten. So they went into the bush and killed.

69

Ndunguru was passionate about his mission, much more so than the sleepy girls who slouched opposite us about theirs. I looked across at them. They were attempting to revive our interest and their appetite for alcohol by edging closer towards us both, pushing their elbows down on the table, touching their breasts and pouting their lips. I caught the barman's eye and ordered, above the tape which had now changed tempo from C & W to ethnic reggae, another round of beers for these brown Bardots. The girls relaxed and settled themselves more sedately in their chairs. Now that commercial honour had been restored, they could concentrate on the drink.

We left the Serengetei. I looked over my shoulder and saw that the two girls had removed themselves back to the bar and the music had been turned down.

'It's been a great struggle to persuade these villagers that there is a future for them without killing elephants, but I think it is beginning to work. Tomorrow you will see.'

I asked Ndunguru about Operation Uhai. Had it been successful in the area?

'They don't like Captain Katali around here,' he replied. 'He's the officer commanding Uhai. He's based up country near the Selous. While he's around the *jangili* are quiet.'

'What happens when the army pull out?'

Ndunguru sighed. 'That is the day I fear. The army cannot stay here for ever. It is far too costly for the country. Uhai has given us a breathing space. Time to build up our own operation, time to persuade the villagers. We can use it to train our own men so they can be more effective, and build up our weapons. We need vehicles, guns, ammunition, medical supplies.'

This could have been Costa speaking, or the ineffectual little warden at Mikumi.

'At the moment we have two Land Rovers. I need at least one more. Nick, do you know what my budget is?'

I shook my head, but he didn't notice. It was a rhetorical question, one that he had asked many people many times.

'Excluding salaries, 300,000 shillings. That's about £3,000. And out of that, 63,000 shillings is all I have to use to patrol the area.'

'Why?'

'Administration costs, that is why. I am responsible for

an area of 55,000 square kilometres. I have told you that already, but what can you achieve with two Land Rovers? How can my men be effective without walkie talkies, radios? I need a helicopter. It's the one way of patrolling this area. Planes can't land everywhere. We have swamps and forests and mountains in the Selous.'

We had reached the Angoni Arms. My head was pumping and my back was sore. My room and its complement of mossies were waiting for me. Ndunguru was going home. In the Land Rover.

'We are lucky in Tanzania,' he shouted across at me as he heaved himself into the cab. 'It is a backward country. You would say Third World. I say we are lucky. We do not have breathalyser tests in the Third World.'

He pressed down the accelerator pedal, and as the vehicle moved off, kicking dust into the night, he flung, from the cab window, a thin, stiff, cardboard file.

'Bedtime reading,' he shouted above the noise of the engine.

It was a court record. A criminal case. I flicked the pages, unable to take in the names of the five accused, and ready to leave it until the morning. Then I saw the charge – ivory poaching – and the number of tusks involved. Eighty-nine. Value: 5,610,000 shillings (£22,000).

And there was something else that kept me from sleep. The accused and their jobs. These men weren't from the bush. They were members of the anti-poaching unit.

It was Ndunguru who arrested them. He'd been tipped off that a vehicle, a Landcruiser, registration TZ84277, was carrying tusks and was somewhere on the Songea–Tunduru road. The poachers, he was warned, were armed. It took him two days to find the vehicle, and, when he did, he discovered who they were. One of them surrendered a sub-machine gun with 30 rounds of ammunition in his pockets.

Inside the back of the Landcruiser, beneath a roof-high pile of hides and skins, was the prize Ndunguru knew was there: 89 tusks, wrapped in cow and goat skins. He also pulled out of the back green jungle combat uniforms.

The men's defence was weak. They too, they said, were following a lead from an informer which took them to Nyam-tumbo, a village I was to come to know quite well, to a hotel called the Argentine Guest House, to a town called Tunduru, a town built by slaves, and now in thrall of lions, man-eaters and middlemen.

The file made extraordinarily complicated reading, considering the amount of alcohol I had consumed that night. But it demonstrated that not only were some of Ndunguru's colleagues involved in poaching, but professional liars too. One of the poachers had the temerity to suggest when he was charged a few days later in the police station at Songea that he expected to be called as a prosecution witness. The trial took place a year after the arrests, and on 12 April 1990, two of the gang, the men who were members of the anti-poaching unit, were sentenced to twelve years. The other three were acquitted.

The sub-machine gun with its 30 rounds of ammunition, the jungle combat uniforms, the 89 tusks, and the 38 hides and skins were confiscated by the authorities.

I dreamed about that file that night. I dreamed I was in the Argentine Guest House in Nyamtumbo. I dreamed of *jangili*, but not of court cases. I dreamed of skinny old men whose shadows were swallowed by the silent bush. I dreamed of village cronies and their furtive dealings with men in uniform by the sides of lonely roads. I dreamed of Ndunguru and his gun.

When I woke, men were knocking at my door. The sun was splintered on the cracks in the window glass, and a gecko was stapled to the ceiling.

SEVEN

The Beast of Likuyu

The purple streets of Songea were suffering a heavy bout of perspiration. The potholes in the roads leading from the Angoni Arms to the HQ of the anti-poaching unit where Ndunguru was based brimmed red with the overnight rains and the people on their way to work or market trod carefully, attempting to keep their feet dry and their clothes clean as the heavy trucks and buses revved up their engines for the day's drive to Iringa or Dar or Tunduru.

Songea. 7.30 a.m. The dawn came later in the south. Now it was greying the sky, rolling back the night to give anyone who cared to look a glimpse of the peaks which encircled the town.

Songea had woken not with a yawn but a hustle. This was the one time of the day when Songea didn't look weary. Give it another couple of hours and Africa's lassitude would return. But, for the moment, people were on the move. The market place was a chaos of colour. Stallholders stood, alive and expectant, on the lookout as Songeans ambled past their merchandise – garish shirts, the sort that made you blink in the departure lounge of an airport on a summer weekend, trousers, shoes and sandals, all plastic; zinc buckets, radios, meat, bananas, nuts, cobs, corn simmering on a charcoal stove; a boy, ten or eleven, in rags with no shoes, preparing eggs for breakfast. Buses heaved up clouds of dust as the drivers pulled in opposite the market, the long, dark journey from Dar way over. Now yesterday's newspaper would be available for today's Songeans.

The travellers shook themselves awake and tested the ground with measured stamps. One yawned as he waited for the reluctant driver to unravel the mesh of ropes that bound the luggage to the roof. People were shouting, some gesturing for silence so that they could hear the breakfast news from a tinny radio that was fighting the babble. I could smell the freshness of the vanishing morning, but sweat was running off men's faces now, and the flies were starting to attack.

It was early enough for the askaris at the headquarters to present themselves for parade and inspection. They were lined up on the square patch of grass round which the anti-poaching unit had built its offices, toting their rifles and responding catatonically to the drill sergeant, a stringy stick of malice with one eye and a bellow that I'm sure could have been obeyed in Tunduru, 266 kilometres to the east.

Ndunguru saw me watching and walked over. 'How's the head?' I asked him.

'Fine. Tonight we shall go Tanzanian. Konyagi!'

Kibasa and Bigurube were preoccupied with breakfast. It would be their last chance of food before Dar, for they were leaving today by plane for the city. Bigurube had been recalled for the wages-run, his weekly hop round the game parks of the Selous to pay the men. We would not see him again, he said, until we reached Kalulu, the village that was furthest from Songea and nearest to the Selous, and the last in the pay queue. He would try to meet us there and, if we needed transport back to Dar, he would take us. As for Kibasa, it was goodbye. 'I'll see you in the Kilimanjaro,' he joked. 'Chicken and rice at the Summit.' I never saw him again. I often thought of him back in Mikumi, without a job, staring into the bush, his eyes and soul searching for elephants.

Ndunguru waited with me till the drilling was over and called for the sergeant to step across.

Standing next to Ndunguru, I got a closer look at the stringy drillmaster. He was holding a rifle, an antique .303, by the barrel; his uniform was torn, and I could see the black flash of his chest through the rips in the olive-green tunic. If he had been waiting for me in the bush, I would have walked past. He could have been a blade of elephant grass.

'This is Burkard Kayombo,' Ndunguru said, tugging on the tunic of this anorexic Pavarotti. 'He is a hero of the poaching war.'

You know how when you see a cripple or a spastic or someone with a grotesque deformity and your eyes are magnetized to the disfigurement. Each time you force yourself to look away, they revolt and swivel back. This was exactly what my eyes were doing now, obeying my impulses and not my inhibitions. Burkard Kayombo's face was missing on his left side. Instead of a cheekbone, there was a deep crater, lividly stitched together. A purple track of scar tissue wound round the eye and across the cheekbone. He saw me staring and turned away. The socket of his eye was glazed and sightless. Off the barrack square, he seemed a gentle, modest man, who told me that these horrible wounds had been inflicted by a *jangili* gang who had caught him following them.

'I was on their trail, alone in the bush, and had been tracking them for some days,' he told me. 'I had worked out the route they would take to approach an elephant area, and I was so tired, I fell asleep. One of the poachers found me and ran back to tell the *fundi*. They woke me up and held a discussion on what to do with me. I heard them sentence me to death. I really thought that that was the end. The leader of the *jangili* walked over to me and fired at point-blank range. The bullet went into my cheek and came out through this eye.' Burkard Kayombo patted the wound gingerly.

'They left me for dead. So I was found in the bush by some villagers and they brought me back here. I spent four weeks in hospital, but I cannot go on patrol again. All I can do is train the men and tell them never to sleep alone out there.'

He told his story the way soldiers always tell stories. Flat, efficient and tailored to fill just so much space on a statement form. But all the time he talked, his long fingers tortured the two wide creamy bands made from hippo teeth that he was wearing, twisting and pulling the rings until the pain released a stop signal. On one of the rings his initials, BGK, were carved. He was married with three children and earned 3,255 shillings a month as a Game Assistant (Grade Two), and I couldn't see that there was much future for this twenty-seven-year-old whose war was already over.

'You must not worry about him,' Ndunguru told me when the sergeant had marched off to rejoin his men. 'We give no medals out, nor do we expect them to be awarded. His is an example that you can see all over Tanzania. But he is an Ngoni, and they are fighters.'

Zulus, Bantu, Hehe, Chaga, Masai, Germans, British: the Ngoni had fought each of these tribes. They conquered them all save the ones who had white skins and rapid-fire rifles. Songea is the capital of the Ngoni, and the town is nourished on the desperate memories of the tribe's homicidal past. Not that these posthumous glories are all entirely without honour. There is a story about the Ngoni that is worth telling not just because it demonstrates how quickly Europeans were capable of discarding their mantle of civilization and disinterring from their past a shabby and merciless streak of barbarism, but also because it exemplifies the courage, pride and stubbornness of the Ngoni in refusing to admit to the inevitable. The Germans have been gone from this area for more than seventy years now. They still possess the head of Paramount Chief Nbino, and, though no one is certain of its whereabouts, it is probably bobbing sightlessly on a sea of formaldehyde in a glass specimen jar in some Prussian attic. Time and preservative may have reduced that head to no more than a grotesque curio, but the virtues that the Ngoni Chief and his princelings showed that day still survive, and are now being displayed against another enemy – the men of the anti-poaching unit.

This is what happened. The forefathers of Burkard Kayombo had stamped through southern Africa, squashing whoever happened to bar their path. When they crossed the Ruvuma river and reached Songea, their push to the north was halted by an opponent who matched their skill at killing, the Hehe, Kibasa's tribe. So the Ngoni settled for the south and centred their influence around Songea. Everything was fine until the Germans came. The Ngoni resisted the colonists vigorously, but they were wielding spears and clubs against machine guns. The Germans won, and decided that an example should be made of the Ngoni. So, with a rare, terrible yet inspirational flash of imagination, they decided to hang all sixty-three of the Ngoni leaders, suspend their leadership as it were in one swoop from the gallows. This fallen aristocracy were led to the drop, set up outside the German HQ, the boma, and hanged, one at a time, in front of their subjects. As each condemned man waited his turn for death, the crowd encouraged them with tribal shouts and warriors' gestures, and when the executions had finally finished, the Germans went to the Paramount Chief whom they had forced to watch as his flowers wilted in the sun, and declared that they would spare his life.

Naturally, he refused, saying: 'You have hung all my lieutenants. Now you must finish the task you have begun. You must hang me.' Now his head and his courage are bottled somewhere in Germany, and the Ngoni want it back. I can understand why.

You could walk down Songea's purple roads, now dried out by the sun, and pass Flamboyant trees that gave to the ditches in which they grew a sudden and unexpected splash of brilliance. You could pass along the streets and thread your way through blue-black people who saw you and weighed you up with their narrow eyes, but you could not perceive the scoundrels or the profiteers behind the mask. Even so, the privateering traditions of the Ngoni were alive. The Germans may have impressed some sort of order upon the streets, but within the houses and huts, some Songeans were exercising that identical impulse that had brought their ancestors so far from their birthplace in the south. Only, at the end of the twentieth century, civilization had taught them a lesson. Not to kill man, nor profit from his death. No, elephants would do instead.

Where the Germans had failed to make an impact was in the bank. I have spent many hours in African banks, waiting to be served, waiting not to be ignored, signing whole trees of paper until my patience and my right arm went to sleep. But the Bank of Tanzania in Songea must, if medals are to be awarded for bureaucratic obduracy, win the gold.

I had run short of money, and because we were about to leave Songea for the villages, I told Ndunguru that I needed to go. I must apologize if this sounds as if I am describing a reluctant visit to a nauseating toilet, but it is an accurate comparison. You have no choice. So you go and go as quickly as you can. Wallets and bowels are cousins under the skin. They empty. They refill. They are subject to the laws of nature.

It was lunchtime when I made my request. Ndunguru

shook his head and said the bank was closed. I was pleased. I'd go later. I'd borrow money.

'But I know the Chief Accountant. He is a good man. He will fix you up. Come on.'

We drove into the main street, and walked into the bank by the back entrance. This, I knew, was going to be easy. The Chief Accountant welcomed us, and Ndunguru and I sat on the wooden chairs that a clerk had drawn up for us. I took my wallet and passport out of my jacket, and Ndunguru placed his hands and his tin box, the black tin box, on the desk of the Chief Accountant.

Nothing happened.

For five minutes nothing happened. Well, we did chat, and once or twice I twisted my wrist to sneak a look at my watch.

The Chief Accountant was a founder-member of the Circumlocution Office, resentful, officious, bombastic, snail-slow, everything a clerk aims to be. The most devastating weapons in his armoury were two ballpoint pens. One was blue, the other red. In his right hand these banal instruments became Sidewinders, capable of inflicting appalling injuries wherever he chose to aim them. I could see they were now targeted at me and there was no way that I could escape. The system he had devised to cause maximum inconvenience and stress among his customers was, as the most malign always are, simple in its execution and impossible to evade. The blue biro could be used only to sign one particular form, the red another, and so on. Now that doesn't sound fiendish, does it? No, except that this applied rigorously to every piece of paper that I signed and he countersigned, and there were others too, forms which, I believe, no one had seen or heard of before, forms with strange numbers coded across their corners, forms which, for all I knew, meant that I had sold out my house, my wife, my children, my car, and my terrapin. One day the knock on the door would come, and I would open it to see the slight frame of the Chief Accountant standing in front of me, sockless in brown plastic sandals, with his white shirt and grey flannels, a triumphant grin somewhere inside that post-box slot of a mouth.

The Chief Accountant was irritated. He could not find the blue pen, and he needed the blue pen to sign the form that was in front of him. He rumpled through the mess of stationery on his desk. He vanished for a moment beneath a white cloud of flimsy. Carbon paper still has a grip on Africa. It was gliding around the bank, performing precision aerobatics. Currency forms, import regulations, export quotas, internal memoranda, financial guidelines, large print, small print, everything was tidal. Anything that belonged on his desk was on the floor or on its way there. Except for the blue pen. The Chief Accountant couldn't find it. This happened every day. He shouldered his exasperation with a heave and dug deep into the reserves of bumf. Ah, there it was, not on the desk, but in the breast pocket of his shirt, where he had placed it so that he could remember where it was. But did he really need it, this blue pen? Surely the red pen was the one that should leave its showy flourish on this particular form. No, he was right after all, it was the blue that was needed. And so it continued, an unending confusion of red-blue, blue-red, a blur of bureaucracy. And when, several forms later, the Chief Accountant finally did uncover the red pen, he threw it away in disgust, realizing as the ballpoint stabbed into the paper and tore the precious form that he had been betrayed by ink.

All this time the Chief Accountant complained. About his salary, his hours, his responsibilities, and, worst of all, the corresponding idleness of his boss. 'He sits in there, in his big cool office, sweating under the fan, counting the times it turns in a minute, while I'm out here sharing a desk with three others. How can I be expected to do all this work for the money he pays me? I am here from eight in the morning till ten at night, while *he*,' and here he threw a dagger in the direction of the manager's door, 'while *he* leaves at five.'

This, of course, was the song of the civil servant, a standard, softly crooned in shaded offices across time zones, continents and cultures. It had evoked yawns for generations. Put it to music and you'd find it being played on a wet Sunday afternoon on Radio 2 by Benny Green. Again and again.

One hour later, just as the bank was reopening for the afternoon, I left the Chief Accountant's desk, dizzy from the kaleidoscope of colour, reeling from the inertia of the afternoon, and sat in the Land Rover, counting the pile of greasy notes I had received in exchange for a single crisp sterling traveller's cheque.

Ndunguru sat beside me, and when I had finished counting the money, he nudged me in the ribs conspiratorially and rattled his black box.

'Nick,' he said, 'I should have shot that man. We could have been on the road by now.'

The road to Likuyusekamaganga is fringed with sunflowers as tall as country cottages. Imagine driving by a transport café and seeing fried eggs twirled on white plates with all the panache of a fourth-on-the-bill juggler. This is the way they looked, proud and precarious. Our driver's name was Vincent, as it happened.

We drove on terracotta roads through these cholesterol fields towards the Matagro mountains. This was the old slave caravan route from Lake Malawi in the west to Kilwa on the ocean, the town that rivalled Zanzibar as an ivory trading centre. Now the only visible evidence of Tippu Tib's men and their *chikote* whips were the clumps of mango trees and banana plantations which marked out the beginnings and ends of villages, the overnight stopping places of the caravans, and, often, the last resting places of the wretches who could stumble no further.

Whole forests were on the move that afternoon. Each of them amounted to a few trees, staggering along the road a few paces at a time, then pausing for breath and a slight readjustment of the weight, and continuing towards some sightless village. A few years ago, Ndunguru pointed out to me, this road had been thick with trees. Now the villagers who lived near it had denuded both sides for miles. Every one of them, I saw as we passed them, was swinging an axe from her belt. Gathering firewood was strictly women's work. But trees were not only vulnerable because they made fires for cooking and warmth. These people would also hack one down if they saw that an owl had chosen it for its nest. Owls were purveyors of evil. Owls were a bad omen and should be driven away from an area. So if an owl regularly used a certain tree to nest in, or as an observation post, it was bye-bye tree.

It was on this very stretch of road, only two years before, that a colleague of Ndunguru's, a game scout, and an experienced one at that, was devoured by a lion. Does this frighten the villagers who walk it daily to collect firewood, or to take their crops to market in another village, maybe twenty-five kilometres away from their own? Yes. But still they walk because, too often, there is no other way of transporting themselves, and if there were, then it would be too expensive.

In fact, only one lorry came by, packed with sacks of grain, and an exceedingly fat man, who had turned steerage into first class and was riding the bumps and potholes to Songea in a large wooden armchair which he had contrived to squeeze in amongst the grain sacks. He had, in turn, wedged himself into it and sat there, dreaming and dozing, perhaps of Tippu Tib, perhaps of man-eaters. Either way, he didn't wake up when our Land Rover squeezed past.

I was happy to leave behind the venality of Songea, the girls in the Serengetei Bar closing in for drink, the shuttered houses whose shadowed insides had sheltered the middlemen from the glare of the sun and the eyes of the police. To me that wasn't the Africa I had come to see. Out here, on the winding painterly road to Likuyusekamaganga in this shuddering metal box, heading for the villages, there was a sense of freedom, of a society untouched by the present, where strange things might happen beyond the waving sunflower fields. Of that I was sure.

The headman of Likuyusekamaganga greets us with two hands outstretched. I grasp them both, and then, with my right palm open and arm crooked at the elbow, clasp his left palm. I follow through with my left palm. It's complicated, especially for the terminally uncoordinated among whom I number. The greetings are complete. We are seated at a rickety wooden table drawn up in the dusty village square outside the offices of the Chama Cha Mapinduzi, the only party, the Revolutionary Party of Tanzania, the unnatural heirs of this one-party state, through which, in which and without which nothing can occur, or so the politicians in Dar say. But Dar es Salaam is over three days' journey from Likuyusekamaganga, and they are far more concerned here about marauding hyenas which attack their children than about edicts from the CCM headquarters. Even so, we are required to sign the visitors' book. That is a rule strictly observed wherever you go, whoever you are.

Now it is eight o'clock and the moon, striving to glimpse us through a serrated roof of cloud, is silently bouncing a patch of gloom away from the square. I think the formalities are over. In fact, they are just about to begin. First I am introduced to the village committee. I feel my way along the line, trying not to bump any of these worthies. Next it is the turn of the village scouts. It is up to them to ensure that every youngster in Likuyusekamaganga is aware of the wildlife in the area and to report any evidence of activity by *jangili* bands. This is all Ndunguru's doing. He has brought me here to see how his plan to involve the villagers actively in the protection of elephants is working. He has chosen five villages, each of them perched on the lip of the Selous, and, he says, each one of them full of poachers.

I look at the headman and the village committee. They are standing, upright under the moon, silent, staring back at me. They don't look like *jangili*, but what does a *jangili* look like? We aren't expecting a 21-gun Kalashnikov salute followed by an invitation to taste elephant meat. I have taken Ndunguru's word that they were not allowed to hunt now, so a birthright going back centuries had been abolished. Overnight almost. But could a law passed in Dar es Salaam make them give up hunting? Ndunguru was optimistic.

'Captain Katali can stop them. He's been here and to the other villages around and he's seized quite a few weapons. But once the army goes, then we need something else.'

'What?'

Before he can answer, the headman returns from the huddle of the village committee who have been discussing with a degree of animation what is next on the programme that evening. A concert. The headman points to the table. I take my seat.

A group of youngsters, maybe twelve in all, are hopping about from foot to foot in the dust in front of us. They are joined by an ancient, who turns out to be the headman's father. He is wizened, grizzled, and carries the crust of age. Someone put him in an oven a century ago and forgot. Actually he is only seventy years old and is surprisingly nimble on his feet. The group start chanting, swinging from

82

Right: The slaughter claimed whole families, even the young. The *jangili* were confident that they would still obtain a good price for tusks no bigger than a man's forearm (*Alistair Morrison*).

Far Right
Above: Major-General John Butler Walden, the commander of Operation Uhai, the army clamp-down on ivory poaching in the Selous.

Below Left: Alex Byatti, a game scout as mountainous as Kilimanjaro (*Alistair Morrison*).

Below right: No medals for the heroes of the ivory war: Burkard Kayombo was shot in the face during an exchange of fire with a poaching gang (*Alistair Morrison*).

Previous page
The last stronghold: Tanzania's Selous Game Reserve, home to 30,000 elephants. *Inset:* Captain Gerard Bigurube (*left*), the Warden of the Selous, and Ireneus Ndunguru.

Left: Ireneus Ndunguru. His work means that he must go armed at all times.

Far Left
Above: Villagers like these have hunted the elephant for generations. Ndunguru's challenge is to persuade them to start a new life with cash crops like rice and fish. So far, his plan is working.

Below: The Ritual of the Night, threshold to a darker, secret world.

Above: 'Strong Beer' is the nickname for the *jangili* who claims to have killed 10,000 elephants. Now he is an informer.

Right: Her husband was once an MP. Now he is in prison and her house is a shrine: Mrs Ali Yusuf Abdurabi and family.

Far right
Above: Father Ildefons, the Benedectine whose flock in Mtwara no longer carve ivory but wood.

Below: What do you say to a hungry man about conservation? People who are starving will hunt to survive.

Above: The need for meat: Farmer's Day in Mchomoro begins with a licensed buffalo hunt, Ireneus Ndunguru's reward to the villagers for renouncing poaching.

Right: 'If you can show these people who have no money, no houses, no clothes, no food, no hope, nothing, that they do possess a talent, and if you can get them to help themselves, then why shouldn't you offer them this opportunity? . . . They were continuing a tradition that was as ancient as elephants, and now that has all ended' – Father Ildefons.

side to side, and the chant turns into a song. Likuyusekama-ganga's Fred Astaire is crouching now as the backing group of sub-teens introduce an element of mime to the song. He turns ferociously, leaps, and aims an imaginary spear right at my vitals. There is no doubt about this song, this har-mony, this dangerous rhythm. It is all about hunting, killing animals, killing elephants. It is all about appetite, meat, and satisfaction.

No one in the village speaks Swahili. They use a form of the vernacular. Ndunguru translates the words of the song:

> Please come and cheer up!
> We have something to eat!
> We can relax!
> It's a great day!

I make a note to pass it on to Andrew Lloyd Webber.

Likuyusekamaganga is in need of a jolt. And tonight the village is charged with excitement. There is much applause. It drowns the nightjars. For once, under that pale and striv-ing moon, Africa is isolated. The atmosphere around the square is comfortable and intimate and not in the least threatening. I wonder if this is all real, this singing and dancing. Yes, I suppose it is; entertainment is third nature to Africans after food and sex, but how much of a show have they put on for Ndunguru and the tame white man who has come from Britain? I am not suggesting that a strong taste of contempt is lacing the entertainment, but I begin to think of a Potemkin village. Is Likuyusekamaganga really on the Dnieper and not the Mbarangandu? Perhaps I am watching a charade.

As I look at the dancers, the singers, the old man with his stick and his stick-insect legs, I begin to doubt Ndunguru who has assured me that this village of Likuyusekamaganga is a haven of *jangili*. And then I recall the document Costa Mlay had given me, the Selous Census he had told me to read, with its evidence that this village and four others – Kitanda, Nambecha, Mchomoro, Kilimasera and Likuyuse-kamaganga – had in the last three months been raided and had surrendered three hundred elephant tusks. There can be no more than a thousand adult men living in these five villages, yet sixty were arrested and interrogated, two were shot dead and several seriously injured.

There was trouble between the villagers and Ndunguru's men, that was for sure, and now they are having a party. Where has all the bitterness gone?

But there is a truth to report this night. Poaching cases are, according to Ndunguru and the headman, down on last year, and the song these children and the old man have just performed for me is a reflection of the new mood in the village.

'We are dedicating our song,' said the headman, as if it were a Radio 1 request, 'to the new era of joint responsibility between us villagers and the authorities.' My God, this could be Nyerere, the Mwalimu, the Teacher, himself, speaking. 'We have composed a song which reflects our new attitude. We celebrate hunting only for food. *Tembo*' – he waves vaguely into the night – 'is our friend.'

He shakes his head vigorously. All this talk of the 'new attitudes' and 'new ways' is depressing. These new ways and new attitudes are beginning to destroy the villagers of Likuyusekamaganga in much the same way as the new ways and new attitudes forced upon them by the government reforms of the sixties eroded their dignity and independence by replacing the customs of the past with all the dogma and crackbrained cant of the century.

Once every man was armed. Each of them proudly wore a muzzle-loader, four and a half feet of wood and iron, its barrel carefully oiled and its stock lovingly carved. With this on their back, and a home-made cartridge in their pocket, this was their dignity, their independence, their badge of virility. It was also their means of survival, because without a muzzle-loader, they and their families and possibly the village would starve.

Now, under Ndunguru's scheme, and after the crackdown by the soldiers taking part in Operation Uhai, there are no warriors left. At least this is what Ndunguru and the headman are telling me. And unless the villagers are playing a canny game, it has to be true. The hyena, you see, supports their claim.

For two months a particularly vicious spotted hyena had terrorized Likuyusekamaganga. It came at night, out of the bush, made bold or, more likely, desperate by the fact that there were no elephant carcasses this year to feed upon. First it attacked the goats of Likuyusekamaganga. Nine were dragged off by it. And then it turned its attention to the old and the weak and the young. One night it entered the village and padded into a hut, sinking its fangs into the leg of a child. She was halfway through the door before her parents woke and tugged her away. But even the beating they administered that night did not persuade the creature to search for easier meat, despite the precautions the villagers were taking. The men organized a watch, armed themselves with sticks and made sure the fires outside their huts blazed all through the darkness, but the hyena attacked again.

Likuyusekamaganga was helpless. Without its weapons, it could not deal with the crisis as it had in the days when weapons and hunting were allowed. Ndunguru was called in and sent seven game scouts to track down the beast. When it was killed, several hundred villagers came to stare at the bleeding body. Likuyusekamaganga was relieved the ordeal was over, but some men, the older men in the village, shook their heads. It was hard to conceal the shame they felt.

As we leave Likuyusekamaganga that night for Nyam-tumbo, the Village Wildlife Management Committee stand in the village square outside the headman's house and wave to us like saplings in a stiff breeze. We have forty kilometres to drive before we reach our night's lodgings. They have nowhere to go. The past is finally behind them, even though, under this vague and peering moon, it is surround-ing them. Their past is the Selous. Their past is hunting. Their past is the muzzle-loader and meat and a full stomach, and probably a severe bout of diarrhoea. The future is writ-ten in the visitors' book, in committee meetings, in visits from the men from Songea. The future is no longer in their grasp.

EIGHT

The New Super Moscow Bar

The temperature was rising inside the New Super Moscow Bar. Captain Katali flicked the excess of perspiration from his brow, and set about demolishing another Safari beer. Certainly it was sultry and the hissing of the hurricane lamps had begun to shred my nerves. There wasn't a lot to do in Nyamtumbo on a Wednesday night, nor on any other night for that matter, but there was always the New Super Moscow Bar. The Safari was cool, and it was just across the road from the Argentine Guest House where Ndunguru and I had fixed a room. So, too, it appeared had the Captain. All right, it was only a single, but the Argentine wasn't the Kilimanjaro, and Nyamtumbo wasn't Dar, but there was always a welcome there for the Captain, as without exception the keeper addressed him, and rightly so. Captain Katali had been posted to this land of the Ngoni to teach these southerners a lesson they would never forget.

The Captain slammed his Safari onto the table top where it slid on the lees to join the row of sweating brown empties at the bottom. He was not alone that Wednesday night in the New Super Moscow Bar, and not just because Ndunguru and I were there. Nestling in his lap, next to his service pistol, was his constant companion, the *kiboko*, two feet of solid, impenetrable leather stripped off the back of a hippopotamus. The three of them, the Captain, the pistol and the *kiboko*, slouching on the wall bench under the wandering shadows of the hurricane lamp, wouldn't induce a feeling of confidence in the heart of any stranger, and I was a stranger. Not that Captain Katali was expecting guests. His company was already provided – his sergeant, two privates, and the *deriva* outside, waiting in the Land Rover, probably snoring vigorously in the front seat, and even more likely to wake up with a flat battery. The fool, said the Captain, was as dim as the

Land Rover's sidelights, which he never thought to switch off.

There was a woman there too, snuggling up to the Captain, a large woman with hips as wide as the single bed that, I imagined, awaited them across the road in the Argentine Guest House. She was one of the many Malaya in Nyamtumbo, married, probably, to some *jangili* who had this night set off for the bush looking for game. The Captain smiled and said to the sergeant that her husband, whoever he was, wherever he was, wouldn't be lucky tonight, and as he said it his fist opened and he pulled her nearer.

This New Super Moscow Bar with its Safari and its women and its nearness to his camp was the place he could relax, escape Operation Uhai. The pressure on him had been intolerable, especially when he realized that this was the first time in years that he had spent more than a month away from his barracks or his home in Arusha. He had fought in the war against Amin, had killed Amin's soldiers, but that was back in the seventies when the world had fawned upon the army for rescuing Uganda. It had not taken long for that same world to forget. The irony was rich. Victory over Amin had brought ruin to Tanzania. The war had bankrupted the country and forced men like Captain Katali to squander their experience. For ten years he had worn out his uniform and his voice, masquerading as a barrack square, a talking manual.

Operation Uhai had changed everything. Now, here in the Selous, he was putting all that theory into action, led, naturally, by his *kiboko*. He had been here only a few months and he was satisfied with what he had achieved. Not that he mattered. Major-General John Butler Walden was the commander in charge of Operation Uhai. I decided not to tell the Captain that I had met the Black Mamba. The news might make him shut up.

Captain Katali's *kiboko* sprang out of its resting place by its master's thigh and banged the table. Instantly, out of the shadows, a man appeared with more Safaris.

'I would like your job.' Captain Katali was addressing Ndunguru. 'I would like to be a con–ser–vationist.' The Captain rolled the word around in his mouth and laughed, high and piercing and incessant like the nightjars outside. 'You are soldiers and you are not soldiers. You wear the

87

uniform yet you do not kill. I am a professional. I am paid to kill.'

'And you're good at it,' interrupted Ndunguru sharply.

'Yes, that is my job in life.' The Captain swallowed some more Safari, and refused the offer of a cigarette, a Sportsman, from me.

'So why else do you envy me my job?' Ndunguru asked the Captain.

'I like the wild animals. I never saw them when I was a child. Only in books. Now here I see them all. Buffalo, antelope, baboon, eland, leopard . . .'

'Elephant?' I asked.

The Captain shook his head. 'No elephant. Just their dung.' He paused and drank some more. 'I see the men who kill the elephant. I try to catch them. Sometimes I fail, sometimes I succeed. But who is a *jangili*, Ndunguru, you tell me?'

'Everyone round here is a *jangili*, Captain. Everyone. That's the truth, I'm afraid.'

Captain Katali laughed again. 'Now you see why I want to be a conservationist. Otherwise I will end up having to kill them all.'

Ndunguru knew the Captain reasonably well. He had met him two or three times in his travels between his base in Songea and the villages around the southern sector of the Selous, and it had not taken him long to gather from the villagers that the Captain was neither welcomed in their district nor much loved. Certainly he was an efficient soldier who followed his orders rigidly, but he lacked imagination and saw only one solution to the poaching problem.

I turned to the bar and made out, through the dancing shadows, three men. They could have been regulars of any public house anywhere, and stood there, leaning against it. Their bodies talked a kind of Esperanto, two of them deferring to the man in between, their heads bowed slightly, knees crooked, an intensive study in relaxation. But it turned out that the Captain had other ideas swilling around his Safari-suited head.

The men stopped talking. The rapport between them curdled as the atmosphere across the room tensed up. Captain Katali pushed himself upright and kicked the table shrieking across the stone floor. The *kiboko* was in his right hand pointing directly at the drinkers, and as he neared them, I swear I saw the *kiboko* itself stiffen in Katali's grip, almost as if it was steadying itself for the thrashing it thought it was ready to administer.

The men moved fast, dodging Katali's raised arm, and headed for the door of the New Super Moscow Bar, leaving behind a landlord crying out for the money they owed for his beer, and Katali flailing at the air.

'You see,' he said, turning away from the bar and the landlord who was now weighing up the chances of adding their bill to Katali's, 'you see, Ndunguru, what men they are. *Jangili.*' He moved back to his bench seat and rested the *kiboko* on his lap. His men were amused with the goings-on. The Captain could always be depended upon for a few laughs. They were sure that before the night was over, he would provide them with a few more. They sat tight and fingered their beers, hoping for a refill. It would never do to ask the Captain. They would have to wait until he wanted another Safari.

Ndunguru peered in the gloom at his watch, trying not to be too deliberate about it. He made as if to go, clearing his throat and shifting in his seat, but he had not anticipated Katali's next move. The Captain fired off a salvo at the barman who ran in with a handful of Safaris, his men breathed easy, laughed and Katali stretched and gripped Ndunguru by the arm. He leaned towards him and whispered: 'I have information. About a man you know.'

Ndunguru guessed how he had come by it. 'Who?'

'A man from Hanga. I had him in for questioning. But he didn't crack. He met my friend here too.' The *kiboko* leered up at Ndunguru from the side of the table. 'When I interrogate a man, when he meets my friend here, he always talks. When we catch a *jangili*, Ndunguru, we make sure they remember us and we remember them. We *kiboko* them. We smack them where it hurts.'

Ndunguru noticed that the Captain wasn't speaking to him any more, nor was he addressing his men. His whole attention was directed at the whip in his hand.

'Katali, they're tough, these men from Hanga. I should know, I deal with them every week. They know how to play the game.'

'His name is Alensio. Al–en–sio Bero.' It was a name that

had irritated Captain Katali at first. Now, clearly, it was a name that offended.

I asked him how many weapons he had seized. He looked down at his lap for confirmation. The *kiboko* nodded. One thousand and eighty nine, do you hear? Muzzle-loaders for the most part, semi-automatics, Kalashnikovs, but only a few. Do you want to see them, my weapons, these people's weapons? They're all in the camp. But Captain Katali's attention was wandering to his plump Malaya by the door, silent and waiting to pad across the road to the narrow bed in the Argentine Guest House. She had work to do that night.

Ndunguru left with me, but he slept alone, under a blanket in his bare room. He recognized the name and understood immediately how frustrated and angry the Captain felt. He, too, had been trying for years to trap him. He knew that Bero had been involved, possibly with Songea's fallen MP, Mr Ali, but up to now he hadn't been able to gather enough evidence to prove it. The Captain's methods weren't for Ndunguru, and anyway, hadn't the *jangili* already demonstrated that he was a worthy opponent of Katali and his *kiboko*? But there was one fact about Alensio Bero the Captain wasn't aware of. And if Ndunguru had his way, this would remain a secret between himself and Bero.

Bero had turned. Bero had become an informer.

How did I know? That night in the Argentine Guest House and the New Super Moscow Bar I knew nothing more than Bero's name and reputation. I could hardly remember his name, and dismissed it as just another wild story. Certainly I never imagined that within a few days I would come face to face with him in Hanga Monastery.

NINE

Chichengo's Revenge

Captain Katali was an early riser. He and his driver had gone by the time I woke that morning. I had heard nothing, not even the argument of a lazy Land Rover engine failing to meet the first command of the day. So much for the carelessness of the Captain's *deriva*. Clearly he was on more intimate terms with his vehicle than the Captain had thought. All that was left of Katali's presence was the deep imprint of a pair of tyre tracks that had scoured the morning freshness of the red earth outside the Argentine Guest House and spattered the walls, suggesting that the Captain had indeed left in a hurry.

Ndunguru had told me that the first owner of the Argentine Guest House had been an ivory dealer, a successful one at that, who had built this establishment on the proceeds of the trade.

'Why did he call it the Argentine Guest House?' I asked.

Ndunguru looked at me as though I was dull-witted. 'Because he was an Argentinian, I suppose. Why else would he call it the Argentine Guest House?'

Good question, Ndunguru. It was far too early for my brain to consider the motives of some long-dead ivory trader, and anyway I was more intrigued by the truly nauseating colours with which this displaced gaucho had daubed his creation. The effect of the pink and creamy-yellow was pure Walls family block, Neapolitan flavour. Bush Africa gives little and leaves nothing. But the proprietor of the Argentine Guest House had provided Nyamtumbo, this comma on the way from Songea to the Selous, with much more than a one-night-stop laced with the flavour of notoriety. He had bequeathed it a psychedelic layer-cake that reverberated all

91

the way to Buenos Aires. I shuddered, and clambered into the Land Rover.

There is a simple equation about the bush which is worth remembering. The further you venture inside it, the more isolated you become from your intellect and culture. Forget maps. These villages are not marked on them, so you cannot even comfort yourself by searching for a dot and ringing it in blue ink. You may think you can rely on chemicals to preserve the whiteness that sets you apart, but do not be deceived. These salves with which you smooth and cosset your skin each dusk cannot hope to repel the irritations of the bush. They may keep them at bay for a while, but that is all. The marks the bush has left on your punctured arms and legs each morning are proof. Everything that you take for granted, the basics of life, edible food, a clean toilet, hot water, a towel, cool nights, undisturbed sleep, do not exist. There is a gap in expectations, a void into which the intellect tumbles. You become a prisoner of your own incomprehension.

I was feeling that now as we rumbled along on this blue and creamy morning. The further I travelled, the less I knew. My tongue was dry and my skull was hammering and in need of a cool compress as the last traces of Safari skirmished inside my veins. I was armed with neither knowledge nor experience to cope with the bush. I did not possess the tools with which to dismantle all its secrets.

But Ndunguru was keen. He wanted me to see the progress he had made with his village programme. First stop was Mchomoro (pronounced Chomorro), which he described as a 'little Dar es Salaam'. It was a reputation earned by the skill and notoriety of the poachers who lived there. Now he had built a maize mill and persuaded the villagers to change their ways. The army, Katali's men, had seized a number of weapons there. They'd found one hidden in a beehive after one unusually observant soldier had noticed that no bees ever swarmed round it. He must have been a honey lover. Then, Ndunguru said, we would go on to Kilimasera, the nearest village to the Selous and after, if there was time, to Kalulu. This meant a journey of maybe 200 km from Songea, over rough track, on those rich purple roads that clung to the edge of the escarpment.

Travelling with Ndunguru and Vincent the *deriva* was a stop-go affair, for Ndunguru was well-known in this area bordering the Selous, and whenever he spotted someone along the road that he was acquainted with, he would slap the windscreen violently with his open palm, and shout above the engine for Vincent to pull into the side.

A dust cloud lingered over us as he motioned Vincent to stop. I hoped it wasn't going to be another of those days perforated by greetings and offers of hospitality that turned out to be lethal for the bowels. It made me wonder if this was a simple method of revenge for the treatment meted out by my predecessors in the days of the colonial administration. I could imagine what was going on inside the heads of these wayside rustics, their smiles crammed with rotten teeth, their handshakes eager. Their welcome was hideously persuasive, one that worked upon the inability of the British to refuse hospitality, especially when it was being provided by one so obviously ground down by the rigours of meagre living. He'll eat this and may he shit in his pants. He'll taste a mere morsel, and may he shit until there is no shit left.

I wanted to return to Songea. Another village, another chat by the roadside, what did it matter? That menacing talk in the New Super Moscow Bar suggested that everything was sewn up between Katali and Ndunguru, and that the *kiboko*'d Potemkin villages had just put on a show for my amusement and education.

I dragged myself out of the Land Rover and straightened myself so the sweat ran cold inside my shirt and trickled down my back to my bottom. I held out my hand for it to be seized and pumped vigorously by the old boy waiting by the side of the road. He led us into his hut, a shambles of straw and bamboo, hardly four feet high at the entrance. I stooped and entered, trying to avoid the mats of woven leaves that were heaped with rice and coffee beans. The smell inside the hut was pleasant, for the flavour of the coffee had won a war against the pungent residues of last night's perspiration.

He didn't offer me a drink or a titbit from his larder. Maybe he was too poor. Instead, I fed upon his memories.

His name was Damian Madogo and he said after some head scratching that he was fifty-five years old, though this estimate could be out by at least twenty years. Madogo was sparse and bowed, an old soldier who had served the British for a generation fighting our wars in the Seychelles, Reunion, the Comores and Madagascar. I wondered if he had met my father who had also been stationed in Madagascar during the Second World War.

'What is your name, effendi?' he asked.

'Gordon.'

'Gorddoon?' He sucked on his gums, dragging what little air there was circulating in his one-room hut into his head as if it would clear out everything that had accumulated there for the past forty years. 'You say, effendi, that he was a doctor?'

I nodded.

'No, I do not know this doctor, but I will think of Doctor Gorddoon. Was he ever in Chatham, in Kent?'

'No, were you?'

'During the war, for a few years, I was training there with our regiment. Chatham is a lovely place.'

'Where else did you serve?'

'I fought the Mau Mau in the Aberdares. I was a platoon commander. I killed many Mau Mau men.'

'Tell him about the Mpalangozi,' urged Ndunguru.

'Oh, the Mpalangozi.' The old boy crouched forward. 'He was a fine man. Do you know of the Mpalangozi?'

I said I didn't, until Ndunguru explained that the Mpalangozi meant Basil Ionides, the Snake Man, the legendary gatherer of old East Africa who snaffled gaboon vipers and cobras, who picked black mambas like daffodils and slipped them spitting into gunny sacks bound for Europe. He'd even kept a tame puff adder which he liked to stroke on his knee.

'He,' Ndunguru gestured towards the old man, 'he was for many years after he left the army the bearer of Ionides. Mpalangozi means the Skin Gatherer. Ionides took anything. He collected all sorts of skins. Not just snakes.'

I would liked to have said here that Damian Madogo's eyes were growing misty with recollection, but it was the smoke from my cigarette that was causing him to blink back the tears.

'Did you know the Mpalangozi?' he repeated.

I shook my head, thinking that the name carried with it a much more sinister resonance than the Snake Man.

'I was with him when he died. He was here in the Selous

for years, before and after the war against the Italians. He was a good boss. I carried him from his bed each morning and sat him inside the Land Rover.' There was no stopping Damian Madogo now that he had found himself bumping back along the road signposted 'Youth, This Way'. 'The Mpalangozi was a very sick man. Very, very sick.' Here he stressed the syllables, producing in a few words a verbal health card that could have been slung on the end of a hospital bed.

'What was wrong with him?' I asked.

'Diabetes,' said Ndunguru. 'His legs were not working. They were like the elephant's. I took him to Nairobi and they cut them off.'

Damian Madogo sawed at his own leg, the right leg, raising a sudden stench of sweat in the room. 'He was dead then.'

'Do you mean after the operation?'

'No, but it killed him all the same.' Damian Madogo paused for a moment, wiping his armpits and flicking the wet from them on the earth floor. 'He is buried at Madaba, near Nairobi. I built for him a stone.'

'At least a snake didn't get him,' said Ndunguru.

'A snake would have been quicker and more merciful,' replied Damian Madogo. 'I saw that man's last days.'

'What about elephants? Have you killed many *jangili*?'

The question changed the mood. In an instant the old man had taken a side turning, gone down a slip road and was now cruising, foot down, full-beam into the dark night of his memories.

'I've shot *jangili* and I've shot *tembo*. *Tembo* were the vermin then.'

'You see, Nick,' said Ndunguru, 'in those days and maybe up to the mid-fifties, a game warden and a game scout were called Vermin Control Officers. It was their job to protect *shambas* and the crops grown there from the wild animals.'

'How many elephants have you killed, Mr Madogo?'

He didn't waste many seconds working it out. 'One hundred and eighty. I was the boss, the chief game scout, so I always was given the first shot. And,' he said, smiling, 'I was a good shot. Never missed. Well, once or twice, I suppose.'

'What happened when you did miss?'

'I ran. Three times from elephants. That was in Tanga. And once from a rhino in Moshe. That won't happen to you, Ndunguru!'

'And *jangili*?'

'I have caught many and killed many, but not as many as *tembo*. In, let me see, in 1972, I think it was that year, I captured 65 *jangili* in one operation.'

'All together?'

He sat back on his haunches, took a cigarette out of his shirt pocket and contrived to light it with the same hand. What was he like holding a gun?

'I was on patrol in the Selous. At a place called Ngombe. My men spotted *jangili*. There were five of us, me and four askaris. These *fundi* had shot two hippos, four zebra, and two buffalo. They were smoking the flesh.' He spoke as if this was happening now, or maybe yesterday. 'These men were in their camp. There were four of them, but I could see that it was a big camp, and what would four men want with all this food? There must have been other *fundi* out in the bush, so we waited until they came back. Four came back at first. We captured them. Then some more. Until we had all sixty-five in our hands. It was the greatest victory. It was.'

He laughed and began choking on his cigarettes. They weren't Sportsman and he had refused my English brand, patting his chest politely and saying they were far too weak. I supposed his were home-grown.

'Do you have Woody still in England?'

I shook my head.

Damian Madogo and his seven children lived on his pension of 600 shillings a month plus what he could earn from the crops he sold. I doubted if it would double his income, yet for all the poverty of the present, he was a man rich in his memories of a violent past. He had killed elephants and humans. Both he regarded as vermin, but then, in those pink gin raj days, that was what he was paid to do. We left him by the side of the road, a small man standing on the grassy bank that led to his *shamba*, silhouetted against the blue sharp sky.

We stopped again on the road to Mchomoro, Dar es Salaam's nasty little cousin, not to lean against the Land Rover and talk, but to watch the Selous. It was staring hard, right into our eyes, staring in the midday heat, a vast, confusing, confident mass of *miombo*.

Ndunguru walked down to the side of the road, and set off along the escarpment, vanishing into a tangle of brachystegia, acacia and msuku. He was leaning against a msuku, shielding his eyes from the sun, and acting the young Raleigh, pointing his finger at the horizon. 'It's three days' walk from here to Liwale. There are no roads, a Land Rover wouldn't make it. You have to walk, like the *jangili*.'

'Where's here?'

'Masueru. This is the edge. That is the Selous. It is bigger than us, isn't it?' The track we stood on soon disappeared into a tangle of undergrowth. To follow it would make you vanish, too. This was a path directly into the reserve, whose secret was kept by nature which day by day wiped out any traces left by man.

He reached up into the msuku and tugged off some of its fruit. 'Here, try this.'

I ate it. It was bitter and made me wince.

'The baboons like it, you know,' he laughed.

In Mchomoro village, the headman was caught unawares by our visit. There was no visitors' book waiting to be signed, no reception committee, no concert party. In fact, all that was visible of human life was a few scattered workers, laden with bundles of wood, walking back into the village after the morning's contribution towards the destruction of the ozone layer. The houses in Mchomoro were set back from the road, guarded from the eyes of the casual passer-by by clumps of mango and banana trees. If I had not been with Ndunguru and the Land Rover had not jerked to a halt, I would not have known a village existed here.

'Where are they all?' I asked Ndunguru. 'Too busy plotting crimes to welcome us?'

He laughed and said that we would not have long to wait. They would be here soon enough.

The headman found us in three minutes. His name was Haji Makunira. He greeted us affably and apologized for the lack of welcome. 'If only we had known you were coming . . . ' he began, launching into an elegiacal summary of the village's progress under the Ndunguru Plan. Not a word about sin, not a mention of criminal activity, not a

97

sign of anti-government feeling. Resentment? Never. Everything, all the 'old problems', as he politely referred to the
days not so long ago when men from this village slaughtered
elephants for profit, was in the past. And anyway it wasn't
us from Mchomoro who were responsible. No, the *jangili*
were from other villages. 'Now we have strict control on
who comes here. Everyone, all strangers must sign the visitors' book.'

Of course, the visitors' book. But where was it? He must
have seen my smile, read my thoughts, because he interrupted himself and whispered to the man standing by him in
the road who straightaway dispatched himself towards the
huts in the background.

'Yes, we then make them tell us who they are, what they
are doing here, where they have come from, and how long
they are staying.' This headman, Haji, could work at Heath-
row's immigration desk. 'You see, many, many strangers
were coming here from other places, staying in our huts and
poaching. So the village is blamed.'

'Why,' I asked him, 'do they come here in particular?'

'The hunting is excellent,' he said.

'Do you like meat yourself, Mr Haji?'

The question may have been loaded, but its effect was as
devastating as grapeshot. It scattered wide among the group
of Mchomoran sinners now gathered round their leader.
There were a few gasps, a ripple of giggles, and then a
period of contemplation.

The headman threw towards me a strange, sideways
glance, but I could see he was no longer under control.
What had I unleashed? His lips were moistening, his stringy
tummy muscles were tightening. Eventually he spoke.

'Of course we like meat,' he said, looking at me as if I
were an imbecile. 'We are all hunters, but now we can no
longer hunt.' Here he turned his gaze upon Ndunguru. It
was a fearsome gaze, basilisk-like, heaped with recrimi-
nation. Ndunguru shielded himself behind a vapid look.

'Yes, Chief,' I said, quick with the follow up, 'I know that,
but what is your favourite meat?'

'My favourite meat is eland,' the headman spat out. And
then before I could interrupt, 'followed by buffalo and sable
antelope.' He said this rapidly, as if he were sitting in a
restaurant and ordering from a menu.

'But isn't sable antelope completely protected, Chief?'

'Yes.' Mr Haji's eyes have gone completely dreamy. 'Sable antelope is . . .' Mr Haji was searching for words to describe the taste. If only his tongue could have talked for him. 'Sable antelope is . . . so salty. So gamey.'

'What about *tembo*?'

'Never!'

'Not even years ago?'

The crowd have pressed closer, forcing my back against the metal of the Land Rover. It is like a hot iron. The crowd have become hysterical. Their appetites have become unleashed and all of them, like the Chief, Mr Haji, have surrendered themselves temporarily to long and lovely thoughts of fresh meat straight from the bush. This sin, I could see, was truly delicious, as original as the day Eve sank her teeth into that green Eden apple.

The vision that stirred them so vigorously that morning in Mchomoro was beautiful but brief. It ended with the arrival of the visitors' book, carried with a flourish of self-importance by Mr Haji's deputy, Mr Rajabu Karumbeta, who was also the brother of Adam Karumbeta, the local MP and leading spirit of the Ndunguru Plan.

I signed the book.

We drove on, leaving the newly reformed sinners of Mchomoro to their dreams of fresh meat, of salty, gamey sable antelope, cruelly caught in a snare most probably, and then hung until the smell drove the men and scavengers who didn't hunt, the cripples of the village and the outcasts who lurked outside, the hyenas and jackals, wild with an envy which served only to exacerbate their hunger and alienation.

What I had seen in Mchomoro, all that lip-smacking hypocrisy, was a perfect mirror of the problem facing Ndunguru. How could he persuade a people for whom appetite was first nature and hunting a close second to give up poaching and co-operate?

His plan was based on a social contract. If the villagers behaved themselves, and gave up hunting, then they would, in turn, be provided with other methods of raising revenue. They would become fish farmers, maize millers, their women would sew with machines that were manufactured in South Korea. There would be clean water for them to drink, and they could always inform on the *jangili*. But Ndunguru was realistic. He recognized that men like the Mchomorans would always hunt. It was in their blood. Subsistence poaching, he believed, would never be stopped. Impossible.

'These people, they asked me today, if I would allow them to kill a buffalo. Once a year there is a great feast, Farmer's Day, and it was always the tradition to hunt meat and then invite the whole village – everyone, the men, the women and the children – to take part in a great feast lasting all the day and into the night. I would like to give them permission, but it is beyond my power. I will have to ask the Director, Costa Mlay.'

'How will they kill this buffalo if they have no guns? Katali has been here, hasn't he?'

'I think they should be allowed to have at least one gun. A muzzle-loader. They can do little damage with just one, and if we don't allow them one for their own protection, then they will make one. It is easy for them.'

I could understand what he was saying and I sympathized with his dilemma. But could he trust them?

It was in Kilimasera that I began to glimpse the light that was concealed by the darkness of the bush.

This time the visitors' book was awaiting our arrival. I don't know how they knew we were coming. No one from Mchomoro could have relayed a message. Perhaps the explanation was simply that Kilimasera kept its book in a constant state of readiness, each empty column on each exercise-book lined page trained and alert and lethal as any SAS trooper.

Car windscreens could have been cleaned with the headman's face. He wore a mauve three-quarter coat nipped in at the waist and styled with running-board wide lapels. His trousers were not only flared, but decorated in generous large green checks. Had this man emerged from some travelling circus that had lost itself in the Selous? Had a plane carrying supplies from an Oxfam shop vanished into the bush all those years ago? Who knows how these villagers had come by their clothes, but whatever the answer, this headman of Kilimasera was, by strut and pose, proud of them.

As soon as he was satisfied that we had observed the

CCM requirements and provided our details for the book, he launched himself at Ndunguru, firing off a salvo of complaints. His onions, the ones that Ndunguru had provided from seed, had been eaten by worms. Now there wouldn't be thirty sacks to sell at market, more like twenty. And what was Ndunguru doing about it? Then there were the fingerlings in the fish farm, which again Ndunguru had persuaded him to cultivate.

'What's happened to the fingerlings?' Ndunguru asked. This was a routine he knew by rote.

'They've been eaten.'

'What ate them?'

'The *chichengo*.'

'He means,' said Ndunguru, 'the hammerhawk.'

'Why doesn't he drive away the bird?'

'It's not so simple, Nick. Ask him.'

'Chief, why don't you drive away the *chichengo*?'

The chief's leather head shook itself inside the wide lapels. Side to side it went, scraping its scrawny old neck against the stitches in the coat. 'You cannot kill a *chichengo*,' he said. 'It's highly respected here.' He pursed his lips and spat out a thick stream of gob which pattered into the dust at my feet. 'There are frogs in the ponds, Ndunguru, and otters.'

'They feed on the fries?'

'Yes.'

'Anything else?'

'Monitor lizards.'

'But these are not as bad as the *chichengo*, Chief?' I suggested.

'No, you are right, sir. The *chichengo* is the devil. If we kill a *chichengo*, then his spirit will return. It will kill me and all my family. It is a small bird, but it is very big.'

'What else?' sighed Ndunguru. He was toying with the black box, his nails scraping away at the enamel.

'*Tembo*. We have seen many elephants here in the last days.'

'Good,' I said.

'No, *not* good,' the chief shouted. 'They have trampled our crops. The *shambas* down by the Mbarangandu have been destroyed.'

'How many *tembo* did you see?' asked Ndunguru.

101

'One by the river on our side. But there must have been 150 on the Selous side.'

'Did you take a close look?' I asked.

The chief gave me a severe look. 'No. That is forbidden.' He poked a forefinger at the man from Songea. 'He tells us not to go there. But when the elephants wreck our *shambas*, we can do nothing. He, and the Captain, they took away our guns, so what can we do?'

'We have an idea to mine the *shambas* with thunder-flashes,' Ndunguru told me. Thunderflashes! What sadistic teachers masquerading as officers threw at us in my CCF days at school. 'Only there is a fire risk, so we could end up doing more damage than the elephant, and there is a risk to the farmer. We'd need to post a game scout, as back-up with a weapon, so if anything went wrong . . . '

I got the drift. I noticed that I could see daylight peeking through the chief's left ear. A dainty hole, about an eighth of an inch in diameter, had been drilled through the inner part. I pointed to it and all the children who had gathered round us laughed.

The chief was not in the least embarrassed. 'This,' he said, tugging the ear in way of explanation, 'is to prevent scrotal hernia.' His hand moved down, involuntarily I would add, to his groin. A sharp tug, more laughs, and a blank look from me.

'How many children do you have?' I asked.

'Nine.' A pause while the laughter subsides. 'And all from a hole in the ear.'

There are only sixty-three houses in Kilimasera, and I am going to have to stay the night in one of them. The sun is surrendering to the night. Already I can pick up the whine of the evening's first mosquito. I am anxious to leave Kilimasera, but Ndunguru has already decided that it is too late to make Songea that night, and because we have no camping gear, we will have to wait until the dawn before we can leave.

The grass-roofed hut where I will sleep is not quite up to the rigorous if plastic standards of Conrad Hilton. There is no electricity, no shaving point, no mirror, no bed, no carpet, no floor. It lacks amenities like water, toilet, taps and shower. There are none of those cosmetic passports, those

102

miniature plastic bottles of shampoo or bath gel, stamped with the name of the hotel chain whose guest you are, which are never opened, but guiltily packed away in a suitcase only to re-emerge in your bathroom cabinet, as symbols of intercontinental cleanliness.

I have spent days now talking and listening to the harsh voices of villagers who are, according to Ndunguru, playing a vital part in his scheme to save the elephant. But all they want from me is my signature, passport number, date of issue, my destination; they are hungry for these details and they are hungry for food. Some are full of enthusiasm, others spit bile. They are impotent, and their bitterness shows. They are clever, too, in the way all peasants are. They are insular and conservative and they defend themselves.

I am standing here in the open doorway of this thatched hut in Kilimasera, and I admit I am in despair. I do not belong here. An old man is shouting at me, waving his arms. I ignore him, and stay my ground in the doorway. I shall move only when I want to, or when a fresh burst of mosquitoes forces me inside.

'He says you must not stay there. He is telling you to move.' The interpretation of the body language comes courtesy of Ndunguru.

'Balls to him,' I say.

Ndunguru's voice is gentle but every syllable is underscored. 'No, he is right. This is his village. I think you should move.'

'OK, I'll move.' I walk away from the man who stops the side-show the moment he sees his message has got through to me. 'What's all this about?'

'It's simple, but you will never understand. You have broken a lore of these parts. A custom.' Ndunguru reads the confusion on my face. 'A man must never stand at the threshold of a house at night, because to do so is a bad omen.'

'So?'

'So you must do what they ask. It does not matter if you do not believe. It matters what these people believe. You were blocking the door and so the spirits would not be able to remove the souls of the dead.' He shrugs his shoulders. I try to laugh it off as pure mumbo jumbo, then I think of

the horrible revenge the *chichengo* is said to wreak. Fear. I
don't want to sleep alone tonight.

This villager who is responsible for ruining any chance I
have of a good night's sleep is now kneeling down in front
of a tree. He has taken off his rags and the moon is playing
among the beads of sweat on his shoulders. The moon has
won its battle with the clouds, and now it is shining fully,
switching on Kilimasera, polishing the trees and huts and
the blackness that is in between. The night is never silent
in Africa. Nightjars are flitting across my eyes, stroking my
eyelids, brushing the thatch with their Kleenex wings. A
thin glisten on the ground in front of me is for a moment a
stick. Then it moves. A hyena mocks its passage.

The man kneeling in front of the tree notices nothing and
everything. He is at peace with the night. He is home. This
is his place, not mine, nor Ndunguru's.

I am an intruder. I am a voyeur. I am eavesdropping, like
some Sunday tabloid doorstepper, on an intensely private
and personal rite. I feel unclean, but the adrenalin is pumping through my veins as fast as the heartbeat of the African
night. Something strange and private is happening between
this man and the bush. I'm not afraid any more.

TEN

The Mchawi

There may only have been sixty-three huts in this village of Kilimasera, but that morning there was something else there. There was a mystery, and Kilimasera was waiting to reveal it. It was at breakfast – boiled eggs (hard), coffee (black and bitter, and poured from Thermos flasks) and bananas (green and bindingly reliable), which we ate off the bonnet of the Land Rover in the main drag of this one-street town – that I asked Ndunguru to explain to me what I had seen last night. He drained his coffee, unscrewed the yellow stained lid of the Thermos, the teapot of Tanzania, poured out another cup, and pronounced: 'What you saw, Nick, was the Ritual of the Night.'

I caught Ndunguru's quick glance and knew then that I would have to persuade him to allow me to stay. He had already decided to move out of the village as soon as we had finished breakfast and he had checked over the fish ponds down by the Mbarangandu. The plan was to drive to Kalulu, the game scout post inside the Selous, and see the airstrip which the warden based there had built.

I had seen a man strip himself of his clothes, kneel in front of a tree. That was all. Admittedly the effect was pure theatre, with lighting courtesy of the moon and sound effects provided by the secret creatures of the bush. But who had been the director? And now for Ndunguru to call all this the 'Ritual of the Night', well, surely he was guilty of elevating the banal into something mystical? But Ndunguru was not a man who exaggerated. He was plain-spoken and analytical. He was a scientist by training and an anthropologist by inclination.

'What do you mean, "Ritual of the Night?" ' I asked him.

105

'This is what the hunters, the *jangili*, perform before they go into the bush. They pray to the spirits to protect them and ask them to make sure that their trip will be a success.'

'So is this man I saw last night a *jangili*?'

'No. He is the Mchawi of Kilimasera.' Ndunguru saw my face. 'The witchdoctor,' he explained.

I asked him if he thought the Mchawi would talk to me. He scratched his head and stroked his chin and said, at last, 'Maybe. We will try. I will postpone the journey to Kalulu. This Mchawi is a man I would like to talk to myself. He may be very useful to me.'

We moved our bags out of the Land Rover and carried them back to the huts where we had spent the night. Ndunguru explained that we would have to wait until dusk before we could make any attempt at approaching the old man. He had status in this village and the day for him was spent inside his hut, meditating, or more probably sleeping.

There was no bar in Kilimasera where we could spend the day, no focal point where we could meet the locals. Village life was stagnant. Now that we were no longer a novelty, now that my supply of Marks and Spencer sweet bags had been seen to be exhausted, we were left alone. Only the flies of Kilimasera were taking an interest. There was not even a request from the headman or one of his village lackeys for us to sign the visitors' book again. All we could do was sit outside our huts and devise ways of destroying the day and insects, pick grass, chew it, scratch the dry earth with snappy twigs, and watch the sun rise and climb high over the Selous, or sleep and wake to see the same sun, now higher in the sky, curving lazily and perhaps avoiding the odd cloud that flecked the blue. Kilimasera was teetering on the edge of the world. Kilimasera was a beginning and an end. The villagers ambled by, their heads turned towards us as they passed. They said nothing, though some came close and passed over snoopy, myopic smiles. Women wrapped in tight *katangas* smacked the soles of their bare feet on the earth and brushed past. A cluck of children and hens tottered behind dancing in their dusty footprints. The hens gave up the chase and pecked a ragged line back to their cock, but the children showed more persistence and followed their mothers and aunts and grannies all the way

to the patch of green that marked the beginning of the
shambas.

So much for the Ritual of the Day.

There were no men to be seen. They were asleep, or in
their *shambas*, but mostly asleep inside their huts which
looked so flimsy, any strong gust would blow them away.
They were lying in the shadows, on mats spread out on the
floor, trying to keep cool, enjoying restless dreams of game.
They were waiting for the sun to abdicate its twelve-hour
tyranny, waiting for the cool of the night to open its loins
and receive them. They, like us, were waiting for the
Mchawi.

My bottom was sore, my back a sponge of sweat. The flies
crawled across my lips and left a trail of tender feet that
were never there when I swatted them.

The women and their children, still snapping like pi-dogs
round their feet, are returning. But they bring with them
something other than their own kind. They bring with them
branches, limbs, half-boughs, wounded and torn, uprooted
and prised from the sparse earth. And when they have been
unable to find a length that is substantial, they gather as
many twigs and shoots and sprouts and tendrils as their
backs can manage to bear. They are not at all concerned by
the size, or lack of size, of the individual pieces of wood.
What matters is that the bundle fits and does not fall off.
The effect may be of assumed nonchalance, yet their step is
as steady and as resolute as it was when they left the village
this morning, but why it should be different I do not know.
This is a function as vital as breath itself, and this scene has
been enacted for a collective lifetime, for a hundred thousand mornings. A roister of cockerels welcomes their return.
Cockerels are not stupid. They know that daylight means
food and sex, and that darkness kindles fires and maize and
millet, that rice will be spilt and there will be peckings to
scavenge. Kilimasera is quickly shedding itself of the leth-
argy of day. The huts begin to hum. Smoke rises from a
dozen or more fires, mixing with the languid light, and
conspiring to dilute the final bursts of activity from the dying
sun. The temperature is falling, despite the fires, and with
the coolness comes a lifting of the spirits.

Ndunguru was first to move that evening. He shook himself free of the dust and told me to follow him to the place of the Mchawi. We walked through the village, past the neat rows of blushing huts, whose walls were alive and dancing with the shadows from the flames. I could smell the wood-smoke burning and hear the cracks and splutters, the pops and the whines as shower after shower of sparks lit tracer paths into the darkness. The village children turned into moths, smiling and dancing round the flames, daring one another to dart closer and closer. They flung pieces of twig into the fires and scuttled away at the double. And then they returned to do it again. All this time their mothers were cooking the dinner, standing round the pots or squatting on the rush matting outside their huts, not resting, but preparing the vegetables. And inside the huts, their men waited.

The Mchawi's hut was at the end of the village, slightly set apart from the other dwellings, almost concealed in a banana grove. It was quieter here and darker too. A small fire crackled as Ndunguru led me to the threshold. He beckoned me to wait and set foot inside. I heard him talking and then a silence. He started again and stepped backwards through the door, bringing with him, like an old salmon on the end of a line, a short grey-haired man, stooping to negotiate the open doorway.

I saw him clearly under the moon, and recognized him from the night before. He was wearing the same clothes, the reject maroon and purple sweater and trousers, and this night he did not shout at me. Ndunguru was pointing and signalled me to come forward. I held out my hand and took the old man's in mine. We touched and clasped hands the Tanzanian way, one quick shake, then a grip of the wrist, and then the triumph of an elbow-to-elbow, skin to skin, grasp. He spoke neither English nor Swahili. His language was the local vernacular which Ndunguru found difficult, but he managed to understand us, and that night he told us the story of his life and for the first time the bush in all its darkness lit the fuses inside my mind. He wouldn't talk by his hut, nor did he invite us inside. Instead he marched off, surprisingly smartly for an old man, and we followed.

For a moment I thought we had lost him as the acacia trees closed round us. But he was there, sure-footed as a mule, shifting aside the clumps of bushes that lined the track. We had tramped some hundreds of metres by now and the grass was thin and resentful and tall. It whipped my cheeks and thighs as I pushed on behind Ndunguru and the man ahead. I could not see where I was treading, and by this time I did not care. It took all my concentration to keep my eyes on Ndunguru's back, always round the next bend. I wasn't frightened. There was no time to be. This man wasn't armed, he was old and shaky, and Ndunguru's black box was with him. Ndunguru had stopped and by the time I had caught up with him and was about to ask him where we were, there was no need. The dark green envelope of *miombo* was behind us now. Ahead, just twenty metres or so and perhaps another thirty down a steep bank was the river, the Mbarangandu. I felt as if I had been freed from a hot, damp cellar and was blinking in the light for the first time in weeks. My eyes opened wide when I looked down at the river, seduced by its rushes and gurgles and slappings, as the waters fought the rocks and sparkled in the moon-shine. The Mchawi was sitting on a rock. He knew this place. He had not just selected any rock, but one on which he could lounge comfortably.

I offered him a cigarette which he sniffed and put to his lips. I lit his cigarette and instantly wished I had brought the brandy. Ndunguru exchanged small talk, about the vil-lage and the families he knew there, and told him the news from the town. He explained why I was here and said that I was a professor from England, a lawyer studying the poaching laws. I needed, he said, to know the local customs, the history, so I could write about the villagers with author-ity. It wasn't a lie really.

The old boy was pleased to help. Yes, he would talk about the old ways and about the poachers, but he would name no names and, anyway, a lot of what he would tell me was in the past. He settled himself, cigarette between his lips, knees splayed apart, in his favourite spot, looking down over the Mbarangandu on a moonlit night, and opened up and displayed for a faraway academic his treasure of memories. He talked fast, and seriously, pausing politely for Ndunguru to tell me what he had said, or to explain again to Ndunguru what the man from Songea had not quite grasped. He never once lost his patience or his thread that long night by the Mbarangandu despite our interruptions.

First I asked him about the Ritual of the Night. He laughed as Ndunguru translated, and then he suggested he demonstrate it to us. He rose from the rock and walked down to the river edge and sat under a tree, and then knelt. He was stiff and could not manage the feat in one. Though we were some hundreds of metres away from the village, I could hear quite clearly the shrieks of children still awake and playing round the flames outside their huts. I could hear the dialogue of domestic stress, carried along on the current of the river, the cries of children who refused to sleep and the overwrought imperatives of mothers who had given up trying to persuade them. But the old man, the Mchawi, was not bothered. He made no sign of irritation and gave no indication that at that very moment we even existed.

Above him, the branches of a tree unfolded, casting their spiky shadows on his. He did not cast off his clothes. He drew a square in the dust in front of the tree. It was about twelve inches across. Then he removed from the square any blade of grass, or flower, or leaf that happened to be inside it. He turned and stretched to his left. He was looking for something. Some millet seed. His fingers stroked it charily, feeling the texture, stroking each seed, and then he extracted it from the ground with precision and placed it inside the square.

'It is the finger millet,' whispered Ndunguru. 'He has cleared the ground, the special ground, and now it will tell him if the spirits are with him.'

The man's head was bowed to the earth. He began to chant. Words that sounded strange and powerful rang through the forest, past the acacias, scattering their message through the bush until the sounds were picked up by the river, and amplified in their passage across the water and into the Selous.

'He is invoking the spirits who own the land where he wants to hunt. He is saying he is going to Mgongo, the village where the elder is called the Nkapula, the owner of Mnamigon,' said Ndunguru.

Mgongo, Mnamigon. I repeated the names of these places and of Nkapula, this elder. I spoke these names to myself. They meant nothing, but as they gripped my tongue and forced themselves into my head, each syllable of each word reverberated. They were charged with a magic I did not

110

understand. 'Mnamigon is an area over there.' Ndunguru pointed across the Mbarangandu to the Selous. 'That's a favourite place to hunt. There are elephant and buffalo in Mnamigon.'

The old man hauled himself from his knees and shook the dust of the river bank off his clothes. He puffed his way back up the hill and resumed his seat on the rock. I gave him time to catch his breath and then I asked him what happened next. He told me that he must wait until the dawn to see what the spirits had decided. What they decided was crucial to the hunter. If when he returned the millet was intact, then the spirits were pleased with him and he could hunt in the territory he had mentioned. If, however, ants had eaten it, or a bird had pecked at it, or in some other way the square had been trespassed upon, then the omens were bad and hunting should not on any account go ahead. The spirits had displayed their anger. The safari into the bush was doomed. I asked what the spirits would do if the advice was ignored.

He looked at me after Ndunguru had put the question to him. He stared and said nothing for a while. I held my breath. I was scared that one foolish question would wreck the interview. Finally he blew out his chest, leaned towards me and said that the spirits were *never* wrong. I moved from my rock seat and sat next to him and out of the corner of my eye I watched the moon toy with the currents of the Mbarangandu, and as I talked with this old man, my mind could not escape from the cell it was sharing with the Ritual of the Night, a liturgy older than Christianity, and this man, whose smell was in my nostrils, was its disciple. I asked him to tell me about hunting, but he shook his head and said that he himself was not a hunter. He had never hunted. His uncles and great uncles, his brothers and their fathers, they had been hunters, great hunters, fearless hunters, but he, like his own father and his grandfather, was the Mchawi. But the Mchawi did not need to be a hunter to know about it. He could tell me about hunting, about the men who came to him with their stories of the bush which they exchanged in return for his guidance, almost as a tip, because his advice and prayers and rituals were always paid for with an offering, naturally.

He stayed silent for a while. I thought at first he was

tiring, but then I saw that all his concentration was focused on killing a mosquito that had foolishly alighted on his wrist. He smacked it to death and then rolled up the wings and body and smeared it across his arms. He asked me if I knew the warthog. I nodded. A man came to him once, he said, out of breath, frightened, his heart was pounding and he had run a long way. He was dirty and hungry and he begged to see him. He told me that he had seen a warthog, but had not killed it.

I asked him what was wrong with that.

Warthogs, the old man said, once seen, should always be killed. To spare a warthog brings the spirits down on the man who neglects to carry out their wishes.

I thought about this. I had seen hundreds of stiff-whiskered warthogs in Africa, bristling proprietorially through the bush like apoplectic colonels chasing grouse. Warthogs in Africa were as common as cats in England. Besides, I had also been told that once they were killed, they were about the only game that could be eaten on the same day. I asked the Mchawi what advice he had given to this man who had omitted to kill the warthog.

He said it was simple. He told him to stay at home, wait, perform another Ritual of the Night and, if the omens were good, try again.

His next story was about ants. If a hunter should meet a column of safari ants which are carrying eggs, the spirits are happy with him. He will return to his village with enough meat to feed the family for days. But if the ants have no eggs, then he should go home at once, for he will kill no game.

And there was a special code of conduct which applied when he left the village to go on a hunting safari. A man must order his wife never to cut firewood when he is on a hunting safari. If she disobeyed him, then his life would be in danger. A wife should never talk to a man outside the door of her hut; she should never allow a man inside her hut; she should never allow a man to pass behind her while she is busy with the maize or millet outside her hut. If she did let these things happen, then her husband might well be savaged or killed by the very animal he was hunting. A hunter could tell if his wife was unfaithful, too, he said. When an animal fell over backwards after being shot, the hunter knew instantly that his wife was a bad woman. If an elephant hunter's wife committed adultery while he was on safari, then that meant he had better beware. He would surely die, a victim of his prey.

The *jangili* would come to him, always at night, and always in the hours that led up to their departure for the killing grounds inside the Selous. They would approach him after performing the Ritual of the Night and discuss with him, their Mchawi, where they were going and what they would be hunting. In the old days the hunters would dance and sing. If they were hunting elephants they would imitate the tramp of the elephant, lifting their feet as though great rocks had been fastened to them, and then they would slowly lower them to the ground, tramp, tramp, tread, tread.

The Mchawi stood up, and bending his head and back to the ground, he raised his thin wiry legs in the air so slowly and let them down. He did this a number of times and we laughed. He saw us and smiled too. Then he sat back on the rock and told me about the potions he prepared to keep the hunters safe. Some men, he said, and this happened years ago when he was young, would cut the soles of their feet and slit the tips of their tongues and rub in these magic potions. But today, these young ones, they were not so tough. They merely took the medicine and threw it on the fire, and hoped that the flames would combine with the nostrum and conspire to protect them. They never looked at the fire while the medicine sputtered inside its red-hot jaws. They kept their eyes shut, so that their enemies, the beasts they would attempt to kill the next day, would not be able to see them and kill them. In fact, there were some hunters who used to believe the medicine was so charged with magic that it made them invisible.

Did it work? I asked.

He nodded. He said that there was one famous hunter who swore on his father's cattle that this happened. He became invisible and followed a herd of elephants so closely that he was able to walk right into the middle of them while they were browsing in the grass. He was invisible, but only to the elephants, he added.

And there were some hunters who never entered the bush without the medicine. A father would bring his son for the sole purpose of carrying it, round his neck or waist, in a leather bag. When the hunter saw game, the son must never follow the hunters to the kill. He must stay where he was, sit down and keep a grip on the bag. If he didn't, there could be trouble. The animal might escape. It is the medicine, you see, which is vital, for it is this, and not the hunters, which will decide the fate of the animal. So it must be looked after carefully.

I asked him where the medicine came from. Was it made of herbs?

He shook his head and patted his chest.

From humans?

He laughed. Again he shook his head. From the elephants. The medicine is made out of the heart of the elephants. He laughed again. To become a good hunter, to match the qualities of the animal that he is trying to destroy, to compete with its speed, agility and stamina, its craftiness, its courage, to overcome its might and to subdue its will, a hunter must capture these qualities. But there was only one certain way to accomplish this. He paused and looked at Ndunguru and then his eyes swivelled in the night to me. He was waiting for us to ask him how. But we stayed silent. At last he continued. They must, he said, smacking his lips, eat the heart of the creature. They must swallow a portion of it without chewing, because to chew it into pieces would minimize the dose of courage, strength, ferocity, or guile that they wished to acquire.

He was quiet for a moment. His eyes were fixed on a passing flash of moonlight floating down the Mbarangandu, but his mind, I fancied, if not his stomach, was engaged in chewing that elephant's heart. He spat out a stream of phlegm, which fell a little short of the water's edge, and followed up with an ear-shattering hawk.

He looked up from the river and turned towards Ndunguru and told him with all the authority of the Mchawi he was that elephants never lie. He explained that men still believed they could obtain much wisdom from watching elephants, more than could be acquired from watching men, and after all why should this not be? An elephant is a vast beast that lives long and is not limited in its ambitions. The Selous was vast yet limited. As limited as man, for the men in the Selous had been brought up in the bush, it was in their blood, and so they took note of what the bush had to tell them. They knew little else, and the bush had served them well for years. He thudded a bony fist into his chest. It was a sign that so too had he.

I asked him what he had learnt from elephants and he said without hesitation that there was no one in the Selous, not even himself, who could even begin to grasp the complete mystery of the *tembo*. He knew less than his fathers and they did not know as much as their fathers, and so it went on. There was a little that had been handed down, but the old lore was dying along with the great herds. Now the elephants were scarce, and so were the *jangili*, but they could kill with their powerful and quickfire guns as many *tembo* in one day as his uncles had managed in a lifetime.

So the slaughter in the Selous amounted to the slaughter of a culture? He shook his head. Men and *tembo* needed each other. Men hunted for food and for ivory. Men made sure that by killing the *tembo* there would be enough food for the *tembo*. And besides, men discovered much about themselves from watching the ways of the *tembo*.

He stopped talking again. I had learnt by now that this was his way, that he found it difficult to continue the conversation for more than a few minutes at a time. He was tired and needed to gather his strength. I had also learnt that it did not pay to interrupt the old man too often. He would tell his story in his own time and in the way he wanted.

He began again, now issuing us with a series of commands. It was as if we were two young initiates sent to him to glean the wisdom of the past so that we could cope with the world of the present. Only it wasn't our world and would never be.

He told us never to snap the fingers or click the tongue at a *tembo*, for the elephant, as sure as we were sitting there this night, would charge. He asked us why in his schoolmasterish way, and before we had time to shake our heads and affect a suitably mystified expression, he provided the answer. Because this sound was often the last a *tembo* ever heard. He held out his left arm straight and cocked his thumb. The fingers inside his bent hand gripped tight, and then his little finger curled and his cheeks blew out and his mouth went *boom*. I didn't see it at first, but by the time his mouth popped, I realized he was attempting to imitate a *jangili* firing his rifle.

115

He told us what to do if ever we found an elephant leaping upon another. Go home. They are dangerous and unpredictable in that sort of mood and one of you might well have done wrong to a neighbour; if a pair of elephants are found kneeling face to face, then one of your wives has betrayed you; an elephant which gathers up dust in its trunk and then offers it to another is a sign that your wife has been offered snuff by another man, and this means your marriage is in danger; it's the same when an elephant touches the breasts of another elephant; when an elephant trumpets, there is trouble in your village and when an elephant plasters mud on the face of a mate, there is death.

These were the old tales of the bush that he was telling, of warriors whose eyes and stomachs, spears and *gabores* were fixed on their prey, but whose souls were tuned to a wilder and more mysterious voice.

The old man sighed. I wondered whether he wanted to sleep. But it was an expression, not of physical weariness, but of fatigue with a world that he knew was changing and that he was sure would render him obsolete. I asked him if his son was a Mchawi and he shrugged and shook his head, and said that he was the last of the line. He didn't know his age and it was difficult to estimate. Ndunguru thought he might be any age between sixty and eighty.

Ndunguru nudged me and whispered that I ought to give him something. I passed over a few thousand shillings. He rose from the rock that looked down on the sparkling Mbarangandu and walked away from us, leaving Ndunguru and me alone with the sounds of the night and the river. Before he disappeared, I called out and asked him his name.

He stopped, turned his head, and said softly: 'I have no name.'

Down below, on the river, hippos were blowing bubbles at each other. Across the Mbarangandu was the forbidden wilderness of the Selous. The Mchawi sniffed at it, drawing its smell into his nostrils, and then his lungs, filling his body with its flavours. This red and crumbly bluff was as near and as far as he could reach. Beyond him and his grasp, perhaps as little as two or three hundred metres away, he could see a kind of paradise.

ELEVEN

Miracle in Kalulu

The Mbarangandu is a sleepy river by day. I know, for I have spied its movements from the air, looked down from Bigurube's Cessna, on one tight brown curl upon another, but I swear that that night when I sat and listened to the Mchawi, the river listened too. The flood of words, of recollections, the gush of memories unlocked the waters just below us. They seemed to be encouraged by what they were listening to, as I had been, and for a moment at least I believed the river was flowing a little faster, and with more purpose.

Now, back in the hut in Kilimasera, all I had was my mosquito net and my memories. I had seen a man enter the bush, walk for no more than three hundred metres, and vanish into his past. I had seen a man cast off the rags of day and surrender himself to the indulgent embrace of the night, heard him talk of a time and a place where there are no laws and inhibitions of the day, where man's culture is not feared but despised and ignored, where magic insisted there was no room for reason.

I had seen this man and heard him speak, and I, too, for a minute, had felt the power of the bush. The rhythm of the night had touched that old man's words and I, between dreams and dawn under a mosquito net, was touched as well. My body faded away from consciousness, but all the time my brain was hearing the voice of the Mchawi.

The only laws in the bush are the laws of the spirits.

The bush belongs to the night, and the night is master of the bush.

The night possesses the power and the mysteries of magic.

117

The night understands magic. The night has the strength to resurrect.

The night is a fearsome creature. The night must be obeyed. The night pumps the veins and fizzes the heart.

The night must be respected.

The night is generous to the faithful.

By night, a man can win back his courage. At night, a man can recover his dignity. Through night, a man can accumulate riches. With night, a man can control his destiny.

The night grants independence. The night is eloquent. The night should be listened to. The night gives guidance. The night turns a slave into a master. The night is unpredictable. The night is savage. The night is exciting . . .

Kilimasera was a watershed. I had witnessed a strange and powerful rite, and then luck had played its part, as it always does in this job, and I had managed to talk to this Mchawi. I had gained a toehold and glimpsed inside an arcane world, if only for a brief moment. But what I had seen had afforded me an insight into the massive problem facing Ndunguru and Costa Mlay. This wasn't just about protecting elephants. It was much larger, for I could now see clearly that here was a battle between the old and the new. The *jangili* may have been toting modern weapons, their firepower may have been frighteningly sophisticated, but they were armed with another, more potent weapon than any that man could devise. They were creatures of another time who responded to voices that ordinary mortals could not hear. They were immune to the new culture which they saw as their enemy and imposed by men whose purpose was to corral their energies, destroy their lives and rob them of their freedom. In short, they had no wish to be enslaved by the modern world. They despised Nyererism. They despised the *ujamaa* village or commune, they despised rural socialism. They belonged to the bush; and the men from Dar, the politicians with their utopian schemes for making men equal, and their lieutenants who dropped in on the villages to implement these plans, were not worthy of their respect. There was little, of course, they could do to stop the plans bearing fruit. They grudgingly obeyed their masters' wishes, acknowledged the new order, and went about their lives as if nothing new had actually happened. They joined the committees set up to administer the villages, but when the meetings were over, when they felt hunger grip them, they acted in the way the Mchawi had described and went to their homes and ate from a full pot. And in the pot was game.

Bernard Asayo could change the Selous. He is a frontiersman, all five foot two inches of him. Asayo is the chief warden of the southern sector of the Selous, only twenty-six years old, and in charge of a vast area of uninhabited land.

Bernard Asayo is a builder. When he first came deep into the southern Selous and Kalulu four years ago in 1987, there was nothing in the village save a few huts and an overgrown track fit only for foot, and then just in the dry season. Neither were there money or materials or machinery to construct the houses for the askaris and their families, the school for their children, the armoury for their weapons, the clinic for their sick, the workshop for their vehicles. There was no road. There was no airstrip.

Kalulu was a fiction. It had been invented in an office in some sticky government building in Dar es Salaam. Kalulu was one of Nyerere's babies, a result of his infatuation with Mao. He had visited China during his fledgling days as President and was unlucky enough to have arrived at the height of the Cultural Revolution. Unlucky for Tanzania, and Kalulu, I mean. The first President was impressed. He marvelled at the way Mao had organized his people, and how the Party's control of the country extended beyond Peking and Canton and Shanghai and reached out to grasp the minds of the peasants in their villages. Nyerere believed that what he saw buried in the provinces, hundreds of miles away from the cities, was a compelling blueprint for his own country and he set about importing it. Of course, the result was a catastrophe, but Nyerere was blind to its impact. It didn't work in China and it didn't work in Tanzania.

Out of the loins of this misguided fantasy, Kalulu was born.

Kalulu didn't exist before 1974. And for fourteen years the only regular visitor was the rain. Each year the rains fell and the dank and forlorn grass grew taller and tougher over and around this village with no roads, no hospital, no school, no airstrip, and no maize mill. Each drop of water that drizzled out of the clouds colluded with the grass and dank soil, the bold weeds and trees, to mist out Kalulu, to drown it in a heaving mire of sodden green.

Then Bernard Asayo arrived. Bernard Asayo was a baby of the Nyerere revolution. He was weaned on the Mwalimu's teachings. He had never experienced the rule of the British. He was younger than independence and carried inside him all the contradictions of the new era. He had been taught that this was his country and he was born to build it. But what with? Bernard Asayo's birthright was blighted by bankruptcy, in a country where the one commodity in abundance was ideology, and this, sadly, was no asset.

I stood on the airstrip a few minutes' drive from Bernard Asayo's headquarters in Kalulu and waited for Gerard Bigurube's plane to arrive. Asayo asked me to walk with him the length of the airstrip. Every few paces, he kicked over a lump of earth or removed a stone. This was his airstrip and he had built it without machinery, without graders or levellers, steamrollers or tipper trucks. All Bernard Asayo had at his disposal was one Land Rover pick-up and twenty men, game scouts and a few of the villagers. And he had what no grant of foreign aid could provide. His courage and imagination.

It took Bernard Asayo and his team one month to clear the ground of trees, thirty days of toil, working from sunrise which comes here, so far south, at six, to dusk, twelve hours of sweat-soaked effort, which tore the hands and twisted the back and strained the thighs, to pull up by the roots thousands of trees so that a great wide hiatus, 1,300 metres long by about 70 metres wide, was gashed into the bush. Each tree was extracted by axe and winch and hawser. The work was slow, and painful, and when it was over, when every twisted and obdurate root had been hauled out, then Bernard Asayo had to compact the ground. This he did with stones which were collected from a quarry over forty kilometres away. Over forty journeys, there and back, were made before there were sufficient stones to cover the airstrip. They made a strikingly strange sight, heaped together as they were, in the midst of this wide expanse of freshly cleared red earth. But Bernard Asayo did not allow the men to become overawed by the task that still confronted them.

He gave them axes and hammers, as many as he could manage to borrow from Ndunguru's HQ in Songea, and ordered these twenty men to break the stones. By hand.

Each rock was dragged out of the pick-up and thrown onto the red soil, and then it was sledged into fragments and trodden into the earth. There was no roller, no way of compacting the fragments, so Bernard Asayo drove the loaded pick-up backwards and forwards, backwards and forwards for days across the airstrip until he was satisfied it was hard and would be usable in all weathers. The villagers of Kalulu were astonished. They believed that what Bernard Asayo had built was not possible. 'How,' they asked each other, 'could one man labour so hard and for so many months without tools or machinery?'

They explained it, as they always explained anything they did not understand, by thanking the spirits for their intervention and advice. Nevertheless, the example set by Bernard Asayo proved a turning point in their lives. This man had come to their village to save elephants. But before he could begin to do this, he had saved them.

None of them had been born in Kalulu. They had all been transplanted there, uprooted from villages and settlements inside the Selous like the trees that once grew chaotically on the airstrip. And like the stones that Bernard Asayo and his twenty helpers had crushed, each one, by hand and hammer, so too their courage and their dignity had been extinguished in the move. Kalulu was an *ujamaa* village whose people had once lived and hunted inside the Selous. There was no room for them inside the reserve. No room, politically, that is. And until Bernard Asayo was posted, their existence in Kalulu was ignored and their hopes dampened by the rains.

At the end of the runway I stopped and wrenched out from the hard soil a clump of weeds and grasses. I could hear a faint buzzing in the sky, and looked up, squinting to try and catch the glimmer of wing, of metal, that was Bigurube.

Asayo stood still, his slight figure erect and stiff with pride, his back arched like a bow against the sky. He was the embodiment of a different Africa, not the Africa which held out a hand and grasped dollarsful of aid and then spent it on Mercedes saloons and Swiss bank accounts, but the

Africa which was driven and determined and achieved results with the barest of help. Asayo had been fed upon a diet of dogma, but none of it had he swallowed. He was a practical man who lived in a continent where rhetoric and bombast, and not action, were hard currency, worthy of respect.

Bernard Asayo's inspiration was drawn from the Bible, not the collected works of the former President, for what he had achieved in these last few months in Kalulu was almost miraculous. Kalulu had his imagination to thank.

This was his second airstrip, and, he said to me, there would be others. Slowly, by dint of his will and his hands, Kalulu and the surrounding areas of this vast expanse of Africa that fringed the southern Selous were being bridged. Inside the village, too, the atmosphere was touched by activity. At 7.30 on the morning after I arrived, the game scouts were parading their weapons – antique bolt-action .303s with not one automatic – and their smiles in the thin sunlight outside the Game Post HQ. The sergeant drilled them vigorously, all two dozen askaris, and inspected the turn-out, praising them for the condition of their kit and choosing to ignore those who were wearing cheap trainers or flip-flops made from discarded tyres. He snapped his heels shut and handed over the platoon to Asayo who introduced Ndunguru.

Inside the armoury, a dim, dusty room no more than six by eight, weapons seized from *jangili* were stacked against the concrete walls. There was ivory there too, long curving tusks, ten of them, weighing around thirty kilos each, and requiring two men to lift them outside onto the parade ground. Alongside the ivory was a poachers' kit, a rotting gunny sack filled with all that the *jangili* and his *fundi* needed to survive any eventuality inside the Selous for the weeks that they planned to hunt.

Asayo opened the bag slowly, taking care to spread its neck wide before placing his hand inside. I thought there could have been a mamba inside it. In fact, there was something just as dangerous. A syringe with its needle intact, rusting, and waiting to inject any of us careless or clumsy enough to brush their skin against it.

'I'd throw that away, destroy it,' I said.

'We can't. It's evidence. We just have to be careful,' said

Ndunguru. 'You see, we are not only trying to catch poachers here, but possibly men with AIDS.'

'What do they want syringes for, anyway?'

'These men are like children. They think that a pill is no good. They believe the best medicine is the injection. Give them a jab and they begin at once to feel better. Isn't that right, Bernard?'

Asayo nodded. 'It was stolen, most probably,' he said. 'Stolen from a hospital or medical clinic in one of the villages.'

Asayo picked up the sack and shook it out. Onto the earth tumbled a succession of broken and rusty museum pieces, the sort of souvenirs that could be found in a boy's bedside drawer: razor blades, brass cartridge cases, a few sharp slivers of sticks – toothpicks – a knife that was blunted, an empty sachet of aspirin powder, a leather sandal with a broken buckle, tyre tubes which had been cut into pieces, ready to tie up the tusks, an aluminium cooking pot, an axe, wire mesh to make snares, plastic sacks, empty now, but once full of grain to sustain the *jangili* on their trek. Nothing was wasted. Nothing had been thrown out. The kit was sparse and wrecked with age, but in the bush everything has its use. The kit smacked of amateurdom, innocence, and make-do, but in the bush there is no innocence.

Not all the old ways had vanished from Kalulu, though. Only one of the old huts in the village had a tin roof. It belonged to the Mchawi. Every other roof was thatched. There was a reason, of course. The Mchawi had told the villagers that to sleep under tin was dangerous. They would be visited during the night by evil spirits, djinns, who would lacerate their bodies and invade their minds. I asked Ndunguru if it were true. He nodded. But did he really believe this?

'Of course not,' he said, 'but I remember when I was a child growing up in the far west of the country my father announced with pride one day that he was going to buy a tin roof. My sister and I begged him not to. We were about seven at the time and we were frightened of the dreams that would surely come to us under that tin roof. The Mchawi in our village had made the same threats, you see. We couldn't sleep for days. We stayed awake, we cried in our beds, we talked each other out of sleep. We resisted dreams.'

123

But what about the people of Kalulu? They were not seven-year-olds.

He agreed. 'The real reason for the Mchawi's opposition,' he said, 'is much more basic than evil spirits and bad dreams. It's all to do with status. You see, the Mchawi with his tin roof, the only tin roof in the village, is something special. Not just a peasant. His tin roof underlines his superiority.'

A man of substance, indeed.

Down the street, where the askaris were busy building the quarters for their wives and children, men were slapping mud on the wooden framework of their houses. One side of the street had been completed and there was a rush to finish the other side before the rains returned. The completed houses were airy, whitewashed and neat under the sun. Next to the carpenter's shop where more frameworks were being hammered together there was a maize mill, locked and empty but for the gleaming green-and-red engine, a refugee from some Yorkshire engineering works, maybe the last export from the north of England. I could smell the oil plastered round the casing.

Bernard Asayo was a happy man that day in this village that had been invented, forgotten, then rescued. Here, in Kalulu, inside the Selous, people's hopes were sprouting as fast as their homes were springing upwards. Not far, just one storey, a few feet above the ground, but higher than most men in this wilderness can ever hope to aim for.

Bigurube set the plane down on the airstrip with a skip. The little Cessna taxied to a halt and he emerged, smiling, and carrying a large fish, which he immediately presented to Asayo. 'For your wife,' he said, adding, 'to cook for our supper.'

He had been forced to wait a day at Dar while the plane was being repaired – the radio was not working again – and had that morning been detoured to Beho-Beho, in the northern sector of the reserve, where he had had to pay the men at the game post. Beho-Beho, besides being the site of one of the most bloody skirmishes of the First World War, had won its place in the history books by being the place where Lieutenant Frederick Selous, the greatest hunter of his day, had been killed, at the age of sixty-five, the victim of a German sniper's bullet. But Beho-Beho was also near Lake Tagalala and this was where Bigurube had obtained his fish, a perch, four feet of glisten from head to tail, and fat with eyes that buttoned on to us glumly.

That evening Bernard Asayo's wife served up the fish with, of course, rice, and warm tea drawn out of the family Thermos. She tried her best, offering first sitting to her husband's guests, with Bernard eating last. As for herself, she didn't join us, preferring to remain concealed in the darkness of the yard along with the chickens and washing that hung limp and damp upon her clothes-line.

Bigurube, as Warden of the Selous, was Asayo's boss and clearly pleased with the progress the young man had made in Kalulu. He was a thoughtful man who had held this post, controlling all these thousands of square kilometres, for almost two years. Before his appointment he had been working in the Selous as a pilot, flying between scout camps, paying the wages, delivering parts for vehicles by air, and twice each year taking part in the elephant counts that often took up more than a month, when with two observers he took off at dawn and rested for just a few hours in the heat of the early afternoon before finally landing each day at sundown. He had in his career flown hundreds of thousands of miles and been alone in his cockpit for thousands of hours. He had seen the decline of the elephant from the air, whitened heaps of bones scattered over the vastness of the Selous. He had counted the casualties of this war and tried, as he fought with the rudder and the stick and the wind, to control his own emotions as day after day, and sortie upon sortie, had registered even worse news than the one before.

He had thought deeply about even taking this job, for the Selous was a huge and limitless place whose size and complexity matched the problems that teemed within its boundaries. I asked him why he had accepted.

'I felt very inadequate,' he replied. 'Costa Mlay called me and told me that this was what he wanted me to do. The Selous was my future, he said. Solve the crisis in the Selous and you solve the crisis in the country. Save the elephant in the Selous and you save the elephant for Africa. It was too big a task.'

He was right. Imagine God suggesting to a human being that it is up to him to save a species. You'd laugh.

Bigurube didn't. He despaired. He trembled, and he went home to his wife Adas and his three children and prayed. He sank onto his knees in his small house in Dar es Salaam and thought of Lazarus. 'There I was absolutely in pieces, frightened of the magnitude of the job that I had been selected to do, and then the parable came into my thoughts. I realized then that there was hope. Lazarus became my friend. I often think of him when I'm flying.'

'Now he tells us,' I said.

'No, really, Nick, it is true. I spend much of the day alone, up there, thousands of feet up there. I have had many moments when I have thought that I am not going to walk on the earth again. Small moments which pass quickly. There is so much to do, to look out for when you think your plane is not functioning the way it should, but always I fit in the time to think of Lazarus.'

The next morning I crawl out of my tent pitched next to the ones in which Kibasa, Bigurube and Ndunguru have spent the night and follow my nose across Bernard Asayo's backyard to the hole in the ground discreetly covered with a wooden stopper. On the way I stumble as my feet stub against a pile of soft somethings on the earth. Elephant dung. The elephants have returned to Kalulu. They have come close to us in the night, so close that they could easily have made more than a mess on the ground outside our sleeping area. The dung is still wet and provides an unexpected breakfast for the flies and beetles which would normally have concentrated their attentions upon and in Bernard Asayo's kitchen. The dung is dark and steam is rising from the pile. I shout to wake Ndunguru. Ndunguru shouts to wake the world. Bigurube's sharp head, a towel round his neck, emerges like a tortoise from its shell. The dung is poked and smelt and talked over. The dung makes us smile. Something magical has happened. Something to do with Lazarus. The elephants have returned to Kalulu, and Kalulu and Bernard Asayo, the man who resurrected this village inside the Selous, deserve their presence.

TWELVE

Bwana Mkubwa

The Angoni Arms had run dry of Safari beer; the roads ran wet with early morning rain; the grass had run itself up another inch; the queue in the Bank of Tanzania ran on and the living line ran round the counters and through the double front doors, ran ragged into the street. Time and ivory were the twin commodities that Songea hadn't run out of.

Yet. Time was no longer an ally of the ivory traders, and Songea was still an ivory town.

There were middlemen in Songea, waiting for the army to withdraw, waiting for Ndunguru, the man who had plotted the downfall of the MP and forced the Somalis to flee the town, to relax his grip. Ndunguru had told me that he suspected fifteen men in Songea of being *bwana mkubwa*, middlemen. He knew who they were and he too was waiting, sometimes in the darkness, waiting for them to judge that the moment was now right, to make a mistake which would put them into a jail alongside their once illustrious but now disgraced MP, Ali Yusuf Abdurabi. He, too, had once decided whether elephants would live or die.

The Ishmaels own a trucking business which is based in a village between Songea and Iringa. The chain-link fence that surrounds their compound is a few metres off the TAN–ZAM highway. Settled in the dust, its nose peeking into a workshop, I can see the gutted remains of a Scania lorry. Beyond repair, it had been parked there, and would remain until it had fulfilled its life's function. A lorry does not die easily in Tanzania. And when finally its axle shatters, or its fuel pump collapses, or its suspension surrenders to

127

the potholes, there is another life for lorries, after death. There is no vehicle Valhalla for these, but the stripping of their vitals can keep a fleet grumbling along those red dirt roads for perhaps another 100,000 kilometres.

Even the dust is sleeping this afternoon. Across the yard from the carcass of the Scania, inside the wooden office with its corrugated tin fringe, I see Ibrahim Ishmael stroking the keys of his upright piano. He looks up and across at me, and then returns to the music. I don't recognize the tune. I introduce myself and he asks me in, waving his free hand at the settee. He smiles and the teeth in his mouth compete with the ivory out of which his fingers are massaging the music.

'I am sorry to interrupt you,' I begin, and the music ceases. I have his attention, though perhaps he has had mine from the moment I entered. 'I am on a holiday, a vacation, from Dar and I would like to hunt, and I've been told that you, Mr Ishmael, is it?, are hunters.'

I stop. I have a tape in my pocket and I am fumbling with the on switch (or is it the off?), desperately fidgeting, hoping he will not notice, and the more I fiddle, the bigger the tape becomes, so defying that Japanese genius which shrank it from radiogram to cigarette-packet size. I hope to God that I will not pull it out of my pocket and smoke it.

'Yes, we are hunters. Who told you about us, Mr...?' He pauses, allowing me the privilege of saying my name once more.

'Mr Gordon. Mr Nicholas Gordon. From London, but now I work for a tea company in Dar. Import-export.' I know that sounds corny as a cover story, but I can do no better.

He nods his head and leans away from the piano towards me. I realize he wants me to answer the first part of his question.

'You have a big business here?'

'Yes, we do. We are one of the leading transport companies in Tanzania. Only this week we have signed a contract for three more 44-tonners.'

'How much are they costing you, Mr Ishmael?'

'One hundred and fifty thousand dollars,' he says. 'American dollars.'

'Then you must be a rich man.'

'We work hard. I have my brother and my father to thank for that as well.'

'About the hunting. Can you take me out?'

'This is the wrong time of the year. The wrong season. You should have come here in September. Didn't your friends tell you this?'

'They did, but as I was in Songea, I thought I would see you and perhaps fix something for the autumn, September, I mean.'

'You haven't told me who your friends are.'

'People in Dar. You know, you have a drink in the Yacht Club, or the Kilimanjaro, and you get chatting about this and that.'

'What do you want to hunt?'

'I don't really know, Mr Ishmael. I'd like to take a crack at an elephant.'

'Impossible,' he says.

'Why? I thought elephants were easy.'

'Not now. It is very difficult. I do not know even if we will be allowed to hunt any this year. The Government has not yet decided on the licences. The allocation. And, if they say yes, go and hunt them, then they may well set a limit on the size.'

'I don't want a big one.'

He laughs at the naivety. The sparkle from his teeth overwhelms the sparse jaw that holds them, but, somehow, the effect contrives to work against the sallowness of his skin and makes him unhealthier than he appears to be. He is a lean man, with close untrusting Semitic eyes of brown, and hair that is black and unruly as the weeds in Kalulu.

'Were you born here?' I ask.

'Yes, but I am not a Tanzanian. I am a Baluchi.'

He sees the bewilderment in my eyes. 'From across the Gulf. Iran. We are now third generation. My grandfather was the first Ishmael to arrive.'

'This is a big business you run here. You have done well, Mr Ishmael.'

'Thank you, sir. It is true. Today I have heard that we can go to Dar to collect the latest lorry we have ordered. $150,000. We have trucks that go all over the country and into Zambia and across the lake to Burundi. We even send them as far as Somalia.'

129

Behind him, in a corner of the room, is a fax machine, waiting for a message from one of his truck drivers perhaps. And behind that, leaning against the wall, an example of a more basic communication system, and one that is probably more reliable, given the caprices of the Tanzanian telephone system. It is a blackboard, and chalked on it is a chant of towns, Songea, Iringa, Tunduru, Mtwara, Moshe, Arusha, Liwale, Mbeya, Dodoma, Tabora, Chilesi, Mwanza, Mikumi, and Dar.

He turns and points to the board. 'These are the destinations of our drivers. So I know where they are every day, and almost on the hour. We give them radio phones and if there is a problem we have the fax. It is,' he says, with a satisfied click of the tongue against his teeth, 'the only way to run the business.'

'But trucking is not all you are involved in?'

'No, we are hunters too. We make no secret of it and we have a licence from the Government. I take clients from America and sometimes from your country. I have some Americans coming in the autumn. I tell you it is my first love. And I have taught my son.' He stands and crosses the room to the desk. On it is a photograph framed in silver, of a little boy wearing what looks suspiciously like Yasser Arafat gear, only without the red-and-white check teatowel on the head. The boy is carrying a hunting rifle, legs astride, standing over an antelope which presumably he has just shot. Beneath his forage cap there is a sullen pull on the eyes, not the smile of elation you would expect.

'Is that your son?'

'Farouk.'

'How old is Farouk?'

'Eight.'

'Why is he so sad?'

Ibrahim Ishmael laughs. 'Because he spilt blood on his new hunting clothes. He was very angry. As soon as the boy got back here, he marched in to his mother, tore off his suit and told her to wash the blood away.'

'Does he like hunting?'

'Oh, he loves it, but he is more careful now.'

I see that maybe now is the time to press a little harder. Ibrahim Ishmael looks relaxed. Will I chance another question about ivory? I look at him again. I must keep the

130

conversation going, not allow the pace to falter. I decide to defer ivory.

'You speak Arabic?' I enquire.

'*Aiwah.*'

'*Il hamdililah.*'

'*Calum Arabi?*'

'*Swoyeh, swoyeh.* I spent a year in the Sudan. They knew me there by another name though, my Arab name.'

He leans forward, interested, catching the smile in my voice. 'Mr Fuck.'

'Mr Fuck?' He laughs and touches my knee. Now he is squeezing it.

'Yes, my first name is Nicholas, Nick.'

'Ah, Neek. I see. Well, Mr Neek, Mr Fuck, should I say, if you do not mind, we will have to see about your coming hunting with us in the autumn.' He is still laughing as two sets of heavy feet rhythmically drum up the wooden stairs that rise from the compound into the office.

Two men enter the room. I assume they are the Ishmael father and Ibrahim's brother. The older man is about seventy and his face and arms are as smooth as creamy coffee swirling round in a freshly made white cup. His suit matches his face. It is light brown, silk, and expensively cut. He is wearing a white shirt and tie. He is far smarter than either of his sons who are both dressed in blue jeans and cotton sports tops. Unlike his sons, the old man has lost his hair and just a few whiffs of white flitter round the slopes of his skull.

I stand up to introduce myself, but Ibrahim beats me to it.

'Meet Mr Fuck,' he announces to his father and brother, partners in the business.

I bow, well, not quite. I lower my head and offer my hand to each of them in turn. They take it and shake hands.

'My name,' I say with as much dignity as I can muster, 'is Nick . . .'

'Oh, Neek. Mr Neek. Mr Fuck, ha, ha, ha,' says the brother, joining Ibrahim's joke. But I notice that their father is silent and has, after the shaking of the hands between Baluchi and Brit, sat down.

'Where did you find a name like that, Mr Neek?' asks the brother.

'In the Sudan.'

'These Sudani are very funny,' he says by way of conso-
lation.

'Mr Fuck, Mr Neek, wants to hunt,' Ibrahim smoothly
explains.

'Oh, so you are a big hunter, eh?' says the brother, and
all the time the father is looking towards me, his brown eyes
soft on mine.

'No, but I would like to try. I would like to shoot game.
I was talking to your brother about this possibility, but he
says it is something that is not feasible. Possible, I mean.' I
sit down again next to Ibrahim. Now what? 'I expect you
know the MP here, Mr Ali Yusuf Abdurabi?'

'Why do you ask this?' The father is speaking. Slowly, as
if he is not really prepared to talk foreign to foreigners.

'I am told he is a good man who knows about elephants.
But I cannot find him in Songea and no one knows where
he is.'

'We knew him,' says Ibrahim. 'Everyone in Songea knew
him, but he is a bad man. He was caught by the Wildlife
Department and the police trafficking in ivory and now he
is paying for his madness and his greed.'

'How well did you know him? Did you visit his house
ever?'

The father has stood up. He is trying to say something.

'Did you ever hear stories about him and ivory?'

Ibrahim has taken in his father's nod and is showing me
to the door. He is very courteous in his good-byes. He does
not call me Mr Fuck again.

I returned to Songea through tall and narrow passages of
green, a convenient hedge to mask these Baluchis' secret
trade. Certainly the Ishmaels were living well. The success
of their business was all the more impressive in a country
where stagnation was a growth industry and failure the
norm. But even the Ishmaels, I thought, must be feeling the
effects of the ivory crackdown. The arrest of their MP might
not have come as a shock to them. These things, regrettable
as they were, sometimes happened. But the trial, sentence,
loss of appeal, and subsequent increase in his prison term
surely had a seismic effect on the middlemen in Songea.

That was a warning shot. But it soon turned into a fusil-
lade. There had been the arrest of a Somali middleman and

132

the confiscation of his two Landcruisers. The Ishmaels must have realized that they were fortunate not to have been implicated – though the direction of Tanzanian shillings had far more influence when it came to maintaining a clean record than mere good fortune. They were not the only ivory dealers to have scattered around, liberally yet carefully, those torn and grease-stained wads of cash held together by the warmth of their palms and a fraying elastic band. So too had the Somalis, and the Somalis, all of them, had cleared out of town.

Another factor, over which they had no control, had begun to strangle their business. The world price of ivory had tumbled to a ludicrous low. Only the previous year, before Operation Uhai had even been conceived, before Ndunguru had launched his village schemes and Ali Yusuf Abdurabi had ever thought that one fine morning his free-dom would not last beyond the dusk, the middlemen of Songea would have been buying a kilo of ivory for 300 shillings and selling it on for 1,000 shillings, a tax-free profit of over 200 per cent. No wonder the businesses in Songea, the legitimate businesses, were blessed with a healthy flush.

The middlemen of Songea were waiting. Why should they risk everything, like Ali Yusuf Abdurabi, now the trade was illegal? Well, it had never been considered so before, even though the statute books declared it was, but now there was too much to risk, too much to lose. There had been crackdowns before, and these had never amounted to more than a few days of sloppy searches, the occasional conviction – never more than a small fine or a few months inside – and then dealing had been resumed in much the same way as it had for centuries. The British Government had allowed the Hong Kong carvers to save their businesses by not implementing the ban on exports to the colony for six months. And what had this achieved? Only a massive upsurge in poaching and trafficking.

No, the middlemen would not surrender so easily. They would continue buying, especially now that ivory was so cheap. They would store the trophies, bury them, and wait. Keep killing elephants. If they didn't, if they allowed Ndun-guru and Captain Katali to win, then it would be their loss and their rival middlemen's gain.

I had met families like the Ishmaels before. In the Sudan.

They, too, were Baluchis, and to assume that such a family would not become involved in any business other than ivory and transport would be to ignore their history, their traditions and their genes. The Baluchis brought with them to Africa not only their religion, Islam, but their skills. The Baluchis were carriers, servicing carriers. They were blacksmiths, horse and camel dealers who would, for a fee, transport goods, any goods, no questions asked, across borders. They had arrived in the wake of the railways, and now they commanded the roads. They had come with oxen, camels and horses, and realized the potential of motor transport. They had exchanged their forges and hoofing irons for spanners and grease pits, and as the railways bit deeper into the interior of the continent, so too did the Baluchis, feeding and feeding off the men who built them. They brought the engineers supplies of beer, dried meat, and the comforting moistness of women; they repaired their vehicles, they serviced their water pumps, they oiled their engines, and with the proceeds they sold their horses and camels and invaded the new century on wheels.

Like the Somalis, the Baluchi people spread through East Africa as effectively as the locust. When old man Ishmael settled in Songea – and Ndunguru told me the family had arrived there from Iringa – I guessed that he saw the potential of making money out of servicing the vehicles that the German army was using in the Great War. Here was a town which was expanding, a frontier town where a businessman such as he could prosper. The German boma, the headquarters of the regional government of southern Tanganyika, was the hub of an efficient and burgeoning war economy; there was plenty of transport but not enough skilled hands to maintain it; there were many opportunities to acquire vehicles, bombed-out, shell-scarred lorries, which the old man could repair and annex for his growing fleet. But there was another reason why Songea might have appealed to him more than Iringa. This was Africa, the Africa he most probably had heard tales of from his grandfather, rich, luxuriant Africa, where the grass and forest concealed all manner of riches. The first Baluchis to cross the Gulf and land on the shores of the continent had collaborated with the Arab masters in the ivory trade. These Baluchis were strictly second-rankers, not in any position to finance or even lead caravans. It was left to them to make sure the caravans progressed quickly, quietly and with the minimum of inconvenience and the maximum of profit. This they achieved with the aid of the *chikote*, which they wielded against the flesh of the slaves without remorse and with a certain kind of pride. The Arabs had gone, the slave trade was buried, when Ibrahim Ishmael's grandfather reached Songea, but the ivory trade was still flourishing, and the trade still required men to move the tusks and men to make sure it was moved swiftly and in secret, the Arab way.

It was Safari beer day back at the Angoni Arms. The landlord was rubbing his palms together in expectation of a good night's trade, but I was far too tired to stay the course of the evening with Ndunguru. I hadn't told him where I had been that afternoon, and he didn't ask. I suspected he thought I had stayed inside my bedroom-hut in the grounds and rested after the journey back from Kalulu.

I changed the subject. I didn't want him to question me too closely, and I couldn't be sure that I was capable of burying the secret that deeply or for long. So I asked him about the MP. What were the chances of seeing him, or even his wife? His shoulders rippled and he sniffed and said that that could possibly be arranged, but he had something far more important to tell me. He pulled out a brown folded envelope from his top pocket and fanned it against his breast. 'I can do better than that,' he said. 'Bigurube gave me this at Kalulu, before he flew back to Dar.'

I could see it was government issue and guessed it was from the Director.

'We have permission,' he said enigmatically, the corners of his lips curling upwards.

'Permission? To see the MP?'

'I think it is better than that.' He paused, sipping his Safari. 'Remember the New Super Moscow Bar? Remember the *jangili* Katali was furious about?'

I said I did, but I couldn't recall the name.

'Bero,' he said. 'Bero. I have been given clearance for you to talk to him.'

THIRTEEN

The Poacher's Tale

The man's name was Alensio Bero. He lived in a village called Hanga Monastery, which was about an hour's drive from Ndunguru's headquarters in Songea. Ndunguru had first heard of Alensio Bero soon after he had been posted to Songea for the first time in 1972. The name kept appearing in police reports and the logs of the game scouts, and Ndunguru, fresh to his job as Regional Game Officer, had asked questions about him. Each time he raised the name, his enquiry would be met with a heave from his soldiers who wore an expression that was pitched some way between helplessness and respect. The man was clearly a *jangili*, a commercial poacher, who, according to the evidence in the files, had been involved for many years and had managed, through, he guessed, the cunning the years had given to him, to evade arrest. Bero had been convicted, it was true, but only once, and that appearance in the courthouse in Songea had happened years ago. A firearm offence, Ndunguru believed. He could not quite remember the case, and at any rate, this had all taken place well before he came to the south.

We were sitting in his cramped office in the HQ of the Wildlife Department talking about Bero and, as we discussed his history, Ndunguru turned the pages inside a brown and worn-out file. He looked up, his fingers stabbing at one particular line. Here was the record of Bero's arrest and conviction. I gave up trying to crane my neck to read the lines and walked round to Ndunguru's side of the desk. I peered down at the page from his shoulder and read the copperplate writing that flowed across the page. Fine old-fashioned English writing, the like of which you would only see practised these days on the envelopes of air mail letters from the United States. The entry was dated 1951 and recorded the fact that Bero had been arrested for shooting an eland illegally. The court had fined him 150 shillings, a few months' salary in those days, and, more significantly and far more punitively, it had ordered that his *gabore* be seized.

So for almost forty years, Alensio Bero had been speckling these pages as incident after incident, all of which involved allegations of his involvement in poaching game, was documented in a meticulous hand, and, as the entries mounted up, so too the seriousness of the offences escalated. An eland in 1951 became a buffalo in 1953 and an elephant as long ago as 1967. There were mentions, too, of lions, leopards, hartebeest, sable antelope, okapi, giraffe. But the word that occurred more often than any other was *tembo*.

Why then, in view of all this, was Bero willing to talk?

Bero was fifty-two and this was old. Operation Uhai had frightened him. Suddenly, after years of killing elephants, with no one, not even those in authority, either bothering to stop it or being in a strong enough position to make poaching difficult, there had been a showdown. The army had burst into the Selous, terrorized the *jangili* and the villagers, seized thousands of guns and bullets and made hundreds of arrests. Men had been killed, some of them Bero's friends. The middlemen had been driven out of Songea. But all this was of little consequence when it was set against the collapse in the price of ivory. This was the really momentous change. Two years ago an average-sized tusk, weighing say 20 kg, could fetch thousands of shillings. Now that same tusk would sell for hundreds.

'The man has seen the future,' said Ndunguru bluntly. 'He is a realist.'

It had taken months to make the approach to Bero, and Ndunguru decided to select him only when he had received a tip from one of his scouts who lived in Hanga Monastery that Bero was thinking of quitting the bush while he still had his life. The *jangili* had been pulled in by the Operation Uhai men, Katali's men, for questioning some months before Ndunguru met him, and, true to his record, he had not surrendered an inch. But then the game scout in Hanga Monastery heard a whisper that Alensio Bero's days as a *jangili* were in the past. The men in the wildlife HQ at

Songea laughed when they heard the story. They remembered thinking that if anyone believed Bero, then they would believe the country would have a two-party state tomorrow. But Ndunguru thought he should check out the *jangili*. Just in case. He couldn't go to Hanga village in the old days without arousing the suspicions of the villagers, and, worse, facing their contempt. They regarded him as a government man who was on a different side from them, who did not understand their ways and wanted only to destroy them. But that was before his village schemes had been conceived. Now, after long distrust on both sides, he and the villagers involved in the schemes were at least on talking terms. And this was how he managed to visit Hanga Monastery and spend enough time there to persuade Alensio Bero to work for him.

Bero had been turned. Ndunguru was right. Bero had seen the future and wanted none of it. So now he was sharing his past, which of course included the deaths of thousands of elephants, with Ndunguru's future. Both men depended very much upon one another. The information about the *jangili*'s movements, weaponry, hunting grounds, methods, hiding places, payments, all of these details, Ndunguru was now aware of. And in return, Bero had kept his freedom, and stayed out of the range of Captain Katali's *kiboko*.

We had been allocated a new *deriva*. His name was Boniface, twice the size of Vincent who had been recalled to Dar where he was needed by Costa. Boniface spoke twice as much English as Vincent. This amounted to two words. Safe and sex. AIDS obsessed him, and whenever he was not driving or eating or drinking, which did account for most of his time, Boniface would fiddle in his deep trouser pockets and show me the condom and syringe he always carried. I never did find out if these were the only prophylactics he carried, and how he planned to replace them once used, for there was no doubt he had an eye for the girls.

The demands of Boniface's stomach delayed our departure for Hanga Monastery. It was after eleven by the time he had brought Ndunguru back to the Angoni Arms to collect me, and Boniface was hungry. We toured Songea looking for lunch. It was too early. Ndunguru tried the café at the

138

town's soccer stadium, but there was no food ready. So we went back to the Serengetei Bar, hostessless at lunch time, much to Boniface's disgust, for chicken and rice and some cold, pallid liquid which would have been called gazpacho had it been served up with lettuce in the West End. I passed. Boniface, sitting at his own table, not by preference but because this was the way Ndunguru wanted it, eyed my untouched bowl and reached over for it. He slurped it down and then launched a mopping-up operation with a piece of bread that he had the good fortune to acquire. Then he attacked the pile of rice and chicken, chewing the greasy bones and spitting out the skin onto the plastic table top. I was anxious to leave, but Boniface was more anxious to leave nothing on his plate. He was a messy, noisy, grunter at the table, and after he had carelessly slid his plate to the side and opened his cavern wide to throw a glass or two of water down it, he stood up, as straight as the soft overhang of double belly would allow, wiped his fingers over the swell of pink American University T-shirt that held his insides outside, peered at them, checking they were greaseless, stretched himself, arms above his head, yawned, and finally and most satisfying of all, proceeded to detonate a loud, wet and lubberly fart.

This was the signal to leave for Hanga Monastery. Boniface wasted no time at all, now that his insides were full. We hit the main tarmac road to Iringa around twelve and passed through the toll gates that marked the town borders five minutes later. Boniface didn't stop at them. They were unmanned and Ndunguru explained that the Songea Council had abandoned the idea of making motorists pay to leave and enter the town because it was more expensive to collect the tolls than to leave the booths empty. Half an hour later Boniface turned off the road and we began the bump and roll of the track that led to Hanga Monastery. There were fires burning on both sides of the ruts that we were following. Fire was a major problem for Ndunguru, and I could see in the distance the charred remains of trees and bushes where villagers were clearing the bush so that they could plant their crops. Of course, the fires would only serve to erode the soil, and after one or two harvests, the area would become parched and infertile. The Land Rover jarred and flew, jarred and flew across the ruts, and nosed down a deep, dark and narrow ravine. Boniface yanked on the hand brake and got out. We followed. The bridge was down. He shook his head and kicked a piece of crushed and rotting timber. It was, I supposed, all that remained of the bridge. The river here, the fledgling Mbarangandu, was not particularly wide, but neither was Boniface particularly brave. He argued for a few minutes with Ndunguru, shook his head as if to say, 'well, I did ask for your advice,' wiped his brow with his T-shirt, and drove across, hideously slowly. I watched from the inside as the water lapped the waist of the Land Rover. It lurched out, like a hippo after a mud bath, dripping thick brown liquid, and pleased to be on dry land where it could graze all night long.

Hanga Monastery teetered on a hillside just outside the village. It was a Benedictine house run by Africans who, I believe, had little to do with the villagers. We passed it by, drove through the one street of Hanga, where the only business seemed to be sleeping. The *duka* or store was closed and so too was the Hanga Bar next door, silent under the high sun. Along its frontage there was a shady walkway, but no one was taking advantage of the relief it had to offer. At the end of the street, we reached the end of the village. We turned by the football field, where any trace of grass that once might have grown in odd patches had been baked away. But what the pitch lacked in greenery, it more than made up for with its goal posts complete with netting. I think this was the most sophisticated pitch I had seen outside the towns and cities of Tanzania. I supposed the Benedictines were the benefactors.

Just past the soccer pitch, Boniface turned the Land Rover towards a group of huts and parked opposite a brown, brick-built house with a sloping corrugated-iron roof. There were two sacks of grain sleeping on the hot iron. The house was larger than its neighbours and more solid. Ndunguru walked up to a corrugated-iron double doorway, fastened with a piece of string. The metal resounded to his banging and someone undid the string and let him in. I peered through the Land Rover window and strained to look inside. Ndunguru was standing inside a yard talking to a small, dark man. They shook hands and then Ndunguru called to me.

The yard was about three metres square. It was coated with a thick carpet of mud compacted by centuries of sun.

At the far end, under a rickety tin roof which leant on three drunken wooden posts, three women, who looked to be in their thirties, sat side by side on a long bench that had been covered with blankets. Two of them were nursing babies, one of whom was feeding eagerly from the breast, while the third stared at the occasional wisp of smoke, all that was left of a worn-out fire. A scabby dog, whose ribs were threatening to burst out of its skin, was trying to find a comfortable place in the shade. It curled itself into as near a circle as was possible and proceeded to lick its bottom.

Alensio Bero was busy being hospitable, diving in and out of the house to fetch stools for Ndunguru and me to sit on. He was a little man, five foot three, with nostrils as wide and flared as a pair of sixties jeans. His hair has not turned grey and his teeth were even and clean. He wore a neat, short-sleeved Kaunda suit, which once might have been described as khaki. Now it was frayed with age. The constant enthusiasms of his wives' washdays had not only affected the fabric, but had driven out the colour. Even so, the buttons were not missing and the epaulettes, wide collar and neat afterthought of a bow where lapels would normally be gave him a military look. Then I noticed that the shiny black shoes that covered his bare feet had no laces. Besides the house, there was one other clue of affluence, the large, glittering watch whose elasticated silver strap clung to his wrist jealously. I looked closer when we had sat down on the stools and saw it was not a Rolex, just a cheap Hong Kong import.

He was not in the least nervous about meeting me. I supposed he knew he was safe and was confident that Ndunguru would not renege on the deal and prosecute him. I thanked him for seeing me and told him the same story that I had told the Mchawi in Kilimasera. That I was a lawyer, a professor of international law and was studying the effects of poaching on society. Though I had had the time to embellish my story, I couldn't help feeling how absurd it sounded. But whether Alensio Bero believed it or not, whether the *jangili* understood, he didn't seem to care who I was or what organization I represented. All he was concerned about was his life, the way he had chosen to live it, and the decision he had made to secure his future.

He was born in 1938 in Hanga Monastery, one of eleven

children. There were six sons and five daughters to raise and the only income his father earned was from the peasant farm, the tiny *shamba* just outside the village. He never went to school and knew little about the bush as a child, and possibly he would have remained ignorant throughout his life had his family been smaller. But then his four brothers were older than him, and it was they who helped his father on the land. In 1949, when he was eleven, Alensio started to hunt. He found work as a porter, carrying supplies, and then, when he became more experienced, the weapons of the hunters. The area, so near to the Selous, was flush with game.

'I saw eland, zebra, *tembo*, buffalo, antelopes . . . ' As Bero talked to me, passing through his answers to Ndunguru, he sat on the stool, small and confident, crossed legs just scraping the dust that flourished on the surface of the mud-cake floor. I offered him a cigarette and had to lean towards him to light it. Though it was not yet 2 p.m., there was a cruel draught in the yard which swirled from corner to corner and caused the iron gates to squeal on their hinges. The dog was irritated by the breeze, for, far from cooling him, it was waking him and making him shiver.

Alensio Bero learnt the ways of the bush from the hunters. Of course, at that time, hunting was legal, and he had nothing to fear from the police or the game scouts. Elephants were vermin who destroyed crops and ruined whole villages. And so the game wardens encouraged the destruction of the great herds. If elephants strayed beyond the perimeters of the game parks, then it was almost inevitable that they would be shot. In 1953, one game warden in the north shot over three thousand.

Alensio started as a porter for the game scouts in the area. He was taught to clean rifles, track game, recognize the signs of danger; but, most important of all, he was taught to shoot. He learnt quickly. He learnt that the bush was a cruel place which did not welcome strangers but soon embraced fools. He saw the bush as a living creature which breathed, displayed its anger, and gave up its rewards. The bush was as much part of him as he was of it. He felt happier there, buried beneath elephant grass three metres high, sheltering from the sun and other human beings under the branches of a brachystegia tree. The bush talked to him and he talked back to the bush. He could read all its languages and interpret every nuance. From a mound of elephant dung, or the wounded bark of an acacia or baobab, he could tell much: how many elephants had passed this way, where they were heading, what they had eaten, when they had eaten, what their age was, their size, the number in the herd, and their sex. He knew their habits, their mating grounds, their migration routes; he knew where they played, and how they talked to each other. He knew where they washed and where their babies would be born. He recognized their moods. He knew when to keep away from them. All this the bush had taught him as it had taught generations of *jangili* before him. He owed a little to the game scouts for whom he had portered as an eleven-year-old, but he soon realized that they were limited in their aspirations, and very much concerned with coming home at night, and not breaking the rigid rules the wardens had set. He never wanted to be a game scout because for them the bush was a place to do a job. For him, the bush was a reason for life, a reason which would provide him with a living. He had spent a lifetime in the bush, but now those days were gone. This was a new world he was living in, and the bush had been invaded by it. Even the bush, he had come to realize, was not robust enough to withstand the attentions of men like Captain Katali and his soldiers or the sweet persuasiveness of Ndunguru.

Still, that was the future. It was something to discuss later. First, he would tell me about his past, his glorious past when he was young and at peace, killing in the bush.

He had killed thousands of elephants. Yes, thousands. Actually, he said, he did not know exactly how many. When you've been killing elephants for money for years, it's something you never keep count of. But it amounted to thousands. Whole herds, single bulls, infants, tuskless ones – yes, tuskless, because *tembo* without tusks are far more dangerous. How many last year? He thinks for a second or so.

Five hundred. In one day? This time, he doesn't need to think. Eleven. In the course of one safari? Sixty-two. Two were tuskless and had to be killed. How long was the safari? Two weeks. Sixty-two elephants in fourteen days. Yes, and not all those days were spent hunting. He walked to the

143

Selous hunting grounds for three, and it took four more days to return to Hanga with the meat. Sixty-two elephants in seven days.

He began killing elephants in 1955. But then it was legal and he joined many other official culls. He was a good shot and news of his marksmanship followed him round the territory. He killed elephants as far away east as Kilwa, on the Indian Ocean, at least 600 km from Hanga and two days' bus journey. He moved north to Tabora, another 600 km from Hanga, and there he killed elephants, but licensed hunting was banned in 1973 and after that he killed elephants illegally and for money. A good marksman did not need to travel, looking for work. Instead the Somalis and the Baluchis came to him with money. A good marksman did not even need to own a rifle. The Somalis brought weapons with them as well. Not *gabores*, but powerful hunting rifles, .404s or even semi-automatics. Alensio Bero was considered good enough to be provided with a Kalashnikov. He liked it that way, because it meant that once the killing was over and he was back in the village, contending not with herds of she elephants but his three wives, the evidence of his crimes would be impossible to find. The ivory had either been buried deep in the Selous or moved away from the area, and the Kalashnikov had been returned to its owner. Nothing was traceable back to him, and, though he knew the Wildlife Department suspected that he was involved, there was never anything concrete for them to hold against him.

The Somalis might have provided the weapons, but he was expected to organize the safari. It would take maybe twenty people to carry the supplies. There was maize flour, knives, salt, axes, pangas, blankets, anti-malaria tablets, syringes, if they could be found, and aspirins were helpful. There were women, too, who worked as porters, trekking into the bush, carrying the meat and the supplies. Strict rules applied if they accompanied the men. There was no sex; a man should not even talk to a woman who was not his wife and, above all, this was business, so however heavy the load of ivory to be carried, the women must share the burden equally. They would travel for a month at least, carrying packs that weighed 30 kg when they left the village and over 50 when they returned. But he, Alensio Bero,

144

carried only his weapon, the Kalashnikov. He would march either at the front or at the back. It depended on the number of game scouts he knew to be in the area. He also had to obtain the ammunition he needed. This would come from a variety of sources. The most prolific was from deserters from the Mozambique guerrilla army, Frelimo, who during the seventies and eighties were fighting a war just across the Ruvuma river, only two days' walk away. There were many refugees from this war in the Hanga area, and the Tanzanian Government had actually provided thousands of them with shelter in specially constructed villages. They brought a poke of belongings from Mozambique, but few neglected to smuggle across the border bullets and shells, a currency as valuable as gold. Some of the ammunition he obtained from game scouts, some from the army. And in Songea, it was freely available, if you knew where to go. Five shillings a round, it cost in the seventies. Now it was over 60 shillings a round, but if he wanted ammunition for a .404, then it would cost 800 shillings.

He never wasted a bullet. One shot. One elephant. Two at the most. Unless, of course, there was a problem. Elephants, you see, were unpredictable. He had spent a lifetime in the bush and knew as much about *tembo* as anyone, but however much you knew, you could never fully understand an elephant.

That was why, each time he was about to leave, he filled a cup with water, and then spat it out of his mouth. Then he asked the spirits to guide him all the way to the hunting grounds. And when he reached those hunting grounds, he never forgot to ask the spirits of that particular place for permission to hunt their animals. He, too, performed the Ritual of the Night, in much the same way as the Mchawi showed me that night at Kilimasera. Only Alensio Bero performed it in the bush and mixed finger millet and salt and the parts of the animals that he had shot – the heart, the liver, the lungs, some blood – with strands of tobacco. When the mess of offal and seed and herb was prepared, he requested the guardians of the game to take care of him, and when he was certain that he had observed all the formalities to the satisfaction of the spirits, he called out the names of the animals that he wanted to kill.

The bush was capricious. It lay in the hands of a power

that man, however much he tried, could never harness. If a man understood this, then he had a fair chance of surviving. If he didn't, well, the bush would always beat him. The bush was a fertile ground for omens, and a man must be capable of reading its signs. Dreams carried signs and dreams should never be ignored. Alensio Bero took herbs to make him dream. He went so far as to cut his body with a knife and introduce the herbs, prepared in a potion, into his veins. He slept and dreamt, and if his dream told him that the hunting would not be a success, then however much he yearned for the bush, he stayed at home.

On one safari, he was tracking a lone bull elephant and had followed it for almost half a day. The elephant led him to a water-hole where it took a long and pleasurable bath. Alensio Bero decided to wait until the elephant became tired of the water before shooting, because he wanted to make sure the carcass fell on dry land where his porters would find it easier and safer to remove the tusks. He waited. But what he saw the elephant doing in the water-hole made him forget hunting immediately and turn for Hanga and home. The elephant had pushed its trunk under its belly and directed a jet of brown warm water over its penis. It was cleaning its penis and this told Bero that one of his wives was misbehaving.

Did he beat them on his return? He laughed. A man could beat one wife, but three? No, not three. That would be too much for him. Instead he gave each wife ten rounds of ammunition and ordered them to put their mark on each bullet. The next time he was in the bush he used this ammunition and discovered which of his wives had been unfaithful. The innocent wives were the women whose name or mark appeared on the bullets that killed cleanly. The identity of the adulterous wife was revealed by the bullet that missed its target, not once, nor twice, but three times.

He had often seen elephants performing strange rites and he nodded vigorously when I repeated the Mchawi's maxim that elephants never lie. He had once almost been buried alive by an elephant, and what passed that day still set his heart thumping and his skin dripping. He had gone to the bush, leaving behind in Hanga a sick father. He did not think that the old man's condition was so serious, otherwise he would have stayed at home, but his family were hungry

146

and he needed money to pay the doctor. He saw an elephant, a lone bull. He pumped two rounds into it, but still it would not fall. He fired eight more times and left it for dead. It was his custom to kill, abandon the carcass after marking the spot, and track another, and another, until he felt that his kill was sufficient for the day. As he killed, and tracked and killed, he informed the porters where the carcasses lay. They would go with him to them and remove the tusks when he had finished hunting.

On this particular day, Bero had given up quite early. It had been tough and he decided to return to the lone bull and remove its tusks himself. It was a simple but bloody job. First the tendons round the base of the trunk were severed with an axe, and then if this was done properly and cleanly, all that was required to remove the ivory was a firm tug. A pair of tusks could be removed in less than an hour. So when he retraced his steps and found the place where the bull had fallen, he couldn't believe that it wasn't there, lying in the spot where it had taken the last of his ten bullets. He checked around and made certain that he had come back to the right place. He was certain. The baobab with the bark torn from its left side confirmed it. He felt sick in his gut and his eyes and ears searched for a sign of the wounded bull. But there was no blood, no dung, no uprooted trees or trampled grass.

And then the elephant was on him. It had torn up a tree and was bearing down on him. No time for a shot. He fell to the ground and the elephant laid the tree across his body. Then it moved backwards, away, but not away from him. It tore up another tree and another, and laid them across his body. He realized he was being buried. The elephant was satisfied and lumbered off into the thick bush, and he managed to wriggle free from the little forest he had been covered with. He finished off the elephant as soon as he was on his feet, and as he pumped another two bullets into its brain, he knew with a dreadful clarity that his father had died and was being buried at the exact moment the elephant was burying him.

Elephants were cumbersome. They blustered around the bush, satisfying their appetite for leaves and bark and choice pickings like pumpkins or bananas or maize. They were hefty and irksome. They growled and trumpeted and their stomach rumbles could be heard for miles. But they were equally capable of being quiet too. They could move like mice if it suited them, and this was when they were at their most dangerous. Bero didn't notice the wounded bull until it was too late, and many times he had been surprised out of his skin to see standing just a hand's length or so away from him, an elephant peeling the juicy bark from a tree.

As he talked to me and Ndunguru, the door kept up its creak and the dog, bored with licking its bum, chased its tail or scratched its fleas. The three ladies in the lean-to sat and gave the babies the sweets I had brought. Everyone there seemed happy, except the door. Alensio Bero was in another world. He was back in the bush. The talk of the hunt and the *tembo* had excited him and his fingers jabbed at the air as he emphasized a point, his hands clapped or his fists clenched. He talked quickly with his mouth and his body responded to the words. He had spent over thirty years in the bush and knew he was lucky to have his life, his house and his wives. They were called, in order, Philomena, Esther, and Daforosa. I didn't have the pleasure, simply because they were working on his *shamba*. He spent two days with each of them, and Sunday, he insisted, was a day for rest, for drink, and for abstinence. Despite this self-imposed discipline and despite the amount of time he had spent away from Hanga in the bush, Alensio was the father of nine children.

He reckoned he had killed 500 elephants a year for twenty years. Ten thousand elephants. And what had he to show for it? There were rich men in Dar running around the city in Mercedes saloons. There were middlemen in Ifakara who employed a battery of slouching waiters in their hotels and farmers in Tanga who never farmed. All had grown fat on the efforts of Alensio Bero. So what did he own, this little *jangili* from Hanga whose only gifts in this life were the eyes of a falcon and the cunning of a wild dog? He didn't run a Mercedes, but he had bought a Chinese bike, a Flying Pigeon. He owned a house, this house we were talking in. It was roomy with strong brick walls, windows without glass but shuttered all the same. It had a sloping roof, made of corrugated iron, and there was sufficient room for his extended family. I guessed that up to twenty-five men, women, babies and youngsters lived there. He had food to feed the family and land to cultivate. He had two radios, both Japanese, one large, the sort that would irritate you were you to sit within a hundred yards of it in the park one sunny Sunday. The other was half the size, and he viewed it with a slight expression of scorn. But he was proud of his home, his bike, his big radio and his wives. His house cost him 35,000 shillings (£100), the Maoist bike 21,000 shillings (£60), the Brixton briefcase 9,500 shillings (£27), and the little radio 4,350 shillings (£12). The largest amount he was ever paid for providing tusks by a middleman was 300,000 shillings (about £1,000) and after he had paid the *fundi*, bought the supplies and ammunition, and paid off the owners of the firearms he was using, he was left with just over half, 160,000 shillings (£550). It wasn't much, but to earn that amount on a tobacco farm would have taken him three years.

In any case, in the old days, before the Second World War, there was never any money in hunting. Men killed to survive. There was no choice for most. If they didn't risk their lives in the bush, they and their families would starve. It was as simple as that. He remembered the stories the old hunters told of how they hunted with wire snares. It was a means of killing that pleased many of these grizzled and garrulous men, because it was silent, efficient and cheap. He had seen them operating the snares. He had trudged miles into the Selous to the places that they had chosen to set the traps.

They cut down as many small acacias as they needed. It was hard work, hacking away at these stubborn, wiry bushes under a hammerhead sun. With the branches and boughs they had taught him to build a series of fences, long barriers that stretched sometimes for a mile. It was vital to leave a gap every ten paces or so, for this gap was the neck of the trap. The game was forced to pass through it because the animals found the fences too high to jump, or were deterred by the thorns and prickles, and in the heat or the darkness these gaps made convenient escape routes for them. Each rains the men would allow the animals to run free through the gaps in the fences, bestowing on the creatures of the Selous a false sense of safety, so that when the rains ended the animals would not realize that the reprieve

149

the wet had granted them was over and the slaughter was about to begin again.

And it was here, in these gaps, that the snares were set. He remembered watching the men, his mentors, the men he respected above all others, even his father who was content to stay in Hanga Monastery and work at his poor soil, adjusting each snare with infinite care, and it reminded him of the precision with which he loaded and aimed his rifle. They secured the noose in position in the fence with wild sisal and they tied the fence ends to a tree. If there wasn't a tree near enough, he was told to cut down a log with the axe they had brought and drag it towards the snare, so that the ends could be tied to it.

But what Alensio Bero loved, the most exciting part for him, what made all the bone-aching labour worthwhile, was when the animal stumbled blindly into the snare. Oh, how the tree would shake, as the animal's dying struggle transmitted itself to the acacia. The branches shook and shuddered and shivered and finally stilled themselves as the tornado, all of a sudden, blew itself away. And he could still recall, as vividly as he saw it happen that day, the thrashing of the animal amid the groans and rasps of the tree which itself was fighting desperately to hang on to its roots. How it pleased him! If, however, the sisal had been attached to a log, then often that log would come alive, as the rage of the beast dragged it for hundreds of metres across the bush. The effort always exhausted the animal, as he knew it would, and eventually it sank in its tracks, defeated, and all that was left was for it to expire, the breath stolen from it by the wire.

He owed so much to those men.

But now, in his lifetime, Alensio Bero had learnt that there were other, less arduous, methods of killing than snaring. It had comforted him, especially during these times when the guns, the SARs, even the *gabores*, had been seized, and when it was particularly dangerous to keep a gun, however well concealed it was. There were, you see, always the *mpelelezi*, the spies who reported on men like him to Katali or Ndunguru. A man had to be wary of the *mpelelezi*, even though, in general, the villagers showed their respect for the *jangili*, and they showed it with their silence. Men like him possessed a far more potent weapon than any of these

150

Darboys, these timeservers who loitered outside their huts in Hanga and waited for a summons from the headman's official CCM headquarters. While Ndunguru was talking to them about forming wildlife committees and seducing their children with promises of scout badges and pairs of boots, he provided meat. While the elections for this committee were being held, the cooking pots of their wives and children were bubbling full with sable antelope or eland, and there was joy in their huts. When their men reached their homes – the chairman and the secretary, pleased with their triumph in Ndunguru's election – they would be happier. Of course, they wouldn't acknowledge the irony; they wouldn't permit themselves to recognize their benefactor. This was best left unsaid, so, instead, they would direct their gratitude and that of their family towards the spirits. And then they would bend their heads and hunch their shoulders towards the feast, and eat. Such was the power of a man like himself.

But now the days of the *gabores* were over, and Katali and Ndunguru had this battle won. The *jangili* were defeated, for how could they kill enough elephants without firearms? With poison, of course. There was always the pumpkin, or, even better, the poison arrow. But he had never liked that idea.

A pumpkin, he knew, was the favourite food of the elephant. Elephants could not resist a pumpkin. He had never liked using them, because this was far too easy a method of killing. He preferred the excitement of the hunt. Finding a water-hole and filling a pumpkin with poison was foreign to him. A Somali, a *bwana mkubwa* from Songea, had suggested it to him. He doubted whether the old men would have approved. They hunted to exist. He understood why they felt this way. That thin, leering Somali with his cigarettes and yellow teeth, swallowing Safari straight from the bottle, along with his contempt for the Ngoni, was concerned only about tusks. Middlemen, Bero told me, never thought of elephants as meat, just shillings.

No, if poison was to be used, then smear it on arrows or bullets, but never fill up pumpkins. The old men of Hanga had obtained the *sumu* from a certain tree, the Acokanthera. It stopped an elephant as effectively as a bullet, for once it entered the bloodstream, the *sumu* would find its way directly to the heart. What's more, a supply would last for five years, so long, as they never tired of reminding him, as it was kept in the dark, away from the heat of the sun.

There was another poison, too, which the *jangili* favoured, the one they found in the Strophanthus tree, a poison that was as effective as *sumu* when used on elephants. This potion was thick, dark and tarry, mixed up in an earthen-ware pot by the light of a hurricane lamp, and was easy to stick on an arrowhead. Using it with bullets was far more complicated, though. They would have to drill a hole in the cartridge case through which they would lace a string of sisal already soaked with the poison. But it acted quickly. Even if the bullet missed the heart or brain by a metre, if the bullet struck a leg, for instance, that elephant was a dead animal.

Poison respected nobody and no animal. The *sumu*, con-cealed inside a pumpkin, embraced all who came to the water-hole to drink and eat. So many *tembo* died horribly in this way, all of them shrieking and bellowing in agony as first one crumpled into the mud, then another, and another, and another. A good night for *mali* or tusks, for the *jangili*, for the *bwana mkubwa*. But it was not hunting.

The *sumu* was cruel, but it was silent and at least poison was less risky than hamstringing. This was a method he had never attempted, probably because the old men who killed elephants in this way were long gone like the great herds they pursued so remorselessly. Even so, he had never for-gotten the admiring tone in his grandfather's voice as he clapped his hands in tribute to the nerve of the tribesmen who tracked *tembo* for days, moving silently like the spirits, keeping downwind, until they were so close to their quarry they could reach out and tickle its belly with their hands, near enough to rip from its tail a long spiky hair to bring home to their wives. But these *shujaa*, for warriors they truly were, didn't waste time on such foolish, macho gestures. No, they flashed their pangas in the split-second their skill at tracking and their experience had allowed them, and split open the hind leg of the creature. Then they ran. They knew that their strike was successful when the elephant crashed to the ground, unable to move, paralysed by the severance of the tendon that drove its leg. And if the lunge with the panga failed? He wasn't surprised that so few had lived to tell of their experiences. He had seen the broken body of a hunter, mangled and abbreviated, and fit only for the hyenas.

But that was in the past.

The first jolt came when one of his neighbours was killed. It happened during a fire fight with the Operation Uhai troops. A platoon had stumbled across a band of *fundi* inside the Selous, challenged them, and then dived to the floor of the forest as the *fundi* opened fire. One of his friends did not survive the shoot-out. The second blow, the one that persuaded him that the time had arrived to retire, came the day Katali's men took him in for questioning. The village had been surrounded. There were soldiers everywhere. Each house in Hanga was being searched. The soldiers were even emptying the grain sacks. He had nothing hidden in the house, no weapon or ivory, no money that would give him away. He had never allowed himself to keep any of the tools of his trade in the house or on his land. Other *jangili* had laughed at him and told him that the soldiers would not come, and if they did, then they could be bought off. But Alensio Bero, who had stayed out of the courts and the clutches of the police for almost forty years, always shook his head at them. And here they were, in Hanga village, inside his house tearing it apart and frightening his grandchildren.

He was bundled into a Land Rover and taken to a camp near Nyamtumbo, just past the Argentine Guest House. He didn't talk. He had nothing to say. He knew their methods, what these soldiers could do to a man with a *kiboko*, how they would aim their blows at the joints, the ankles, the knees, the elbows; and then when they tired of this precision beating, the target would switch to the back and the sides; or how they broke a man's fingers by placing between each finger a thin piece of wood which they would then squeeze; or how they would make a prisoner frog jump on the double for an hour or more, jeering that he would never hunt again.

He was too old for all this. The thought of what lay in front of him, the *kiboko*, the punishment, the questioning, it was all too grim. Alensio Bero sat on a chair in the makeshift interrogation room, weighing up the choices. He really didn't have any. The sweat trickled down his chest and made him shiver in the stifle of the room. His shirt was wringing with wet, his wet, fear. And it was at that moment,

153

on that day in May 1990, that Alensio Bero's successful, long and blood-red career as an elephant killer ended. He asked to speak to an officer and when a lieutenant eventually sauntered towards him, he told him that he had information about the *jangili* and would talk. To the Wildlife Department, he insisted. The soldiers weren't at all happy, but eventually they agreed. That there was tension between the army and the civil authorities was no secret. Bero knew of the conflict, and played politics to his own advantage.

I asked him if he was in danger from the *jangili* who had remained underground waiting for the army to quit, so that they could resume the killing. He laughed loudly and puffed out his chest and told me he was not afraid of men like these. He believed that they had some weapons still and he knew for a fact that at least one elephant had been killed outside the village in the last week. There were young boys in the village who had threatened him, sworn to kill him, and he laughed again at the thought of it. Boys. He called them boys. Was he scared of them? Scared of boys! He shook his head. He had known the bush and in return the bush had taught him everything he knew. It had brought him happiness and a level of comfort he never could have expected. And it taught him one last lesson. The past was buried along with the ivory of a thousand elephants, somewhere in the Selous, out in the wilderness. The past was over.

The door creaked for a last time that day. We shook hands.

'Did you ever have a nickname?' I asked. 'Did the *jangili*, your fellow hunters, or the *fundi*, give you a special name?'

'Yes,' he nodded. 'I was called *Mchupa*.'

'What does that mean?' I asked Ndunguru.

'Strong Beer. The kind that shoots straight from the penis.'

FOURTEEN

Hunting Mr Ali

It is 1,091 kilometres from the door of Alensio Bero's house in Hanga Monastery to the iron gates of the nine-storey building in Dar es Salaam where Costa Mlay directs the war against the *jangili*. Every brown brick of Alensio Bero's house is a tombstone, each wall a grave. It is quiet in Hanga Monastery as we leave to return to Songea, untouched like the clean eye of a hurricane. The storm is raging in Dar es Salaam, in the city, amongst sedentary bureaucrats and inert politicians. Their eyes are rooted to their in-trays, to the heaps of files that they cannot see beyond. Their clocks keep pace with their idleness. The files, each day, grow fatter and taller, their appetites never quite satisfied by the constant diet of memoranda, a note from the permanent secretary, a reply from the minister, an objection from the undersecretary, an agreement from the President's Office. The pace of inactivity is furious.

Here in Hanga Monastery, outside Alensio Bero's house, the *jangili* who has quit killing elephants shakes hands warmly with the Regional Game Officer who has won his confidence. It is a bold gesture on Ndunguru's part. It is, if it works, a signpost to a future. But, in the jungle of Dar es Salaam, in the Ministry of Natural Resources, no one is shaking hands on any deals to secure the safety of the elephant. Costa Mlay has a far more complex task in front of him. He is not dealing with peasants, however canny they may be. His prey are the politicians. He must persuade the Government to allocate him more money, more vehicles, more men. In Hanga Monastery, life may be hard, but it is not complicated by political and fiscal jealousies.

155

We drove into Songea within the hour. Boniface was hungry, but Ndunguru would not let him eat. Instead he wanted me to see Ali Yusuf Abdurabi's house and meet his wife. She had remained in Songea after the MP lost his appeal and had been sent to Mtwara to serve his twelve-year sentence. The house, in a dusty, rubbish-strewn side-street not far from the centre of town, would have been the same size as Alensio Bero's had it not been for the untimely arrest of its owner. Ali Yusuf Abdurabi had had some big plans in mind when the Land Rover 110 he was driving (registration number STG 8675) was stopped at Namabenga village on the Songea–Tunduru road at 4.30 a.m. on 8 January 1988 with 105 elephant tusks snug and cool in the back.

There was a half-finished extension at the end of the house, a pathetic monument to hubris, a nudge and a wink to the townspeople who, Ndunguru told me, had skitted at his trial. Breeze-block columns climbed half-heartedly into the blue sky, waiting for a tin roof to cover them, for windows and for mortar. For his wife, who with her six children, daughter-in-law and two grandchildren had to make do with a living room, three bedrooms and a cramped courtyard for a kitchen, it was a daily reminder of lost dreams. Leah William was her name. She was forty years old and spoke English well. She had been brought up in Nairobi and had come to Tanzania with her father who worked as a forest ranger in Mafindi, a town between Songea and Iringa, about 500 kilometres to the north. She had met Ali Yusuf in Mafindi when he worked for the Forestry Department. They had fallen in love. She was a Christian, he was a Muslim, but they had married and they had been together for twenty-five years.

She invited me into her living room whose wooden shuttered windows glimpsed onto the street. I sat beside her on a wooden sofa with no cushions. On her lap sat her new grandchild, Leila, whose mother, her daughter-in-law Marion, stood nervous and rigid at the open door which led out to the courtyard, crossed arms supporting a rich swell of milk-laden breasts. The baby Leila's fingers curled and caught her grandmother's patterned blouse.

On the drab walls, in a dismal attempt to cheer the place, someone had hung a paper chain. Family pictures were dotted below, portraits of her father, her mother, her husband, Ali Yusuf Abdurabi in the parliament building, Ali Yusuf Abdurabi being sworn in by the Chief Justice, meeting the President, greeting his constituents, by his car, on his wedding day, with his children, refereeing a soccer match. But there was no picture of Ali Yusuf Abdurabi in court, nor in prison. There was no picture of the smart Land Rover 110 in which he was arrested.

This room, ten feet by ten feet, with its concrete floor and caged wire windows, was both her prison and her shrine. She believed passionately that her husband was innocent, that he had been the victim of a conspiracy, and that he would be pardoned by the President, one day. But until that day came she would have to make do with looking at his image on the wall, and prayers.

She handed the baby Leila back to her mother Marion, and flip-flopped across the room to a small wooden table. From it she took a photograph album. It was cheap and battered and bound in red-fringed velvet. She leafed through, pausing at the pages which gave, she said, a complete history of her husband's career. But, like the portraits on the walls, the snapshots stuck inside the black pages of the album bore witness to a lie. At the back of the album, four or five pages remained black and blank, waiting for her husband's release before they could be filled.

Ndunguru told her that we were going to Mtwara and there was a possibility we might see her husband. I asked her if she wanted me to take anything to him. She went to the table in the middle of the room and sent her eldest son, seventeen years old, to fetch writing paper. While she was waiting, a gust of wind blew through the half-open front door, sending a plastic stem of pink flowers tumbling to the floor. She wrote the letter by the light of the open door, for though it was mid-afternoon, the room was dark. There was an electric light, but maybe she could not afford to use it in the daylight hours. Then she sealed the letter in a flimsy air mail envelope. I got up to leave and she handed me a tiny red New Testament. She asked me to give it to her husband along with the letter.

She had seen her husband just once since he had been imprisoned. He was weak from diabetes. Now I was leaving, she was talking fast, each word almost an invitation to stay on in the room with her. She told me about the hotel she and her husband had owned. She had been forced to sell it. She told me about the people who came to this house seeking his help and advice: her husband was a popular man in Songea, and he had helped the young in the town with his soccer team. It was called Maji-Maji after the Ngoni uprising against the Germans in 1905–6 and had won the championship twice. Her husband, she said, was never a rich man; his only income came from his salary as an MP, just 4,000 shillings a month, and the hotel. She told me of the night he was arrested; how he hadn't come home; how she had heard from a neighbour the next morning that he was in the police station in a police cell. She told me that no one believed his story; that people, like the wind, changed their minds about him. She had been sick in hospital for two months after his trial, worn out with shame and septic abscesses. It was God that kept her alive and in hope. She told me that her husband was innocent.

Outside on the concrete step, a crowd of children with swivelling eyes stood round the Land Rover and watched, intent as royal bodyguards. Except for one boy who blew at a tin whistle but could not find a tune.

Ndunguru was quiet. I knew he felt bad about seeing the MP's wife, because it was he who had been responsible for the arrest. So why had he visited her? Why had he told her that we might be visiting her husband? There were, he explained later that afternoon in the Angoni Arms, some unanswered questions about the MP's case. Who, for instance, had provided the information that had trapped him? An informer, I said. He agreed, but who informed the informer? Was the source a member of a rival ivory ring? Why would they want to give information about the MP? Because, Ndunguru said, he believed this man was really a small-time gangster and he was getting in the way of a much larger gang. He shook his head and moved towards the door. 'We had better get going. You must pay the Angoni for your room. We have a long way to drive.'

I asked him where we were going. It was now four o'clock. It would be dark in less than three hours.

'Mtwara. To try and see Ali Yusuf Abdurabi.'

Mtwara was a port on the Indian Ocean. It was over 600 kilometres from Songea and the road, Ndunguru said, was rough for most of the way. How rough? He grinned and

158

rubbed his bottom and said I would feel this part of my body for days after the journey.

He was, of course, correct. Except it wasn't a sore bottom that I remembered for days afterwards. Boniface took the road out of Songea and headed towards Tunduru, 350 kilometres to the east. The rutted track mirrored the fire of the blood-orange sun. It was a familiar route, the same one that had taken me with Vincent earlier in the week to Nyamtumbo, Mchomoro and Kilimasera. Tunduru was twice as far. I asked Ndunguru why we were in such a hurry.

'Because I have asked Costa to contact the Prisons Department asking them to allow us to see the MP. It has to be done fast. The Government is changing and there will be a new Minister of the Interior. He may well not let this happen. Costa knows the present Minister well and so it can be arranged. We must be in Mtwara by tomorrow morning.'

As we drove away from Songea, leaving the dusk to settle over the softening shadows of the town, Ndunguru began to tell me the story of the fall of the district's most celebrated citizen, the man who, with luck, I would be seeing tomorrow in Mtwara. Night closed in on us, the rest of the world vanished. We were lifers, locked in a tin box that was bearing us into the deep. Through the shroud of dusk that masked the windscreen, the twin beams of headlight picked out the ruts that curled towards us like silent oncoming waves, rolling on, always in front of us. They ruled us, these miles of ruts; we slid, we lurched, we shivered in our seats, we lunged and plunged, but we never quite went in the direction we wanted. Sometimes, the great lines smoothed themselves to nothing, and Boniface, an optimist, pressed down his foot on the accelerator and relaxed his grip on the wheel. Once or twice, I leant forward and caught the speedometer needle flicking around the sixty kilometre mark. But never for long. The chaos of the track always reasserted itself. As I listened to Ndunguru, I wondered if we would ever stop. I wanted to smoke, but slopping around behind me in two orange drums was about fifty litres of diesel. We had kept the windows closed because of the dust cloud that travelled alongside us, and, at times, the fumes of the fuel were powerful enough to make us gag.

The story of the MP's downfall began, Ndunguru said, in

the office of Superintendent of Police Simon Dau, the Officer Commanding Songea Urban and Songea Rural Districts. It was 4 January 1988 and Dau had on his desk a piece of paper informing him that the MP for Songea, Ali Yusuf Abdurabi, was planning to drive to Lusowa village to pick up a consignment of ivory. He would be using his official vehicle, his Land Rover 110, and he was going to make the journey on the fifth, the following day. Dau had suspected Abdurabi of being involved in illegal dealings with *jangili* for some time and the information he had received that morning made him determined to set up an ambush and catch the MP with the tusks.

But it didn't quite turn out as he expected. On the fifth, he answered a phone call in his office and heard a voice say that the trip to Lusowa had been cancelled. He asked for a reason and his informer told him that the MP knew that the police were aware of his plan. There had been a leak. Dau locked away the note he had made and put the ambush on ice. There would be another time, he knew, but what really concerned him at that moment was the leak. Who had passed on the information to the MP?

He didn't have long to wait. On 7 January, Dau's informer telephoned him again. It was on. The MP was going to pick up a cache of ivory the next day, not in Lusowa, but in Ligunga, a village on the Tunduru road, the road that we were bouncing along now. Dau knew he had to move fast. The informer had told him that Ali Abdurabi would be leaving Songea that afternoon.

Superintendent Dau was convinced that his source was telling the truth. He had been proved right in the past. But the information given to him was very flimsy. Dau did not know how many men would accompany the MP to Ligunga; he did not know whether they would be armed. Ligunga was about 250 kilometres from Songea, and though it might take six hours' hard driving, Dau did not know how long they would take to get there. All he could do was hope they would not delay their journey again, and that his men would not be outnumbered. He asked his Inspector how many men were available. He was given the answer that he expected. None. He managed to extract three, Sergeant Dominic, Corporal Bakari, and Constable Jeremiah. He briefed them hurriedly and told them to drive immediately to Namabengo village on the Songea–Tunduru road, set up a road block and wait for the MP's Land Rover. They were to stop it, search it, and look for elephant's tusks.

It was 9.30 that night when the three officers left Songea with over 200 kilometres to drive on mud and rut-pocked tracks. They arrived at a point in the road near Namabengo where they could see both ways for some distance and set up the road block, dragging branches and large stones into the middle of the track. Then they sat in the police Land Rover and waited. Corporal Bakari was in the front and held his rifle ready. At 4.30 a.m., a Land Rover approached. Constable Jeremiah, the *deriva*, switched on his headlights full beam. Bakari, sitting next to him, saw the driver of the approaching vehicle stop, then suddenly rev the engine and reverse. He pushed open the passenger door and charged after the MP's Land Rover, all the time shouting for it to stop.

Bakari levelled his rifle at the windscreen of the Land Rover. The driver took the hint. He braked so hard that the vehicle skidded off the road and into a ditch. The door opened on the passenger side and out stepped Ali Yusuf Abdurabi, his hands held up, high above his head. He was angry, and yelled above the noise of the wind that he was the MP for Songea and was returning from a safari. Bakari ignored him, just telling him to sit down. He pointed the rifle at the side of the road and nudged the MP towards it. Then he ordered the other men out of the vehicle. There were three other men in it, a *deriva* and two more in the back. When Jeremiah and Dominic looked inside, they were for a moment overwhelmed by the sight of so many tusks. The vehicle was crammed with them, almost up to its roof.

It was then that Abdurabi offered them money. A million shillings if they released him. They shook their heads and drove back to Songea. Dominic drove the MP in his Land Rover with the tusks and the other two police officers took the remaining three men.

It was past dawn when they reached Songea. Dau arrived at the police HQ soon afterwards and set about counting the tusks. There were 105. They weighed 498 kilos and were worth 2,490,000 shillings (£10,000).

Even when Ali Yusuf Abdurabi stood in the dock at Songea Courthouse, he believed he had a chance of acquittal.

161

He addressed the jury confidently, telling them he had been the people's representative in Songea since 1985. He had been elected by the people and had served them well. No one could accuse him of being idle. He was a diligent member who conveyed their concerns and their worries to central government in Dar or parliament in Dodoma. He then read out his duties as an MP as laid down in the constitution of Chama Cha Mapinduzi. Yes, it was true that he had toed the Party line, but was that a crime? Among these duties, he said, he had been entrusted to carry out the decisions of the CCM, and one of these was to encourage the public to give information to the police about anyone they suspected of dealing in ivory. And this was precisely what he had been doing. This was why he had been wrongly accused. This was the reason for his humiliation by the police.

You see, it had all been one dreadful mistake. He had received information that a middleman called Yusuf Mohamed wanted to hire his vehicle to transport tusks. Now he knew that because his vehicle was an official government Land Rover, the middleman believed it would be unlikely to be stopped by the police. For that reason, and that alone, was he approached. He hadn't done this for gain, nor out of greed. Why should he, the MP for Songea, a successful man, risk everything for a vehicle load of tusks? Of course, he had meant to tell the police about this middleman and how he had planned to trap him. In fact, he had actually gone to the police HQ and sought out Superintendent Dau to brief him. Anyway, nothing had happened. This middleman postponed the trip, and he was surprised when the idea was revived forty-eight hours later. This time, he had no chance to tip off the police so he decided that he would make the journey himself along with his driver and Yusuf. He felt that it would be dangerous to allow the driver to go so far into the bush at night without his protection. Even so, despite the hurry, he told his nephew to go to police HQ and tell Superintendent Dau what was happening. Then, at around 5.45 that afternoon, he left for the Mfaranyaki Hotel in Songea, a Somali-run establishment, now no longer in business, where he met Yusuf Mohamed.

Immediately they set out for Ligunga, driving for six hours until they reached the village at around 10.30 p.m. They

162

parked some way out of the village and turned the vehicle round so that it was facing in the direction of Songea. Yusuf Mohamed, the middleman, left them in the vehicle and disappeared into the bush. He was gone for an hour.When he returned he was with some other people, about four, he thought, and each of them was staggering towards the Land Rover, their arms weighed down by tusks. There were so many of them that there was not enough room in the Land Rover to fit them all in. Two tusks had to be left behind because they were so large. When the Land Rover was full, they left for Songea. The MP was nervous. He had all the evidence he needed now, the trophies, the middleman and an accomplice. Now he had to choose the right moment to strike. As the Land Rover approached Namabengo village, he told Yusuf Mohamed that he was under arrest, and in the custody of Ali Yusuf Abdurabi, an MP. It was then that he saw the headlights of another vehicle suddenly being switched on in front of them. He was blinded and shocked, but he thought that this could be the police and that his message to Superintendent Dau had got through. His driver panicked, dazzled by the headlights, lost control of the steering wheel and the vehicle ended up in a ditch at the side of the road. He reversed back onto the track, but by this time the police were chasing them and waving their guns.

He didn't expect to be arrested, nor endure the humiliation of having the muzzle of a police rifle pointed at his head. But, all the same, he got out of the Land Rover, held up his hands and made no fuss. He still thought that this was all part of Dau's plan and that the three officers had been told to go through the motions of arresting him to protect his integrity. It wasn't until he heard one of them demanding 1,000,000 shillings as the price of silence that he began to realize everything had gone horribly wrong. Of course, he refused to listen to such talk. An MP cannot be involved in bribery!

Ndunguru finished the story, smiling in the darkness, as he described how Ali Yusuf Abdurabi addressed the court, displaying all the authority and majesty that he could muster. But the act had not been successful. The evidence against him was overwhelming, and when he was sentenced the court was packed with men and women who had once been his supporters and who now were baying for justice.

They were, the MP said, sadists. They laughed and jeered and cat-called as his defence counsel listed the reasons for leniency. His client had suffered from diabetes for two years; he had heart disease; he had nine small children (his wife told me it was six); he had an old mother and an aunt who depended upon him; he had been an outstanding contributor to his country's development; he had ceased to be an MP now that he had been convicted, and that was punishment enough. As the list of his values grew more florid, the noise in the courtroom subsided to a hush, but Ali Yusuf Abdurabi hadn't, it appeared, noticed the change. He stood upright in the dock and stared the rabble in the eye, defiant and sanguine until he was led away. Maybe Ali Yusuf Abdurabi thought that his nine-year sentence would be quashed on appeal. It wasn't. In fact, the jail term was increased by another three years.

I asked Ndunguru about Superintendent Dau's part in the ambush.

Ndunguru shook his head. Dau, he said, was cleared of any involvement by the judge during the trial. His evidence was compelling.

'Remember, Nick, Dau had his own informer. He didn't need the MP to tell him anything. The allegation that he received a tip-off from Abdurabi's nephew is not important. In Africa, if an uncle, an influential uncle, tells you to lie, then you lie. This is an African family in action. And why should Abdurabi have decided to go miles into the bush at night with a stranger, without weapons, collect 105 tusks, and then decide to arrest the men he had travelled with? It is beyond belief.'

I put my notebook back inside my pocket and felt the warmth of the little red New Testament which Mrs Abdurabi had given to me that afternoon. I wondered if her husband would ever see it.

Where we were, I couldn't tell. Ndunguru looked at his watch and thought that we would make Tunduru by 8.30 p.m. Another hour at least.

We passed Namabengo village, see-sawing over the track. Boniface was tiring and emitting huge deep sighs that he hoped would persuade Ndunguru to let him rest. But Ndunguru ignored him and tapped on the window to show me the exact place where the ambush had occurred. There was nothing to see, not even a nightjar playing kamikaze with our front fenders. I strained my eyes for a pinhole of light. Tunduru must be near. I risked lighting a match. Eight forty-five. No lights. I knew this was a race, that we had to be in Mtwara early the next morning, but I could see Boniface was tired, and I did not think that he would last out. Ndunguru disagreed. He shook his head slowly and said that we would eat in Tunduru, let Boniface sleep for a couple of hours and then start again. He wished he had brought tents with him, so that we could have slept by the roadside, then he thought better of it and said perhaps it was just as well he hadn't. This was lion country. Man-eating country.

Only a few years ago, in 1986, a game warden, a man Ndunguru knew well, was eaten by a lion *inside* the town of Tunduru. It was an old lion, starved to the point of desperation because much of the game that once thrived in this part of the Selous had been driven away by *jangili*. There were few elands, and even fewer antelope and kudu on which to pounce. Lions are notoriously lazy beasts and the game famine had made them not only hungry but increasingly feeble. Human beings became their target. They took forty-eight people between 1985 and 1988 along this very stretch of road. Twenty-eight men, women and children were severely mauled and were fortunate to have escaped with their lives. Like the game warden, who had been charged with bringing an end to the reign of terror, many of the victims were dragged down on the baked-earth streets of Tunduru and part gorged in the town itself. Some bodies were never recovered. Fragments of others were found in the bush. The death of one of their men forced the Wildlife Department to send in a well-armed force. They solved this appalling problem in the only way that was possible. They shot dead forty-six lions.

But this wasn't quite the end of the story, for nothing ever turns out neatly in Africa. The townspeople of Tunduru and the villagers living nearby could not be convinced that the lions were really dead and that their three-year nightmare was finally over. They were shown the carcasses of the man-eaters only to stare at them in disbelief, while one or two of the less cautious among them prodded the corpses with a toe, shook their heads, muttered a few words, and walked away, certain that here powerful and dark forces were at work, and nothing, not even a .404 shell, could prevent the spirit world from preying upon them.

Tunduru was a one-street town, larger than the villages I had visited nearer Songea, but it was still a single row of scruffy shops, squalid bars, miserable-looking guest houses, and flimsy huts, all capped in straw, the more substantial government buildings constructed with bricks. Cashew nut trees ran the length of the street, looking like a row of giant horse chestnuts, and conferring in the dark an incongruous sense of English spa-township. But there was no electricity, and the vision of the locals, possibly because of their isolation, or their poverty, or both, certainly did not extend to erecting any dwelling or business beyond a single storey, or just possibly because there was not a ladder to be had in Tunduru.

Boniface pulled in outside the New Small Amigo Hotel, which was neither new nor friendly. It was, however, small. If the Land Rover had had four legs instead of wheels, he could have tied it to the wooden railing that ran alongside the place. Outside the wooden boardwalk, a small boy was cooking omelettes and chips in a few litres of sunflower oil. His oven was a bucket of red-hot coals, his kitchen a wooden table, his sink another galvanized bucket of greasy cold water that could have passed for days-old cold tea. Occasionally, when his customers' demands for food were low, he dipped the dirty plates into the bucket and swirled them around for a second, no longer, more in hope than hygiene.

I watched him make my omelette. He took the eggs, smashed them into a cup, flailed them vigorously with a spoon and emptied the yellow liquid into a blackened pan that sat smouldering on the coals. He left it there and prepared the chips which were swimming around in a pan of oil. The omelette sizzled, the chips drowned. When the omelette was ready, he rescued a plate from the washing-up water and plonked the omelette on it. Then he found another plate, wiped it on his shirt, and laid it on top of the omelette. So my omelette was going to be cold. Now for the chips. There was much steam and spluttering and then out of the frying pan they emerged, grey and slippery as beached whales.

I decided I would eat my supper at a table inside the hotel. I chose one and ordered *chai*. It came immediately, poured from a large cylinder by the bar, where soft drinks or tea or coffee were on offer. My tea came in a cup and saucer, but the sophistication ended there. The cup was filthy, stained brown by a thousand tea drinkers before me, though the tea was hot, thick with sugar and overflowing its saucer, precisely the brew that had maintained the morale of Londoners in the Blitz, God help them. A large, glittery radio perched on the corner of the bar and competed with the hissing of a hurricane lamp. No one seemed to be listening to either. I ate the omelette which slipped down, helped by the film of grease, but I left the chips. There were a few more tables, covered like mine with red table cloths, where men, no women, munched at their food. Boniface was absorbed, his eyes a few inches from his plate. Ndunguru had finished his meal and was checking the Land Rover. A girl screamed 'Hold On! Hold On!', but it was only the cassette playing on the radio. The boy behind the counter was smiling at me. He had, I guessed, chosen to play the tape especially for me. Perhaps it was this girl's piercing voice which had called out to the lions of Tunduru and drawn them into the town. Perhaps not.

Though it was past nine o'clock, the New Small Amigo Hotel showed no sign of closing for the night. It survived on passing trade, on any other vehicle that was following us from Songea. We had, in fact, seen nothing on the road for over 400 kilometres; no buses or trucks or government Land Rovers, no men on bicycles, not even women or children on foot. I heard the owner of the New Small Amigo talking to one of his customers in Arabic, and I greeted him with an *'il hamdililah'*. He asked me where I had learnt to speak his language. I told him in the Sudan. He rolled his eyes and clicked his tongue. Then he shook hands. He was a small, merry-looking man, with a barrel chest and no hair save for a mean outcrop under his nose. I asked him why he wasn't going to bed, back to his wife. He laughed and muttered a few *inshallahs*. Allah would surely send other travellers to him. I shook my head and told him the road was deserted. But he was an Arab and Arabs are charged with optimism, or is it fantasy?

Ndunguru was waiting for me in the Land Rover. We were going to take a break and use the time to let Boniface rest for a few hours. We left the main street, drove towards the end of town, took a right by a truck stop, which like the New Small Amigo was staying open in hope of business, and bounced along a track until Boniface parked outside the town club. I followed Ndunguru inside and sat back in a large, dully lit room and waited for beer. I wanted to ask him about the prison visit in the morning, whether he thought we had much chance of seeing the MP, but he waved his hand at me and jerked his head towards the sound of the radio. No one else in the room was interested in Radio Tanzania's world news at nine. The few men at the tables across the other side of the horseshoe bar carried on with their Monday night's desultory chat. The newscaster's voice faded and crackled and regained its vigour, a hostage in the struggle waged between short wave and static. He was detailing the changes in the Government. So far he had not mentioned any new Minister of the Interior, which was good news so far as our proposed visit to Ali Yusuf Abdurabi was concerned.

Ndunguru sipped his beer and talked. He talked about the Party, the Government, he speculated on the identity and policies of the new Cabinet. He discussed the way the Party had lost touch with the people, which it now described as the 'common people'. He had been a member of the Party for many years, one of the first of his generation to join, but I sensed that he now believed that the Party he had grown old with had itself grown out of its usefulness. For all this muted criticism, he was a great defender of the President but contemptuous of his ministers. He was convinced that the nation was being bled dry by a glut of bureaucrats and that there were not enough men of action. He considered that maybe now was the right time for the country to introduce democracy and establish a two-party state, but this would mean, of course, that the Party would have to cede control of the army and make it responsible to the people, not to their masters.

I could see that Ndunguru was a capable politician himself, despite his inexperience and distaste for the ways of Dar es Salaam and its political jungle. He had been persuasive enough to win over thousands of distrustful and resentful villagers to his way of thinking, perceptive enough to realize the value of a man like Alensio Bero whose knowledge of the bush and of the *jangili* was now a weapon as lethal in his hands as a Kalashnikov was in a poacher's. He wanted to stay in Songea and finish his job. And then be posted to Dar? He shook his head firmly and drained his beer.

At the counter a hurricane lamp shone its heat and yellow light onto a sign which read *'Malipo Kwanza'* – Payment First. The bar girl was yawning and clearing the tables. Then she stacked the chairs. It was time to go. Twelve-thirty. The night was velvet, perforated by a million pinpricks in the Milky Way. It was fresh outside after the closeness of the club bar, but we soon forgot about that as the perspiration seeped out of our systems on the bumpy road that led to Mtwara. I'd forgotten how uncomfortable the Land Rover was as soon as it had stopped in Tunduru. Now every pothole and rut, each rise and fall, jerk and shudder, brought the pain back.

Tunduru was asleep by the time we left. Africa was asleep too. We were the only people on this entire continent awake and on the move. But people in Tunduru did not sleep soundly. They were, two years after the last of their neighbours was eaten by lions, still dreaming a nightmare. They were believers in spirit possession. They were convinced that men inhabited the bodies of those man-eaters, and even when the game scouts showed them the bodies of the lions, they could not be persuaded otherwise. They took the death of the district game warden as a sign. How could it be that the lions would choose this man? Was it not obvious even to a fool that this was intended, that this man who had been ordered to wipe out the lions, must be killed because it was he who posed the greatest threat? It was certainly clear to the people of Tunduru, if not to any stranger, that this was the case. Lycanthropes were abroad. The roads were deserted, lonely, and dark, and all that I could see was the white dust that spilled off the deep ruts in front of the Land Rover, that and the dark bulk of Boniface, who never spoke.

Moths flew into our headlights, intent on suicide. We could hear nothing above the roar of the engine as it argued with the road. All that seemed to be out there in the black of the night was the Selous, grim and challenging. There were, out there, among the brachystegia and acacia, and the Watta tree whose glorious yellow flower was concealed by the dark, wild animals and potent myths, each one involved

169

with the other, each one independent and strong, feeding and flourishing on the night.

There were a hundred or more kilometres of rough road to drive before we hit the tarmac at Masasi, and then another 250 kilometres to the Indian Ocean and Mtwara. Boniface decided to sleep. He pulled the car to the side of the track, switched off the lights and sank his head onto the wheel. There was a silence inside the tin box, broken only by the whine of a mosquito that had, I suspected, accompanied us all the way from dusk, and the hoarse grumblings of frogs somewhere off to the left of us. I stretched and searched for a place to sleep, but failed. I was conscious all the time of the mosquito and wondered whether the chorus of frogs meant that Boniface had chosen to rest up next to a swamp. I wanted to get out and smoke a cigarette. But, out there, was Africa, mythology and death, waiting.

The sun rose at a quarter to five. Now, with the pink tips of dawn showing, the Land Rover was running smoothly. We had reached the tarmac road, a thin, hard, straight strip that cut the bush in two, neatly and efficiently. The tin box was travelling at 100 kilometres an hour, and at last there were no bumps to keep me awake. I was heavy-lidded, but conscious enough to dismiss from my mind the anxiety that Boniface was driving too ferociously.

A scream flung open my eyes. The bush was rushing past at about 100 miles an hour. Bits of trees, branches, grass, whipped across the windscreen. Everything was grey, not green. My hand clawed at the door handle. I stayed rigid. The Land Rover was behaving like a rhino. It had charged off the surface and down a steep ditch. Boniface was asleep. At least I hoped he was. Another scream. Ndunguru. Boniface recovered from his paralysis, regained control, and braked until his foot had almost disappeared through the floor.

We walked away from the Land Rover, leaving Boniface to check the seals on the diesel drums in the back. I felt large raindrops on my face. They were soft and comforting. The front wheels of the Land Rover were perched on the edge of a deep ditch about twenty metres from the road. Another few metres . . . I climbed up to the side of the road and walked down its edge. Approaching fast from the direction of Tunduru were two pinpoints of light accompanied by a steadily growing muffle of thunder. I dived back down the culvert and felt the earth tremble as a two-trailer truck whipped along on its way to the coast. Those hotel men in Tunduru must have got lucky after all. Following in its wake of fumes and spray mixed with dust, a woman, supporting a large pannier of vegetables, strode effortlessly past, on her way to a market, somewhere ahead of us. The dawn was gone now too, but the sun had failed to join it. The sky was grey and unfriendly, even though the raindrops had been swallowed up. I realized how fragile life could be. As we huddled round the car, Ndunguru told me he had had a dream a few nights ago in Songea. He had dreamt that he and I had been in a Land Rover. We were in a hurry, and had driven through the night. The Land Rover had crashed, and the fuel cans on board had exploded.

'Did we live?' I asked him.

'It was just a dream,' he said. I decided not to press him.

There was a village a few kilometres up the road. It was Naganga. We thought of breakfast, tea or coffee, a banana, perhaps, but there was nothing there on sale. We drove on, past whole areas where the road and the bridges over the Ruvuma which formed the border with Mozambique to the south and its tributaries, the Mambi, the Mkundi and the Mutumnadi, had been washed away by the floods that had devastated this south-eastern corner of Tanzania in the spring. They had been the worst floods in over fifty years and hundreds of thousands of villagers had been made homeless. Often there was no road on which to drive. The tarmac abruptly ran itself into a wall of rich, red mud, a God-made mountain of thick, clammy earth greedy to feed on more road and determined not to allow us passage. Boniface was nonplussed. He merely shook his head for the hundredth time since we had left Songea all those hours ago and aimed his flat nose at the bush, sliding the Land Rover round the mud mounds until he found a bridge that had been repaired or one that had been completely replaced by a mesh of steel and oil drums and wooden planks which, from all its groaning and swaying, appeared to be far more nervous of our transit than we ourselves.

Every kilometre or so on that road to Mtwara we passed vehicles that had broken down, buses with painted slogans

171

on their sides that evoked the wisdom of the Koran; or tankers with infidel messages, exhorting those who happened to be stuck behind their tail for hours, to 'put your faith in God', proving that a belief in the deity, whoever He should be, was no nostrum for mechanical failure. There were lorries that had shed their loads of maize, leaving sacks to soak up the rain that was running now across the roads and down into the ditches on either side. There were burnt-out pick-up trucks, rusting Mercs with no windows, the carcass of a tractor that had died a thousand breakdowns ago. And each little disaster was signalled, not by the orange and red cone that flourishes along the length of the M25, but by the leaves and branches of banana trees which were laid out at intervals of every ten metres or so up to a hundred as a courtesy to other drivers.

It was nine when the Indian Ocean, slate grey and joyless, announced this was the end of Africa and we followed the flat, seamless sea all the way to Mtwara. I was expecting that life would resume here. I thought there would be hot showers in the hotels, maybe braised steak, Safari beer, Konyagi, sailor-talk, prostitutes, Somalis, ivory trade-offs, a market selling fresh tropical fruit, all greens and yellows and shouting, where all the garishly patterned shirts in the south-west of Tanzania would come together and swap gossip. But all I could see was a new church, grey-white and pushy as it tried to touch the cloud-base. Beyond this were the squat, functional offices of government: the police station, the Wildlife Ministry, and next to it, the headquarters of the Prisons Department.

We climbed the stairs, shaking off the fatigue of the ride from Songea with each step, and were shown into the office of the Prisons Chief. He shook hands and Ndunguru asked him if there was a message for us from Dar. He looked as blank as the wall behind him and about as interested. He shook his head. There was no message. Permission to visit the MP? Of course, he would allow us if it was in his power, but it wasn't.

We would have to wait.

FIFTEEN

Holy Father, have you Sinned?

Had there existed a brochure entry for the Beach Hotel in Mtwara, it would have consisted of maybe one line at the most. The imperfection of most of its amenities and the limitless deficiency of the more basic, the squalor, the languid service, would surely have conspired to defeat the guile and finesse of the most accomplished copywriter. That line would go something like this: 'Ocean views for the select in rare comfort – great sunsets, tropical rhythm.'

The copywriter, of course, would have Tipp-Ex'd over the gecko shit on the bedclothes, the holes in the mosquito nets generous enough to accommodate a warthog, the brown and pinguid water stagnating in large drums into which guests were required to dip themselves at wash time, the lavatories piled high with take-aways for the swollen flies of Mtwara, the broken glass in the windows, cracks the size of fault lines in the ceilings. And that was without going into the shortcomings of the staff, who seemed as if they were not of this planet. But the view was beautiful. This hotel was dipping its grubby toes off the edge of the continent into the slate-flat ocean that stretched lazily all the way to India. Three thousand miles of Africa, bush, rivers, mountains, *miombo*, red earth and plain, jolted to a halt here at the Beach Hotel, Mtwara.

We ordered beer, which arrived without an opener. Ndunguru said, while we were discussing the bottle-opener famine, that Ali Yusuf Abdurabi could not have been sent to a more suitable place for his incarceration than Mtwara. I told him that I thought the jail had to be more comfortable, cleaner, and better run than this hotel, but he just smiled and stared at the ocean.

Mtwara was always a big ivory area, even before a port was constructed. It was near the old Arab settlement at Mikindani Bay where the ruins of the slave market could still be seen.

The first slaving routes were established from the coast into the interior, either through Tunduru and west to Congo, or along the Rufiji river delta just fifty or so kilometres to the north. From Mtwara, the slaves and the ivory they carried would be sent by dhow to Zanzibar, and this was how the trade had continued up to this day.

'You could say,' Ndunguru added, grinning, 'that our MP has at last achieved what he always wanted to become. An ivory king.' He paused. 'But in an ivory tower.'

At last we were sipping our beer. Lunch, I reasoned, would happen sometime in the late afternoon.

I had already been disappointed by Mtwara as we drove through it earlier that morning, but then I was always a sucker for a big black blob on a map. Where was the port? There was a dock of sorts here, and I had seen one large revolving crane unloading a single container ship, across the road from an import-export office, which was run by a cheery Asian who told me that if there was room on the Texaco plane, I could scrounge a lift to Dar es Salaam the next morning. This hardly seemed the sort of shady place where ivory was being smuggled out of the country, but then Mtwara didn't possess quite the same sinister and exotic ring as Casablanca.

'There is a priest here,' said Ndunguru, almost divining my thoughts, 'who was suspected by the army and the Department of being involved in some way in ivory dealing. He was raided.'

'Is he still here?'

'Yes, he runs the mission. He is a Benedictine – Father Ildefons, a German. He is very influential. Someone told me he is building a new stadium here.'

I emerged from the coma brought on by all those hours in the Land Rover and shook myself free of the disappointment of not seeing our MP. I asked Ndunguru to take me to Father Ildefons instead. He agreed. He would like to meet the Benedictine too. Perhaps he could be of some use.

Boniface, of course, was nowhere to be found. He must be eating. He was caught fork in hand in the kitchen, the top of his head just visible behind a massive pile of rice and chicken. After he finished, he walked out to the verandah where we were drinking our Safaris, caught my eye, and gestured me to give him a banknote. I asked him what he needed it for as the 1,000 shillings vanished into his fist. I needn't have asked.

He grinned and drew from his left trouser pocket a syringe and, from the other, a condom. They were still intact.

But first, before Boniface had the opportunity to savour the sullied flesh of Mtwara, Ndunguru told him that he was going to see God. Boniface may not have understood the humour, in fact I am certain that it was beyond him, yet unintentionally Ndunguru had come close to the truth. Father Ildefons may have been suspected of being a sinner, but what I saw that day and the next, when I visited and talked to him and saw how inspirational his presence was, led me to believe that Mtwara was blessed enough to possess its own resident saint.

He is a tall, stoutly built man with a white shock of hair and creased grey eyes. He is wearing a blue shirt, fawn flannels and sandals with socks peeking out of the toe holes. He has spent the last twenty-five years in Mtwara, and twenty-nine in all in Tanzania. He speaks Swahili and English fluently, but with a heavy North German accent. He has built this mission with its church, hospital, workshops, schoolrooms, nursery, its kitchens, dormitories and children's playground. And beyond the mission grounds, he has built the church which I had noticed on the drive into the town. There is a hostel which he has established, to house the young men who come from the countryside beyond Mtwara looking for work. It isn't much, he says, but at least it is a home for them. There is a tractor station, too, where blacksmiths, welders and mechanics learn to repair vehicles, a garage, and a builders' co-operative, so the poor can be taught how to construct a house for their families from bricks and straw which they make themselves at the co-op.

Inside the mission, beyond the white walls that lead to Father Ildefons's office and the refectory, is an interlude of green sitting with some pride above the puddles. Here and there it shows signs of severe bruising from the tread of man and tyres, but for the most part it represents the neatest and healthiest piece of lawn I have seen since leaving London. Set to one side is a wooden shelter with what looks suspiciously like a see-saw inside it. For the children, Father tells me proudly.

He is showing me round the mission, pointing unnecessarily to the fizz of activity inside. This is the kindergarten for 700 children. One of the 700, bolder than the others, or quite

175

likely a little nearer, reaches for his hand. He takes it. Priest and child are smiling now and he walks, lopsidedly with the child, who can be no more than five years old and whose head brushes his knee, towards a classroom. Everyone inside stands for Father Ildefons. There are, he explains, five classrooms for the little children, with twenty-five teachers. He bends and kisses the child and pats her bottom away back to the other 699. Another room, this one full of sewing machines, gleaming new, each one operated by a smiling mama. They are, says the Father, making clothes, some for themselves or their relations, and the rest they can sell. They make a living this way, like the carvers.

'Carvers?' I ask.

The Father looks at me. He points to his Land Rover and we jump in. He is taking me to see the carvers. It is not a long way, just a few hundred metres round the back of the mission, but still within its boundaries. I see a straggle of tree trunks, chained together, each one marked with red paint. These marks show that the wood has been bought legally, the Father tells me. The Father buys it himself, and hands over the raw material to a team of carvers who are chiselling and sculpting intently under a banana leaf shelter inside a small compound. They are telling the story of their lives, the Father says.

He pats at one young man and whispers a few words. This man works with his father. He points to an old man, who is dwarfed by a carving three-quarters complete. He has transformed a child of the forest into an artefact for the hallway, or a foyer, or a boardroom. Now this is no longer a relic of a hardwood tree. It is part testimony, part homage to this old carver's past. It is almost a chair now, decorated with likenesses of his ancestors, who are harvesting the cashew nut. Such a scene brought good omens for the harvest, but now it will bring good money for this old man. Next to him, another younger man is digging into the bark of a much smaller piece of trunk. On it, he has gouged out the figure of a witchdoctor, beating powder in a mortar. It's a cure for a bad stomach. A six-foot log has been restored to life. Now it is no longer a dead piece of timber. It tells the story of one man's family. That man, says the Father, will earn 60,000 shillings for that (£240), less the money the Father has paid for the wood. In Germany, he calculates, it would sell for five thousand Deutschmarks (£1,800). A piece like this takes three months to finish. They work with no sketches, no plans, just their memories.

Once these men carved ivory, the Father tells me. Now they work in wood.

The day the army raided the mission still makes him tremble. He is angry as he talks to me about it. He loses his English and tries to compensate for his sudden stroke of inarticulacy by resorting to German or Swahili. It was 3 June, he thinks. He disappears from the room for a moment trying to find his records in his office. He comes back empty-handed, and clearly nervous. Ndunguru, who while I was touring the mission has failed to reach Costa Mlay on the mission's telephone, and I are sitting in the Father's living-room easy chairs. Behind the priest a small crucifix hangs from the wall. Otherwise there is little decoration.

Three soldiers came to the mission at dawn and demanded to see Ildefons. He went to his office and two soldiers who were armed were stationed outside. He was told not to move. At 6 a.m. he was expecting to take mass. He was told to stay where he was. The District Commander of the army arrived at nine o'clock. He was polite but insisted that the house must be searched. He said he was looking for ivory. The priest said they could look where they liked. The soldiers went inside the church. They went to the wood carvers. They saw what they thought was ivory. But it was the bones of pigs which the carvers were using to make teeth for the effigies they were working on. The priest suggested they go to the docks where two of his containers were waiting to be shipped to Germany. He sent twenty people to help the police search the cargo. Some ivory was found.

In one container labelled No. USA 2210-2526155 there was nothing incriminating. Just carvings, wooden carvings. The search moved to container No. 2210-200210-2002211. This one contained one big box bearing the name Brother Petrus. In it was one large drum, and two candlesticks made from ivory. In another large box, the soldiers found 52 pieces of ivory and 5 bangles made of ivory. In a bag, there were 72 pieces of necklace made from ivory, and one big piece of ivory. In another box there were 32 pieces of ivory, a complete chess set. This box was labelled Dr Stefen Pastor. In another box there was an ivory bowl. This box was labelled Mariane, and bore an address in West Germany. In a fifth box, addressed to a doctor in West Germany, there were 34 pieces of ivory, and wrapped in a blue-and-white cloth there were 4 ivory bangles and one other big piece of ivory. The ivory from Father Petrus's box weighed 16.60 kg and was valued at 33,000 shillings; there were 150 grams in the doctor's luggage worth 3,000 shillings. Both finds amounted to nothing of real value. They were souvenirs, some years old. Even though what the army had uncovered amounted to no more than £150-worth, and despite the fact that the contraband was addressed to men other than Father Ildefons, the army scented they were on the brink of a major discovery.

The news of the find, of course, brought more soldiers, and this time they weren't playing with a priest, but with their guns. Not that the macho charade frightened the Father. He was taken away from the mission to the army HQ outside the town. He made a statement which an army stenographer took down. The first sentence read: 'Father Ildefons had in his container . . . ' and then proceeded to list every piece of ivory that had been found, regardless of whose name or address was on the label. The Father refused to sign the statement. He was moved from the army HQ to the police HQ. He was granted bail, and the soldiers left him. The following week he had to report each day to the police station, and was on the point of postponing the vacation to Europe which he had arranged months before. His passport had been seized and he was now concerned that his work permit would not be renewed. The authorities, however, had looked into the case and were satisfied that he had been wrongly accused. Even so the Father believed that people would think he was running away and then he considered the point and was reassured by the feel of his passport in the inside pocket of his jacket. After all, he thought, no one flees a country with his passport. They leave without it. And by now he had been told that he had nothing to worry about. The Government had closed the file. The bishop had been informed of the raid and he fully supported the priest. Father Ildefons was told that he was welcome in Mtwara and that his return would amount to proof of his innocence.

He is breathing heavily as the details of the raid, the interrogation and the searches of the containers and the church seep out of him. I can see the sweat trickling down his forehead, making salt tears across his cheeks. He wipes his brow and runs his hand through hair that looks like yesterday's snows. Above us, the fan clacks its way round the room for a thousandth time, but it moves no air.

'But you do admit that you once dealt in ivory, Father?' I ask.

He shrugs. The colour returns to his cheeks. He pulls at his collar. 'I stopped buying ivory the day it was declared illegal,' he says. 'Of course, I bought it when it was legal, but everything I did was legal.' He uses the words 'legal' and 'illegal' constantly, but I can see he is struggling with English. 'None of the ivory I bought was acquired illegally. I have a community behind me and a bishop above me. I have the Order as well, so what I do wrong will reflect on the community.'

'So why were you raided, Father?'

He draws a breath and stares at me with those grey eyes. 'There is a man in Dar es Salaam. He is after me. I think you have met him.' He pauses and waits for me to answer.

I ask him if this man is Tanzanian.

He shakes his head. 'This man who you say you do not know has a . . . ' He clears his throat and searches for the word.

'Vendetta?' I suggest.

'Yes, he has a vendetta against me. He is sending his spies down here to Mtwara, asking questions, telling the bishop about me. It is not right.'

'Why don't you see him?'

The Father smiles and relaxes in his chair. 'See him! I have asked him to come here and talk to me, but he will not. I think he is a coward. He is not an honourable man.'

'But this doesn't explain why he is doing this to you. Why you, Father?'

The Father does not know either, but he believes that some of the elephant lobby has run out of control, like the old, solitary bulls who with age and lack of contact with the herd turn rogue and rampage through crops and men and their own kind.

I know men and women like this from the wildlife lobby. I've listened to them in England, in East Africa, in America. They are muscular conservationists who look down a long,

long way from the high ground which they believe they alone have the right to occupy. Their minds are made up. Their hearts have no room for doubt. Their convictions dictate to them that there is no other way, and whoever opposes them is viewed with contempt. They make enemies easily and possess the arrogance to brush this off. To the muscular conservationists, a priest like this is an irresistible and compelling target. He is not a man whose motives need to be analysed, but a source of evil whose power and influence must be destroyed.

As for the evidence against Father Ildefons, I came across a dossier after I had left Mtwara which revealed more about the amateurish methods of those who compiled the 'evidence' than about the criminal activities of Father Ildefons. I read over thirty pages which first laid out the facts about the Father. His real name: Reverend Manfred Weigand. Nickname: Father Ildefons. File number of Immigration Department: MTR/DN/102 MTWARA. Date of birth: April 22, 1932. Town of birth: Konigshofen, West Germany. First entry to Tanzania: 1960. His father: Josef Weigan *(sic)*. Date of birth: June 9,1889. Town of birth: Koenigshoffen *(sic)*, West Germany. Then the dossier gave out personal details about Father Ildefons, or was it Rev. Weigand or Weigan? Height: 180 cm. Colour of eyes: grey. Colour of hair: greyish. Occupation: priest. Languages spoken: Swahili, Dutch and English . . . and so it continued.

Then I read an interview with a former MP in the Mtwara area who alleged that the Father, now described as Father 'Fonz', tried to bribe him. One day, he says, the Father brought him a sewing machine for one of his wives. The MP refused it and sent it back, asking why he had been given it. He was offered no reply. He added that 'many officials have been given sweet presents in the name of Merry Christmas'. He then went on to describe in general terms how the illegal trade worked in the area.

I could not see any evidence at all of Father Ildefons's involvement here. He had given an MP a sewing machine! He had given presents at Christmas! The linkage was to say the least circumstantial.

There was information purporting to come from Father Ildefons's driver, who was described as a 'sincere and trustful' man. Of this driver, the dossier alleged that 'he walks and drinks alone. He does not prefer drinking in a group and he has no proper girlfriends.' The information, in fact, comes from a friend of his girlfriend of three years' standing. And it is this friend of a friend of the Father's driver who has alleged that the driver makes secret trips into the bush, carrying with him 3–5 million shillings, which would fill the back of a Land Rover with banknotes, to pay the men from whom he collects the tusks. The friend of a friend of the driver has quoted the Father advising the driver to 'make sure that not a single word of my activities goes out and I shall pay you in plenty. Do not worry about the police and other leaders, I know how to handle them.'

The dossier alleged that this driver was 'the most trustful of all the confidants of Father Eidelfonz (*sic*). He adapted him when he was very young and so far Paul has two houses and he a Mawia by tribe. — — has two VW combis of yellow colour. These two vehicles are usually used in the collection of ivory from different areas (*sic*).'

Then the dossier went on to allege that 'there is a rather shocking information that Father Eildelfonz (*sic*) processes a fake note printing machine at West Germany (*sic*).' It goes on to add, with an unusual note of caution, that 'this information needs more elaboration from other independent sources'.

There were other allegations, too, that named names. Father Ildefons was building a government officer a 'very beautiful' house in Iringa; Father Ildefons had given a 'lot of presents including a video and TV set' to a policeman; Father Ildefons was building the main stand at the town's Saba Saba stadium at a cost of 'six million shillings', and this was slated as the venue for the forthcoming CCM celebrations. This was what Ndunguru had told me. I had asked the Father about it, congratulating him on yet another example of his municipal benevolence.

The Mtwara stadium. Father Ildefons is incandescent. The grey face is the colour of an Easter-tide altar cloth. (Remember I have not yet seen this dossier. So when he begins to wave his arms and behave more like a Latin than a Saxon, I am at a loss.)

These people, these spies, they are saying that their priest is paying millions for their new stadium. He slips into the third person. The hurricane is not yet spent. He slams his

181

hands down onto the wooden arms of the chair. It is a gesture more of resignation now than fury. 'All I am giving is the price of a gate. That is all.' He takes a breath and asks us if we would like a drink. He goes out of the room and brings back, before we have the chance to talk, two cans of Coke, ice cold, flip-tops. He settles back in his chair.

'*They*' – a heavy emphasis on the word – '*they* accuse me of giving videos and TV sets and *they* say I have built houses for policemen and government people, but I tell you now, this is not true. There is no TV here. There are no videos. There are no houses I have built. Yes, I have helped out policemen and government officials. I have helped these people with school fees. If a man says he would like to send his child to a school and he cannot afford it, yes, I would help that man. This is normal. It is not bribery. This is God's way.'

He is talking about *ujamaa*, the African way of life where the extended family reaches out and gathers in help from distant relations, so that blood, however thin, runs deep. Christians, I suppose, would describe it as *caritas*, or charity, or our love for one another.

Ndunguru has taken no part in the conversation up to now. I can see he is intrigued by the Father, and by his view of Christianity, and now that the storm has subsided, he mentions in his gentle way the name of a priest who, at the time, I had never heard of. He says, almost in a whisper, 'Father Erio. Tell me what happened to Father Erio.' It was a name that was mentioned repeatedly in the dossier. There were many misspelt pages on the case of the unfortunate Father Erio.

Father Fidelis Erio is fifty-nine years old. Two years earlier, he had been facing a judge and jury in the High Court in Mtwara, accused of economic sabotage and organized crime. The catalogue of events that had brought him from the pulpit to the brink of prison were set in motion on the night of 3 May 1987, when the police raided the mission in Mchuchu, a village three hours' drive from Mtwara. Acting on a tip, they found inside a padlocked hut 224 tusks valued at 9,320,000 shillings (£37,000). Erio, who was in charge of the mission, was arrested. He denied that the tusks were his and said that a man named Aziz, a Goan of mixed race, had approached him and asked his permission to store some ivory in the mission. At first he refused, but he agreed when some weeks later Aziz asked again. He said he changed his mind when Aziz assured him that the tusks would be on the mission premises for a very short time. Despite two witnesses saying that they had seen a man who was called Aziz in the mission talking to Father Erio, and despite an extensive police search, no trace has ever been found of Aziz. Erio was sentenced to one day's imprisonment. On appeal this was increased to five years. He was released after three months.

Ndunguru finishes recalling the case of Erio. He sits back. Nothing is said. Then Father Ildefons breaks the silence.

'Father Erio is an old man. He is almost blind. He takes drink.' The Father acts the drunk swigging at a bottle with his hand. 'He is like this in the morning. It is too bad, but what can you do? He knows no other way of life and no one will throw him out. He is a poor man and has nowhere to go.'

He is saying that Father Erio did not see the tusks. He was either too drunk or too blind, or most probably both, and he was naive enough to allow the shadowy Aziz to dupe him. Plausible? Not according to the judge at appeal. But Erio is a poor man, a drunk, and simple, according to one of the witnesses. He had not benefited personally from his involvement in the ivory racket, but I can feel now that the Father's patience is on the point of expiring.

Why, he asks me, do you not ask questions about the big people? He leaves the room again and comes back, out of breath, holding a newspaper cutting. He thrusts it at me.

'Seventy Tonnes of Ivory Smuggled Out Last Year,' the headline reads. The story in the *Tanzania Daily News* reports the Inspector-General of Police disclosing that two ships had smuggled this amount of ivory the previous year through offshore islands between Zanzibar and the Tanzanian mainland. It was ferried to 'undisclosed Gulf states . . . where it was traced to the Far East'.

I agree with the Father, but suggest, gently, that there would be no ivory smuggled out of the country if there were no elephants killed.

'Elephants die,' he says, confidently. 'Elephants die. Human beings die. All over the bush elephants die. So why shouldn't their tusks be of use?'

183

'Twenty thousand elephants were slaughtered in the Selous in ten years. That is a massive scale of death, Father,' Ndunguru replies. 'Are that many people dying?'

The Father's look tells me that neither of us do understand and neither of us will ever understand the world. His world. And he has made up his mind about it a long, long time ago.

'First let me tell you that as soon as it was a question of survival of the elephants, I stopped the carving. Now let me tell you this. I believe that to export raw ivory is a terrible thing. It is a sin. What I bought legally gives me no moral problem. None of the ivory I bought was acquired illegally. I have tried to encourage people to carve it. Then they make a beautiful object. I believe ivory is very precious and it gives our people here the opportunity to show their skill. You see, if you can show these people who have no money, no houses, no clothes, no food, no hope, nothing, that they do possess a talent, a gift, and if you can get them to help themselves, then why shouldn't you give them this opportunity?

'A carver will work on one piece for six or seven months and from that one piece he will be able to buy a house. In Dar, the carvers were getting 25,000 or 30,000 shillings for their work. A man would come round to their factory each Saturday to pay them. By Tuesday they had drunk their wages. But here, my carvers were proud. They worked hard. They loved their work. They were continuing a tradition that was as ancient as elephants, and now that has all ended.'

People still come to the mission and ask for him, he says. 'Father, I have something for you,' they say darkly. But he throws them out. Does he inform the police?

'No. It is not my way.'

He asks us if we would like another Coke. He doesn't wait for an answer, but fetches two more cans. As we fight with the ring pulls, he draws himself up in his chair and says: 'Now, let me ask you both a question. What do you say to a hungry man about conservation?' Theatrically, he emphasizes the point by patting his stomach and waits for us to field the question.

It is difficult to answer. What can you say? What has Ndunguru said to the villagers in Kilimasera or Mchomoro who want to taste meat or who complain that their fingerlings are dead?

He waits while Ndunguru explains his village programme,

and hears him out, and then he nods and says that he has families, like every priest, in his parish, who are very poor, families to whom he gives money so that they won't steal.

The Father is well versed in the arguments for and against. He tells us that when he was last in Germany he told people who were worried about the effect that car exhaust pollution was having on their health that he, Father Ildefons, knew the answer. So what were they going to do about this? They shook their heads, as one does when faced with someone who claims Ultimate Wisdom. Some said they would buy lead-free petrol, as if that would save them. Send your cars out to Tanzania, he suggested. That will save you. He laughs. A point has been scored. 'I have my conscience. They have theirs.'

Ndunguru asks him how he can assist the conservationists. The Father thinks and says he would be very interested to start a crocodile farm if someone from the Wildlife Ministry would explain what to do. And he would like to educate youngsters about wildlife by showing natural history films in the mission. 'I want to build up this country. I don't need a cent in my pocket. All my needs I get from the community. Now I must go to mass. Thank you, gentlemen.' The Father shows us out of the mission. He has given us most of his day.

There is one final word from him as he shows us to the gate. 'These accusations that have been levelled at me,' he says. 'Bloody nonsense.'

That evening, back at the Beach Hotel, Bigurube was waiting for us. He had flown in from Dar with his easy cackle and bad news. We would not be able to visit the MP. The change of Cabinet we had feared had taken place. There was a new minister, and now no chance of obtaining permission to go inside the prison. The journey had been wasted, all those pea-in-an-empty-pod hours through the night for nothing. I thought about Ali Yusuf Abdurabi's wife, and the way she had pulled up a chair and settled herself at the table in the middle of her sitting room just two days before, and in the midst of strangers composed herself and her thoughts and written a message to her husband. I felt in my pocket. It was still there, damp now and worn like a 200 shilling banknote that had been passed from hand to hand a thousand times. I knew it wouldn't be read by him now, nor would he see the tiny red New Testament she had entrusted me to give to her husband. I handed them to Ndunguru.

That night, in my gecko latrine of a room, I gave up worrying about the mosquitoes of Mtwara which were said to be immune to any prophylactic yet devised by man, and I thought hard about the Father. Certainly no one could deny that he was a sincere and compassionate man. He had admitted that he had dealt in ivory up to the moment it was banned. He had dealt, he said, for the good of his people. I had seen the benefits of his energy and vision, his refusal to be defeated by the inertia of Africa. The mission with all its components – the hospital, the schools, the workshops – was clearly a force for good, most probably the only force for good in this town. He had stopped dealing in ivory as soon as the ban was announced. And he had transformed the ivory carvers into wood carvers.

His activities had brought him much satisfaction. But they had also brought him trouble. There was no proof of his having any improper connection with Father Erio other than that the half-blind, permanently drunk priest from Mchuchu mission was also a Benedictine. Even so the army had raided his mission in Mtwara and arrested him. He was cleared of any involvement whatsoever, but this man must have made as many powerful enemies as he had influential friends during the twenty-nine years he had spent in Tanzania, a land where whispers fly and lies grow fat with age and heat and telling. Father Ildefons was an honest man. He was not frightened to brandish unpopular views; and to judge wanting to save humanity as old-fashioned and out of favour was ludicrous. He had made a choice which had appalled many of the muscular conservationists. People, he believed, were more important than elephants. He should not be judged by Western standards, nor by the cosy morality of campaigners who see the single issue as the only issue.

The ends, to Father Ildefons, justified the means, though this is to question whether he really, honestly, understood the complexities surrounding the means. I wondered whether he was aware that so much killing was going on in the bush, so much money was being transferred, with the crack of a *jangili*'s Kalashnikov, from a tusk into a bank account of some Somali middleman. Did he realize that the carving of ivory into exquisitely refined sculptures was more than just a way of providing his people with a living and a chance to reclaim their dignity? That his decision to encourage them to carve was also generating the demand in the ungodly world outside the mission for more and more of this rare, elegantly proportioned and delicately fashioned material? He had been to Germany. He had installed carvers there. He had seen the way the prices had escalated. Or perhaps it was the hunger he saw each day as he travelled round his parish, the pain written across young faces, that convinced him there was no choice.

There were many half-truths and whole lies told in this country, but Father Ildefons had decided long ago where to draw the line between fact and fantasy. To this humble and determined man, who had spent his life working quietly in a corner, the answer was clear. People – those poor, starved, ragged, hopeless people – would always come first.

SIXTEEN

Sign Here for Flat Beer

The bar boy at the Kilimanjaro Hotel waited while I signed the hotel's 'flat beer' form, took it from me, and scanned my signature. His chin scraping across the starch on his white tunic as his mind grappled with the piece of paper. For him, this was not a question of beer but simply of shillings. The signature, however, appeared to be in order, and, showing his satisfaction with a return to insouciance, he dragged himself off towards the bar. Hopefully, he would return with a beer that possessed at least one faint throb of life.

I had flown out of Mtwara that morning with Bigurube, leaving Boniface to drive Ndunguru back to Songea. We had arrived at Dar's international airport at about midday, sandwiching the landing of the Cessna in between the only other take-offs of the day, a Boeing 707 on its way to Nairobi and another Cessna, airlifting hunters into the bush. Bigurube taxied past the passenger terminus, past the fraying fuselage of a long-grounded Dakota, and parked his Cessna outside a Tanzanair hangar.

Now I was in the Kilimanjaro, Mtwara's vicissitudes forgotten, with swordfish steak and fruit salad cohabiting inside my stomach, and I was struck by how similar the fortunes of the Kilimanjaro were to those of Tanzania.

This hotel, opened in the sixties with all the handsome promise of a tall, young man, well set-up and armed with a string of qualifications, was a reflection of what had happened to this country over the last thirty years. The two had been born at the same time, but the shine and energy of the early years had long gone, to be replaced by diffidence and a kind of helpless enervation. The vigour, the red blood of the nation, had gone flat too, like the beer. Of course, there had been massive transfusions of cash from the World Bank, but where this had gone to was a source of conjecture among many Tanzanians. Certainly, the villagers scratching the miserable earth of a bush *shamba* had not seen a cent.

I could sense, though, through meeting men like Ndunguru and Bigurube, Costa Mlay and Kibasa, Bernard Asayo, Major-General John Butler Walden, Father Ildefons, and even Alensio Bero the *jangili,* that perhaps, at last, the nation was drawing back from an edge. It had looked over the precipice, drawn breath, and stepped back. They were men of practical experience, highly educated, and I include here Alensio Bero who may not have been able to read or write, but was raised and taught by the bush and was as shrewd as the Director of Wildlife, Costa Mlay. Each of them shared a vision about what the future should be. Each of them was anxious to mould that future with his own hands. Their lives had been touched by the fate of the elephant, and their fates, though they may not have been aware of the fact, were inextricably entwined with the fate of their country.

Though the goal was the same, they were fighting on different fronts. For Charles Kibasa and Costa Mlay, the enemy was inertia with its battalions of brown files and arsenals of memoranda, waiting to booby-trap them, and the theatre of war the pale green offices of government ministries. For Ndunguru, Bigurube and Asayo, the struggle was altogether more complex. They did not know who was on their side. Their work had brought them to the bush and before they could attempt to succeed, they had had to come to terms with the bush and the men and women who lived inside it. Before they could preach the new ways, they had to understand the old. This truth, unlike the politicians in Dar, the social engineers who had framed their dogma from Chinese textbooks, they knew.

The General in his polished brogues, and the *jangili* in his shoes with no laces, had been enemies all their lives. Alensio Bero owned no fine-tailored uniform with golden stripes seaming the trousers and golden epaulettes on his shirt, but nevertheless he wore all the authority of a general. Both 'Black Mamba' and 'Strong Beer' were soldiers. Both were marksmen. Both were hunters. Both were respected. Both were feared. Both were leaders. Both were lovers of the bush. The General may have won a victory, but Alensio Bero had retained his dignity. Father Ildefons had triumphed, too. He had been cleared of any suspicions about illegal ivory dealing

189

and this victory had ensured that his people were safe from hunger.

Only Kibasa was a loser. He had fought the bitterest battle and his enemies were implacable. He had fallen foul of his own, and was now paying for it. He told me that he was going to resign because, even though he had been reinstated to his position in the national parks, there was no future for him there. He was regarded, he said, as a troublemaker, and this would always overshadow his career. In the end, he had just been sacked. He planned to build a guest house in Mikumi village with the money from his commuted pension and perhaps show visitors round the area, taking them into the areas between the Selous and Mikumi, following the migration routes of elephants and other game. But how he would afford all this, and pay for his children's education, I could not fathom. His pension amounted to around £1,200 and this sum reflected sixteen years in government service.

So would the elephants be saved? It seemed likely. Elephant mortality through poaching had been reduced dramatically after the intervention of the army in the Selous. The demand for ivory had evaporated now that public opinion had decreed that it was taboo. Men like Costa Mlay and Ndunguru were tackling the future with a vigour and a determination the country had never quite experienced before.

Yet, already, there are signs of disenchantment with the moratorium on ivory dealing. The lobby in favour of restoring the trade is active and powerful. It rests its case on the successful 'farming' of elephants in Zimbabwe, South Africa and Zambia, where efficient policing of the reserves and management have combined not only to protect the species but also to exchange illicit killing for efficient culling. Costa Mlay believes that Tanzania must wait ten years at least before the elephant is ready to be 'farmed' in such a way because it will take that long to set up an effective management system and to restore the herds to the numbers they once enjoyed. He is not going to follow the example of Kenya's President Moi and set fire in a Hollywood-theatrical gesture to the thousands of tusks that line the floors and walls of the Ivory Room on the outskirts of Dar. Instead, he wants to build up the stocks of ivory and release them onto the world market in ten years.

The great herds are roaming free, and relaxed, in the vastnesses of the Selous. Alensio Bero, and men like him, are content, inside their homes. They have seen the future and they know it does not include their like. But already the elephants are leaving the reserve and treading the migratory routes their grandfathers and fathers knew so well. The elephants are reclaiming their past. Sadly, this path will lead them, inevitably, in the direction of a *shamba* with its mouth-watering banana plantations, maize and cashew nut trees. This is the future for the great herds. Already some elephants have caught up with it. And it means only one thing for them.

SEVENTEEN

The Buffalo Boys

Remember Mchomoro? Those ragged villagers standing by the side of the road that dashed through their lives, the purple rain-sloshed path that connected them to civilization in Songea and led, the other way, out of the village, towards the Selous? Remember the way their sad eyes kindled out of a misty memory the fire of food? Remember meat? Remember the headman in his oversize jacket and ragbag trousers licking his lips at the thought of what he could no longer enjoy . . . sable antelope . . . eland . . . buffalo? Remember hunting?

I had been back in London for six months when I received Ndunguru's letter. In that time, I had written three articles in *YOU* magazine detailing the stories of the men who were trying to protect the elephants, and was astonished at the response. Over £100,000 was sent to the magazine, and with this money I set up a trust fund and began dispatching uniforms, vehicles, boats, radios, musical instruments (Tanzanians are a very musical people, and in the bush at night, I thought, they could pass the hours playing the keyboards I had acquired.) And then the letter from Ndunguru came. He wanted me to go hunting with the men of Mchomoro. Farmer's Day was imminent. He said that they would kill a buffalo and feast that night when they returned to the village. Of course, they would have to pay for the privilege. Six thousand shillings, but the money had been saved, and the villagers could not wait for the day of the hunt. It would be, he said, a reward for them, a prize for not poaching. I could see the point too. If these villagers were to co-operate with Ndunguru and his team, if the poaching was to stop, something had to give. The villagers had made sacrifices. They had surrendered their weapons and, with them, their means to protect themselves. But they had also ceded to the authorities something far more precious. They had lost their past, and hunting was one simple way of reclaiming it.

I wrote back, telling Ndunguru that I would come, provided the permits were issued by Costa Mlay. This time, I wanted everything to be in writing.

Bigurube was waiting at the airport to fly me to Songea to meet Ndunguru. He also showed me the permit. It was signed by Costa and allowed the villagers to hunt not only the buffalo, but warthogs, eland, and puku.

But nothing in Africa is that simple. By air, Songea is about 800 kilometres south-west of Dar, three hours' flying time. I had expected to be sitting on the terrace of the Angoni Arms by midday, drinking Guinness out of the cans I had brought with me. This trip I had anticipated the Safari famine in Songea. But I had reckoned neither on the rain nor on the Mbarika Mountains. Bigurube put the Cessna down in Ilonga, a tiny game-scout post to the north of the mountains. Soft rain enveloped the airstrip, blotting out the Mbarikas. There was no chance, he judged, that the Cessna would be able to climb over them and fly on to Songea if the clouds persisted. They did. We had to stay in Ilonga until the weather improved. The village was no more than a dozen or so houses. Only six were brick. Many of the mud huts had been abandoned. There seemed to be more chickens scratching at the wet soil than human beings. Bricks, softened by the damp, lay half-broken on the earth.

A Toyota Landcruiser was parked next to the game scout HQ, three rooms, which housed the radio, the armoury and an office. There was a wooden table, two chairs, that's all. No typewriter, no filing cabinets, no in, no out-trays. We were on the edge of the Selous, beyond bureaucracy. Outside the HQ, a grove of mango trees rose with dignity into the low clouds, dwarfing the metal post that supported the solar panel which powered the radio. Bigurube had raised Songea and had spoken to Ndunguru. The weather, he was told, was closing in down south. He walked outside and climbed onto the roof of the Landcruiser and scanned the clouds. He shook his head. He was resigned to staying in Ilonga.

He saw me taking a sip of water from a bottle and said he was glad that I had brought it. There was cholera in the villages nearby. As soon as I heard him, I wanted the clouds to sweep themselves away and leave Ilonga, but instead they grew more louring. Thunder boomed to the south, around the Mbarikas, and the rain grew more intense.

We pitched the tents under the mango grove, and as night fell down upon us, the fruit bats twittered and shrieked as they launched wave after wave of sorties on the mangoes. They sounded like a madly squeaking set of bed springs. I woke at two the next morning, shivering inside the tent. The rain was crashing down and I could see flashes of lightning burst out of the night. All night it rained. In the morning it was still raining. I crawled out of my tent, sick of the sounds of cocks crowing and men hawking, pulled on my boots and slopped through the mud to the pile of bricks and tin that housed the toilet. The hut was behind the HQ and inside cockroaches emerged from the hole in the floor, pleased, I believe, to see a human being, waiting eagerly for breakfast. I couldn't log.

Outside the open door of the HQ, Ilonga was swimming. The little green tents were surrounded by water and their reflections were mirrored in the mud. Inside I sat by the door and stared at a pullet which had sought shelter from the rain underneath a bench that had been drawn up outside the hut. My boot prints were perfectly reproduced on the concrete floor. Behind me, on the wall, was a calendar for 1991. It showed a photograph of the flooding in the south, a town whose main street was awash with a torrent of white water. In the background an impatient line of people were picking their way to safety across a makeshift series of planks, supported by chairs and tables, tin cans and bins.

Ilonga was the sort of village that no one was destined to leave. It was Sunday and Ilonga was in need of hymns and psalms and those grim, grey piles of stone and slate that make a chapel. Ilonga needed to hear a deep-voiced preacher combating with violent and awful prayers the offerings from the sky. It was 12.30 that afternoon before Bigurube decided we could fly. Raindrops purred in the short airstrip grass, but he could see the break in the clouds, and for the first time the ragged outline of the barrier that had condemned us to a night in Ilonga.

Tanzania had changed all right. There was Safari beer in the Angoni Arms. The manager was ecstatic, clutching four bottles under his armpits, two more in each hand. I shook my head and showed him a can of Guinness. The smile faded. I asked him if he could bring a bottle of Konyagi. This time he shook his head. No Konyagi. Only Safari. No Konyagi in Songea. He banged the bottles onto the table. I waved them away. He was intrigued with the Guinness and pointed out the rusting sign nailed to the terrace wall. 'GUINNESS GIVES POWER' it said. He had seen not a trace of it in years.

The manager went away shaking his head, unable to believe that his consignment of Safari had been snubbed, leaving me with Ndunguru and Bigurube and a girl with short legs and a high instep who lay in a lazy model pose along the length of the terrace wall. She didn't work in the hotel. She said she wasn't a local either. There was nothing more to her. She was merely a part of the furniture of all such African establishments, docile in the afternoon heat, yet bristlingly contemptuous of the notice that stared at the back of her head: 'The Management Reserves the Right to Refuse Admission'.

Ndunguru's Landcruiser was carrying tents, camp beds, blankets, sheets even, a folding chair, the sort that could support the ample bottom of a Hollywood director, a wooden table, a crate of soft drinks, a crate of beer, three bottles of Konyagi he had hoarded, three rifles, and a wooden chest in which he had stowed eggs, salt, knives, powdered milk, tea, coffee, bread rolls, a tin of strawberry jam, uncooked beef. Amid all this, the chaos of camping, next to a couple of fuel drums, we sat, Ndunguru and I, bumping and crashing all the way to Mchomoro.

The village was waiting for us. They had been waiting for several days now and their impatience was matched only by their appetites. The village secretary greeted me. He was the man who still licked over the memories of meat and the hunt and the pot. He said he would organize some men to come with us, good men from Mchomoro who had not been allowed to hunt or set foot in the prohibited areas of the bush for years, or at any rate since Captain Katali and his men had arrived in the area. I asked about Katali. Was the Captain still here? No. He was now in Mbeya, hundreds of kilometres away, not far from Lake Nyasa. The Captain's task was over and Operation Uhai had been wound down. Did the villagers miss the presence of the Captain? No reply. Just a smile here and there among the crowd who had surrounded the Landcruiser parked outside the village chairman's office.

There were fifty men there, all of them clamouring to come with us, and there was one girl, whose broken-toothed open grin masked the blankness in her eyes. Next to her was a bearded man in his thirties, sewing skull-caps as he stood, one finger a living cotton reel wound round with white twine, holding in the other hand a long thick needle, the kind that grannies wielded when darning socks was the rage. He asked me my name, motioning me to write it on a piece of paper. I printed the letters and he took the paper and my pen and put down the needle and twine. 'Nicko-louse,' he muttered. He peered at the letters and wrote underneath them the figures 50, 300, 30 and 60. Then he cancelled out the figures. I looked at the paper. All that was left besides my name were the numbers 2 and 6. He added them together. He told me that I must come to his house so that he could consult the books he kept there. I asked him if he was the Mchawi, but he shook his head and said that he was the Mganga, the witchdoctor who cured the villagers, not cursed them.

The house was down the road a few hundred yards. He led me into his consulting room. No appointment necessary with this Mganga. No white coat either. He was wearing a dark blue shirt and light blue slacks. His feet were scraped into sandals. Nor was there privacy. The door was open and his children, eight of them, none of them over ten, peered in at me. Beside him on the hard earthen floor on which he and I squatted were three thick volumes, bound in red morocco, piled one on top of the other. These he did not consult. Instead he fished behind himself and produced a tattered paperback the size of a school exercise book. He opened it, impatiently flicking the pages as if he was searching out a telephone number. I saw that each one was covered with lines and columns of Arabic numerals.

'I am not up,' he said. 'I am not *up*.' He pushed his face up from the floor where the book was resting and his close-together black eyes and button nose inspected me. 'I was not more than standard six.' His fingers point out the numbers.

'You have,' he said, jabbing in the region of my trouser belt, 'a bad stomach.'

I shook my head. I did, as it happened, have a slight feeling that were I to stay in this dark cramped hut no more than six feet square for much longer I might be sick. The breaths and sniffles of the children outside the door were unnerving; the pungency of the chicken shit which littered the floor of the yard outside the room was cloying like someone else's aftershave. But the Mganga was oblivious. He asked me my mother's name. I wrote it down. His hands worked boxer-fast, calculating the numbers, cross-referring in the book. 'I am most anxious about your mother Meery.' These were his exact words. 'Djinns,' he said. 'I see them standing at the side of the roads. They are invisible, but I feel their presence when I pass them by.' I told him my mother was in hospital and that she was very ill. I began to feel sick in the stomach, the sweat popped on my brow. I wanted to get out of the room, away from him and his books and Arabic calibrations, away from the penetrating gaze of his eyes and the whispers of the children in that doorway. But something I saw in the book made me stay. It was a pencil drawing of a woman and it looked to me to be the scribbling of a child. It was on a loose piece of paper and stood out from the lines of figures. I asked him what it was.

'It is a spell. A man asked me to kill this woman. I must put these words,' and here he turned to another book and showed me a page with an identical drawing labelled with what he said were the words of a spell.

'Does it work?'

'Yes,' he said. 'If you want to kill a man or a woman, you must put these words next to a drawing of that man or that woman. Then you bury the paper or put it on water.'

I asked him why there were no words on the drawing I had seen.

'I do not like the man who brought it here. He is not a

good man. I asked him why he wanted to kill the woman and he will not give to me a good reason.'

I asked him what the words said.

'The day, the time, then they can be dead.'

Outside the room in the yard that was overrun with chickens and children, there was a wicker basket turned upside down. The Mganga saw me looking at it and lifted it up. Underneath it was a Msharifu tree, a bush really, about three to four feet high. He plucked a leaf and chewed it. He told me this would make him dream. And when he dreamed, the Mchawi would visit him.

I walked up the street with him, back to Ndunguru, back into a world of Landcruisers and cigarettes. I told Ndunguru what the Mganga had said about my mother and asked him whether he thought this man was a Mchawi.

Ndunguru shook his head over and over.

'Possibly he is. He's been a poacher, I know. He was arrested by Katali's men. They *kiboko*'d him, but he would not admit to anything. Then the askari with the *kiboko* wanted to give him a few more strokes. He hit him and the *kiboko* snapped and struck the askari right in the eye. After that, everyone here believed he was a Mchawi.' Ndunguru went on to tell me that the *jangili* did visit the Mganga's house and seek his magic, but they had fallen out with him because they had promised him a house in return for a magic potion which would guarantee that they could deliver the ivory safely, a potion that would make them invisible. He gave them it, but they never gave him the money for the house.

That afternoon in Mchomoro there was another disappointment for the Mganga. He wanted to join the hunting party. Ndunguru said that we already had enough villagers. He didn't want him with us. Neither did I.

The place Ndunguru chose to camp was about fifty yards from a river, at the bottom of a ridge that curled round the remains of a mountain top. We had driven for two hours from Mchomoro, leaving the road after half an hour and then following an ill-defined path that climbed towards the mountain top through trees and saplings which, if they happened to be in the way of the Landcruiser, were brushed aside or thwacked down. They reared up in front of us and reached out to stroke the windscreen like lost souls drowning in a sea of undergrowth, their thin, elastic trunks and limbs scraping along the underside of the vehicle. Wave after wave of these little trees succumbed to our advance. When one of the saplings proved too resilient and stood its ground, one of the villagers would solve the problem instantaneously with the axe he carried. Three strokes here, one there, four here, and the path ahead was clear.

We reached the camp at dusk. I sat on the director's chair, watching the men – there were four of them – unload the vehicle and set up the tents. Round me stood crates of drink, camp beds fastened with string, a canvas tarpaulin, the camp bed legs, suitcases, tentpoles, the table, grain sacks, an adze, a saw, an axe, the three rifles propped cosily in the fork of a tree trunk, the blankets, two hurricane lamps, a spirit stove. Out of the disorder they created a home in thirty minutes.

One was pushing his face close to the pile of dry twigs and bark he had collected, blowing gales of breath into the hot embers that were forming into a fire. Smoke from the kindling trickled up towards the trees. Another pumped the spirit stove until it putt-putted into life. Sometimes it missed a beat and he had to begin again. Another scrubbed potatoes. Another fetched buckets of water.

Three of them went off to the nearest Mohoro tree and performed the Ritual of the Night. They stripped to the waist and called out to Kyombe, the god of this particular area. They begged him to protect them and left a pinch of salt on a leaf in a square of ground. They asked Kyombe to prevent lions, leopards, snakes and buffalo from harming them. Ali led the prayers. His voice was loud and confident and drowned for a moment the sounds of the forest. It seemed that even the crickets, the frogs, and the bee that had been buzzing round my face were, for a second, listening too. It felt damp in the forest. The sun had sunk and the moon was just a sliver, a slice of lemon in a tonic sky, waiting for the blackness to shine through. Orion was in the sky, only briefly, for the clouds came early that night and robbed us of the stars. I hoped it wasn't an omen for the morning.

It is six-thirty. Time to rise, to unzip a new day, to crawl into the morning forest mist. Already the men are up, sharpening their knives; one is chopping down a tree. He believes there is a honeycomb in it. Ali has revisited the Mohoro tree and declares the auspices to be good. I look too. The salt has not been touched. The leaf is whole. The square of earth it sits in is unmarked. The men hear the news and set to sharpening their knives again. In the night more villagers have come. Some have walked, others been picked up by the Landcruiser. There are now twenty of them here, but who will hunt? Ndunguru says ten including me. The others will stay in the camp, and prepare for the return of the beast, they are that confident of killing it.

We set off at seven-thirty. Ndunguru divides us into two parties. I am with Ali, the disciple of Kyombe, Juma Althuman, Saidi Mponja, who carries an axe and a knife, and a game scout I had met before in Kalulu. His name is Romanus Alois Hionde. He is tall and as wiry as a sapling, a man who has caught many poachers and earned the nickname Salaama Hakuna (the man the *jangili* hate). He is the only one of the four who is wearing boots, though there is a large hole in the left toe cap. The others are barefooted, except for Ali who wears flip-flops. Hakuna, as he is called by everyone here, carries the .458. It is a powerful rifle designed to bring down an elephant. Ali is given the double-barrelled twelve-bore shotgun. Ndunguru, in the other group, has his pistol and the .3006.

We are walking along an elephant trail, no more than two feet wide. It roams around the ridge, and looks down upon ravines and valleys on each side. There is plenty of elephant dung on the path, some a few days old. Huge footprints cross at intervals. There are paw marks too. Leopards, Ali says. He is second in line behind Hakuna and his hole in the boot. Behind these two guns come the *fundi*. Me, Saidi and Juma. Every so often, these two reach for their knives and sharpen them on a rock. It is an hour before we pick up the tracks of a buffalo. Hoofprints and caked dung. It is old, possibly, says Ali, one day old, and doesn't particularly arouse the interest of even the flies.

We press on, this time down a ravine, through dense bushes, saplings and trees, into a valley. The grass is high here, higher than me. Only Hakuna is taller than the grass. More tracks, this time damper. I can see that whatever hap-

pens these men are going to kill a buffalo today. Their eyes
are down, their noses up. They possess wrinkling, thinking
noses, noses that know. Often there is disagreement, but
voices are never raised. These hunters work in whispers and
signs and whistles. They are speaking another language, not
Ki-swahili, but one far older, born out of our primitive past.

Another climb through the brachystegia up to the ridge
and then a plunge down into another valley, narrower this
time. The sun is up now and I am hot and beginning to
think that maybe they are being too optimistic. Where is this
buffalo? All I have seen is day-old dung. Each pace forward
I take, I pray I will not step on a mamba, black, green, who
cares. I look ahead at Ali's maroon T-shirt, the gun he holds
behind his shoulder blades, one hand on the barrel, the
other on the stock. In my mind a mamba rears, six feet
above the ground, its tongue licking the tops of the grass. I
am thinking of pain, paralysis, foaming lips, lockjaw, the
journey to Songea. But by the time they got me back, it
would be too late.

Halfway down a ravine, Ali turns and looks down at a
tree trunk. Something dark and shiny is wedged in its fork.
He fishes his hand in. A snake? No, it's his flip-flop. Then
Hakuna stops and points. Ali points. I stop. Juma and Saidi
point. Their fingers call me away from a tree that is directly
in their path. I move off, treading over mines. I stare at the
tree and make out something brown or black hanging from
one of its branches. A wasps' nest. I feel cheated.

We are in a swamp and the pace quickens. There is, in
front of us, a muddy patch of ground, chewed up as if a
company of tanks had laagered there overnight. The buffa-
loes have been here. When? Last night, I gather. There is
silent debate about which way to go. Ali points to the left,
Hakuna to the right. Saidi and Juma take sides. But Hakuna
insists he is right. I stay well out of it, glad of the pause. We
follow Hakuna through the swamp and up another ravine,
puffing to the top of the ridge. There is time for a smoke
now. I offer cigarettes around. Each of them takes two, one
to smoke, one for the pocket, and for the first time it crosses
my mind that I have never hunted before, never killed
before, and these men, smoking my cigarettes, these four
ragged, black, sweating, pungent strangers, can't wait to
kill, nor eat. The knives rasp against the rocks on the ridge

top and the rifles lie at their sides. If the mambas don't strike first.

In the next swamp, there is a water-hole, oily brown, motionless under the sun. There is no creature round it that I can see, yet Hakuna and Ali and the others are high on something. They are peering down at the mud. Buffalo dung. But this time it is fresh enough to please the flies. Ali sticks his big toe in among it and leans down and sniffs deeply and contentedly. We squelch round the edges of the pool. One of my boots slips into the mud and my knee vanishes for a second. I pull it clear, knee, calf and boot, with a sucking sound. My socks are wet, my shirt is damp, my head is hot. The bottled water I have has gone sour, but the boys steam on like muggers through the swamp, up the next ravine, along the ridge, stopping only to sniff the air and toe-test the dung.

It all comes to an end three valleys, three swamps later. We have been walking five hours now and I have no idea how far we have come from camp, or in what direction we are heading. The sun is overhead and I am too tired to work out where my shadow is falling. But the boys are happy. Crossing the last swamp, there is no chat. Their movements are quick, their gestures flash like fireflies in the night. They don't have to wave their fingers any more. Their eyes are telling them what they are thinking. The boys belong to the Ndendeule tribe. They are closing in on the *mbogo*. Their name means the Arrogant Ones. *Mbogo* is their word for the buffalo. *Mbogo* means Fierce One. Now here in the corner of this swamp, with a ravine ahead of it, and a ridge above, the Arrogant Ones have finally caught up with the Fierce One.

The buffalo is grazing. It is wide and long and a female. Its trophies catch the sun when it moves its neck. It must be from this distance of maybe fifty metres the length of a car. It bellows, raising from within its ample stomach a V-12 roar that sends the thought of mambas racing out of my mind. I keep back, well back, positioning myself with the axeman, Saidi, on the slope of the ridge overlooking the swamp. It is just as well. The two guns go forward. Now the only sound between them, whistling. They circle round the beast and I lose sight of them below me. The silence is close, inside my ears, the silence of the mad.

A branch snaps some ten metres below, at the edge of the swamp. This is like pulling a Christmas cracker knowing it's going to explode in front of your eyes. When the explosion comes, the thunder of the .458 rumbles on and on through valley after valley, losing its resonance until all I can hear is a faint vibration in my skull. Saidi and Juma rise and cheer. We shake hands and the knives flash along with their grins. We stay where we are. This is the dangerous time. A single shell, even from a .458, rarely kills a buffalo, even a neck shot. More likely it will stop it. Buffalo have been known to sink to the ground and stay there, bleeding and apparently dead, until the hunters approach. Ndunguru told me that once he saw a buffalo knocked down with a neck shot force itself to its feet and charge at him. He fired three rounds but it still rushed forward. He had no more bullets and all he could do was move three steps sideways towards a tree. The buffalo matched his move. He was so close he could see the tears dripping from its eyes. He didn't realize it at the time, but there was another warden standing behind him who finished it off. What had made it so difficult to kill? It was a female, a pregnant female, and this must have endowed it with a supremely powerful will to survive, a determination that matched the name *mbogo*.

We hear a whistle from the edge of the swamp and charge down the ridge. I am last now. Saidi and Juma want to see their supper. My foot is swallowed by a gaping hole in the hillside and I tumble the rest of the way down into the swamp. I am still ten metres or so behind the others when another shot rolls round the valley. The kill.

Now all I can hear are the flies, angry and intent, greedily feeding on the pools of blood, bright scarlet mixed with black. Ali is standing on the carcass, waving the twelve-bore. He holds his hand up to me, inviting me to join him. He is disco dancing on this dead beast, shuffling his flip-flop feet on this mountain of meat. I decline, not out of propriety, but from fear. I can see it is still twitching. I back away. The noise of the flies is intense. The boys are smiling. The boys are killers now. The job is done.

Not quite. Saidi brandishes his knife and says 'Mimi', and no one is about to stop him. He wrenches back the head to expose the neck and slices the steel blade neatly and efficiently through hide and gristle until the blood spurts out, spills carelessly onto the earth, and offers the flies feeding on the bullet wounds a richer harvest. Then he moves to the rear of the beast and reaches for the tail. It is long and hairy and will, I suppose, make a man feel rather dignified as he whisks away the flies. But the amputation of the tail is a sign of possession. He hacks through more gristle and then waves it round his head in his jig of triumph.

Ndunguru had heard the first of the shots and had set off in the Landcruiser to find us. It took him two hours. Two hours in which we walked along the ridge, following a path where leopard and elephant, buffalo and eland had trod the night before. Not that any of us cared. On that trek back, there were no whispers or whistles, no finger signals. The boys were talking, discussing the feast they would prepare that night, and the feast the village would share tomorrow. When Ndunguru saw the carcass, he estimated it weighed half a ton, which meant that each family in Mchomoro would share a kilo of meat. I hadn't thought about how the buffalo would be brought back to the camp until Ndunguru told me that we were heading back to the site of the kill. We had met about a mile from the camp. The Landcruiser was gingerly picking its way down a steep earth bridge that separated one ravine from another.

Two vultures were exercising their rights of scavenge, and all along the belly of the beast the flies had been busy laying eggs. A fertile topping of cream snaked along the flanks, setting off the dark tan of the carcass. The boys set to work with their knives. They were quick, professional and as their knives worked, their hands were stained in blood. First the right hind leg was severed. Then the foreleg. A knife slit open the belly, releasing along with a fizz of air, as if opening a lemonade bottle, a rich and unpleasant smell of intestine.

The boys grinned.

'That's what you would call a gamey flavour,' said Ndunguru. 'They are always talking about it.'

Next Saidi raised his axe and began clouting away at the ribcage. Then the head was severed. Limb by limb, the animal was dismembered and carried up the ridge to the Landcruiser. The boys in the camp had prepared a green tarpaulin which they had sprinkled with salt as a kind of funeral bier. The limbs were flung onto the tarpaulin. The head, the ribs, the spleen, the heart, the lungs, the liver all followed. Three hours ago this butcher's window slopping around on a green tarpaulin in the back of the Landcruiser was a buffalo, feeding earnestly on the grass. Now all that remained was a squelch of entrails, the rumen, and a pool of blood fast drying in the shadows of the afternoon sun, hardly a meal for the scavengers of the night.

It was almost dark when we arrived back in the camp. I could see by the light of the fire the men had lit that a roasting platform the size of a snooker table had been lashed together. I stared through the gloom and smoke at the forest and realized that there were a few less trees standing that evening. They had also made a rustic bench for us to sit on. It would have looked at home in any suburban garden centre. The men placed the choice cuts on the fire and hung the rest of the meat on the trees that were left standing. Then they went to the Mohoro tree and thanked Kyombe, the god of these lands, for protecting them from the leopards and lions and snakes. They didn't mention wasps. Ali knelt at the base of the Mohoro and offered to Kyombe a plastic bowl which contained bits of liver and kidney and heart. Kyombe said, 'No, boys, you have it.' Ali thanked him and pushed the bowl in my direction. I took direction from Kyombe and said, 'No thanks, Ali, you have it.' Ali took it, flung back his neck and swallowed the contents of the bowl, licking the blood off his fingers as the offal slithered down his throat. The feast could now begin.

'*Chonde, Chonde, Pepaie,*' they chanted. 'Please, please forgive us our sins if we have done something wrong, something against your wishes.'

'*Asante sana kwa kutupa mboga,*' they chanted. 'Thank you for this buffalo. It will keep our larders full.'

The boys clap hands and conceive with their palms and their fingers and their feet a rhythm that emerges only out of Africa.

'*Fundi Mwoga!*'

'*Kuliya Ndetema!*'

It is a rap as old as time itself. Hundreds of thousands of men have sung songs like these, sung them for centuries, their feet stamping in front of sparky fires, their voices fuelled by full stomachs and the memory of the day's battle to survive. 'A coward hunter runs away, but when the *fundi* is going to die, he sees a vulture.'

I ate my buffalo steak, fillet of course, well done, tasting like prime beef. The men guzzled theirs, satisfied at the end of the day. Saidi grabbed the tail and whirling it around his head began another song. No other place, no other world existed. One year ago they poached elephants, these boys. Today the elephant was safe.

I walked away from the fire and the boys of Mchomoro, walked beyond the tents to a spot in the forest where I knew I would not be noticed. I was carrying a bucket of hot water. I unlaced my boots, peeled off the damp socks, the blood-flecked shirt and muddy trousers I had worn that day, and stood naked in the night. I poured the water over my head. Africa washed itself out of my body.